P9-EEK-725

JAVA FOR BUSINESS

Using Java to Win Customers,
Cut Costs, and Drive Growth

JAVA FOR BUSINESS

Using Java to Win Customers,
Cut Costs, and Drive Growth

Thomas Anderson

VAN NOSTRAND REINHOLD

I(T)P®   A Division of International Thomson Publishing Inc.

New York • Albany • Bonn • Boston • Detroit • London • Madrid • Melbourne
Mexico City • Paris • San Francisco • Singapore • Tokyo • Toronto

Copyright © 1997 by Van Nostrand Reinhold

 Van Nostrand Reinhold is an International Thomson Publishing Company. ITP logo is a trademark under license.

All rights reserved. No part of this work covered by the copyright hereon may be reproduced or used in any form or by any means—graphic, electronic, or mechanical, including photocopying, recording, taping, or information storage and retrieval systems—without the written permission of the publisher.

The ideas presented in this book are generic and strategic. Their specific application to a particular company must be the responsibility of the management of that company, based on management's understanding of their company's procedures, culture, resources, and competitive situation.

Chapter 15 Mitsubishi: Java in Silicon © 1997, Mitsubishi Electronics America, Inc. All rights reserved. This material provided by MELA is published with the prior written permission of MELA. No warranties, express or implied, are granted by MELA as to this material. Broadcast or republication is not permitted without MELA's prior written permission. "eRAM" is a trademark of MELA. "eRAM-enabled" is a servicemark of MELA.

Java, HotJava, Javasoft, JavaOne and JavaBeans are trademarks of Sun Microsystems, Inc.

Reuters and the dotted logo and the sphere logo are house marks of Reuters Limited. Reuters is a registered trademark in more than 25 countries worldwide.

Netscape Communications Corporation has not authorized, sponsored or endorsed, or approved this publication and is not responsible for its content.

Netscape Communications Corporate Logos, are trademarks and trade names of Netscape Communications Corporation.

All other product names and/or logos are trademarks of their respective owners.

Printed in the United States of America

http://www.vnr.com   Visit us on the Web!

For more information contact:

Van Nostrand Reinhold
115 Fifth Avenue
New York, NY 10003

Chapman & Hall GmbH
Pappalallee 3
69469 Weinham
Germany

Chapman & Hall
2-6 Boundary Row
London SEI 8HN
United Kingdom

International Thomson Publishing Asia
60 Albert Street #15-01
Albert Complex
Singapore 189969

Thomas Nelson Australia
102 Dodds Street
South Melbourne 3205
Victoria, Australia

International Thomson Publishing Japan
Hirakawa-cho Kyowa Building, 3F
2-2-1 Hirakawa-cho, Chiyoda-ku
Tokyo 102 Japan

Nelson Canada
1120 Birchmount Road
Scarborough, Ontario
M1K 5G4, Canada

International Thomson Editores
Seneca, 53
Colonia Polanco
11560 Mexico D.F. Mexico

2 3 4 5 6 7 8 9 10 QEBFF 02 01 00 99 98 97

Library of Congress Cataloging-in-Publication Data available upon request.

Java for business : using Java to win customers, cut costs, and drive
     growth / Thomas Anderson, editor.
          p.   cm.
     Includes bibliographical references and index.
     ISBN 0-442-02517-3 (pbk.)
          1. Java (Computer program language) 2. Business enterprises-
     -Computer networks–Case studies. 3. Web sites–Design and
     construction. 4. Internet programming. I. Anderson, Thomas, 1950-
     HF5548.5.J38J38 1997   97-14574
     650'.0285'5133–dc21   CIP

Production: Jo-Ann Campbell • mle design • 213 Cider Mill Road, Glastonbury, CT 06033 • 860-657-2156

To Janice, Justin and Sarah

CONTENTS

FOREWORD

Early in April, 1997 we kicked off our second Java developer conference, packed with 10,000 Java developers. Their enthusiasm and innovation, along with that of the 400,000 or so other people around the world now developing Java programs, has made this the most quickly diffused and embraced software technology ever. The language is about 700 days old at the time of this writing, and it is in 45 million or so browsers and other Java-enabled devices, enables 100,000 or so Web sites, has several hundred books written about it, and is taught in over 150 universities. Dozens of companies have developed tools to build Java applications; thousands of companies in turn, large and small, are using Java to build everything from games to full-scale transaction processing systems.

The case studies in this book—the first on Java that takes a business case study approach—are an indication of Java's business utility. A programming language, no matter how elegantly designed, is only as good as its applications. It is exciting for us to see an office productivity suite developed in Java and delivered by a Java-based broadcast medium.

It is also gratifying to see how Java is practically used to help investors, shippers, communicators, patients, bankers, auctioneers, engineers, scientists, and others. The use of Java at large and small enterprises in a wide variety of applications validates its openness and portability. Java is having and will have a tremendous effect on how businesses communicate, distribute, and grow.

I am frequently asked about the reasons for Java's rapid success. Clearly there was a need for a network-centric language and runtime environment with the explosion of the Internet and intranets over the past four years. But why Java as opposed to any other technology?

Because Java is:

- Open

- Portable

- Safe

- Scaleable

- An industry initiative

- The best language for rapid development of network applications.

One of the fundamental factors in Java's immediate ascension to de facto standard is that it shares the philosophical principles of the Internet in that it is based on open protocols. The source code can be licensed, a binary version of the Java Developers Kit can be downloaded and used to create applications with no charge to the user, and the specifications for all the application programming interfaces for Java are fully published.

One hundred companies, to date, have licensed the source code to implement the JDK on their platforms.

Today, there are really three sets of open standards that drive the new paradigm of network computing: tcp/ip for connectivity; html/http for access to static information; and, of course, Java for access to dynamic content or applications.

So how does Java accomplish this Holy Grail of computing, in which applications can be written once, and run on any computing device? It begins by compiling the source code to bytecodes, a neutral format that can be delivered over the Internet or any other network. On the platform side, a "virtual machine" interprets that code to run within the underlying hardware or software architecture. Hence, any device with this virtual machine can run Java. The "VM" has been ported to myriad devices large and small. So when we say "write once, run anywhere," we aren't kidding.

Imagine a world in which automakers operated as computer makers do, and you'd see signs on the road that point to "GM gas, 2 miles;" or "Ford gas, 5 miles." Silly, isn't it? Yet, customers of computers have been beholden to their supplier under this very business model for dozens of years. Java breaks this operating system lock-in to become the universal fuel for computing. Developers can write applications once and eliminate porting from their overhead expenses; customers can buy applications over the network or in stores without worrying about the platform the application runs on.

To ensure compatibility, licensees, who have implemented the virtual machine on their operating system or other software or hardware architecture, are required to pass over 8,500 tests. For developers, a new program called the 100% Pure Java Initiative will educate and train them to write applications that are tied to no one architecture, because they will use only Java. Applications tested and certified will be eligible for a special logo and marketing programs from Sun.

Delivery of executable code over a network is nothing new. But what really differentiates Java from other contenders is its ability to deliver this code safely. Java does this by verifying the bytecodes before they run. With other technologies such as ActiveX, once the code runs, the user has no control over its destiny. The program can access file systems and memory, it can erase the disk, it can cause untold damage. The bytecode verifier within the virtual machine "sandboxes" the application to do only things it should do and nothing more. Java is the only environment that has this capability. In addition, the code can be authenticated to verify the place of origin is a legitimate and desirable place from which to receive code.

In today's world, the desktop computer is but one device we use to access information. Every electronic device, it seems, is now controlled by a microprocessor and this microprocessor, in turn, must have some "intelligence" through software. Java is the first platform to be able to scale into devices as small as "smart cards," credit card size devices that can actually store values, and to scale to devices as powerful as mainframes and even supercomputers. For programmers, this means a new market that is far larger than the desktop computer market of today. Devices such as smart cards and PDAs and cell phones will sell in the millions and hundreds of millions of units and require thousands of new applications.

One of the major factors in Java's success was its early release on the Internet. This enabled thousands of developers to work with the language creating Java applets, applications and tools. These early adopters validated Java's benefits, found the bugs, and provided valuable feedback to us to help us build the right set of application programming interfaces to make Java the fully robust environment it is today.

In addition, as we have evolved the Java platform, we have had great assistance and collaboration from the entire computer industry. Today, over 30 companies—including IBM, Apple, Novell, Netscape, Oracle and many others—are helping us refine the set of programming interfaces that define Java as a platform.

And finally, Java as a programming language enables all kinds of businesses to be more productive. With Java, developers can write code faster than with any other language. Developers report five to ten times the productivity with Java! This is a real cost savings for any independent software vendor or information systems manager within an enterprise organization.

The whole notion of deployment itself shifts with Java. The language, and the use of the JavaBeans component model, enables a new way to build applications, reuse pieces of software for rapid development, and new ways to deploy networks as distributed components over a network. Pay-per-use becomes a feasible marketing strategy. Transparent updates are possible and are being done now. Barriers to entry are lowered for innovative software start-ups; distribution and revision costs are lowered for software behemoths; MIS managers reduce their distribution and version-control costs.

Java will indeed enable businesses to win customers, cut costs and drive growth. This is just the beginning.

Alan E. Baratz, Ph.D.
President, JavaSoft
Sun Microsystems, Inc.

CHAPTER 1

USING JAVA TO WIN CUSTOMERS, CUT COSTS, AND DRIVE GROWTH

Thomas Anderson

Java™ is Sun's new programming language and computing platform. Java applets have animated the Web, and Java has made the new NC, or network computer, possible. Java's utility for business goes beyond these innovations. This cross-platform language works with all major computer operating systems—UNIX, Windows, Macs—simplifying development and accelerating deployment of business applications. Java runs on mainframes, workstations, servers, PCs, NCs, and consumer electronic devices, expanding the scope and simplifying the integration of a business network. The language was designed for the network, and has built-in security features, increasing its utility for electronic commerce. Early limitations of Java, including a lack of development tools and run-time speed issues, are quickly being overcome. The language is maturing rapidly and now has all major Information Technology providers behind it and an estimated 400,000 developers working with it. What can it do for business? Early business adopters from different industries have seen significant gains in developer productivity. Practical customer applications have been deployed successfully, and with positive customer response. Business applications are expected to rapidly increase in number in 1997. As a network-centric language, Java opens up entirely new ways of com-

1

municating with customers and colleagues, and new ways of distributing and updating data and software.

In August 1995 I was in the small, windowless office of Sun's then Webmaster, Hassan Schroeder. Business colleagues I had come with were outside the office, patient but anxious to move on to the next meeting. Hassan had this tumbling character on his screen. Would I like to see some links to some chemical models? As a former chemist, I had lingering affection for chemical structures and models and a subscription to *Science* that will not die. I took Hassan's mouse, clicked on a model, and it filled the screen. Cute. Nice. Balls in space. I had seen this before; I had commissioned multimedia molecular animations; I had paid thousands of dollars to create images of complex molecular structures for annual reports and technical marketing literature. But I moved the mouse, and I moved the molecule, and I could turn the molecule around and it was simple and elegant and quick, and I was amazed.

Close on this epiphany, I read an article on the flight back to Boston, in *Forbes ASAP*,[1] by George Gilder about this new Java language and what it would mean for the future of computing. The message was astounding: you could do *this* with *this?* Gilder's writing was powerful; the case was made with anecdotes, facts, and fervor, with continuous surprises and revelations, with endorsements by Marc Andreesen, Gilder's interviewee in the article and power behind the opening of the Web with his Mosaic and Netscape Navigator. I felt like Keats reading Chapman's Homer for the first time, "like some watcher of the skies/when a new planet swims into his ken; Or like stout Cortez when with eagle eyes/he star'd at the Pacific—and all his men/Look'd at each other with a wild surmise..."

Chemistry and Keats: I was hooked. We could "Javatize" our Web site: we could run off and start a Java business, make Java-powered network presentation software, quicken our initiation into electronic commerce, become part of this revolution, apply it, make it work for our business.

Then the plane hit turbulence, surmise, something.

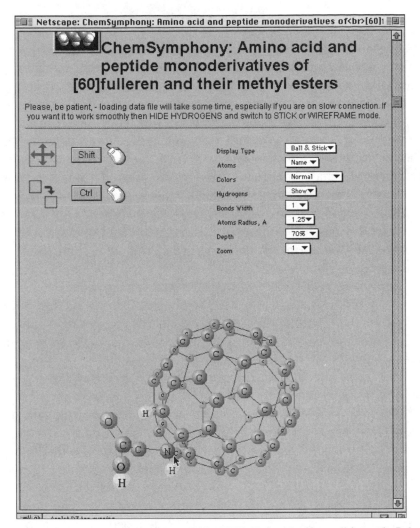

ChemSymphony © Anatoli Krassavine 1995–1997 Published by Cherwell Scientific Publishing http://www.cherwell.com/cherwell/chemsymphony/. Used with permission.

Figure 1-1. Molecular modeling is a perfect application for Java: highly graphic, lots of variables, and value for a high degree of interactivity and involvement on the part of the user.

PARADIGM FATIGUE

Businesses outside the software and computer industries are jaded: call it paradigm fatigue. Ephemeral productivity promises unmet, always later. Internets, intranets, extranets. Pick a technology horse today and tomorrow you are wrong. Ten thousand dollars or more per year for each of your knowledge workers to be desktopped, internetted, and wired to each other. Dueling presentation packages. Incompatible documents. And the critical attachment to a customer e-mail that cannot slip through the firewall, no matter how much you electronically grease it.

Dutifully, network "clouds" are drawn on overheads for you. Experts push salesforce automation, executive dashboards, and data warehouses full of video training programs that your company does not have.

Success stories break through this wall of jargon and disbelief. Everyone in business is aware of the Federal Express on-line tracking story that cut out thousands of "Where's-my-package" phone calls a day and resulted, along with incredible cost savings, in an increased level of customer satisfaction.

Everyone in business knows the Netscape story: how fast it grew, who the players are.

Everyone in business has succumbed to the overall Internet story. They see the URLs on television. They hear about the several hundred thousand visitors to their company's site. Pointcast has seeped into Executive Row. Get me my stocks! Get me my competitors!

The skeptics strike back: stories of Internet misuse, of companies blocking Pointcast access, of firewalls being closed to Java applets. Never give your credit-card number on-line. Our customers will never buy that way. It is only high school kids visiting our site. Our systems don't talk to each other. We need a magical training program, another task force, a new consultant, a chip in everyone's brain.

The proclamations and rush to judgments are safely ignored: what sticks are the stories, naming names, naming companies. This happened to X. This happened to Y. We should do this because they did this. We should watch out for this because they got burnt. Look out, our main competitor is doing this. The iterative, conservative business ethos, built on precedent and practicality, is fueled by stories. Tell your senior management what your best customer wants delivered and transacted on-line and chances are you have won the latest budget battle.

Do you tell them about technology, about the means to the end? Do you mention Java? Do you run the risk of drawing clouds on overheads? Are you talking to them from the Barksdale side (CEO and President, Netscape) or the Andreessen side (Senior VP of Technology, Netscape) of your business brain?

JAVA TIME

More than six thousand people attended the first JavaOne Conference in San Francisco in the last week of May 1996. The staging was impressive: sports stadium-sized video screens, ramps and girders, colored lights, smoke. The Java gods in denim shirts. Free backpacks. Geek cafés. Long lines snaking through the Java bookstore. Break-out sessions with hard copies of slide presentations grabbed and clutched by information-starved hackers, programmers, and venture capitalists. There were technical tracks, design tracks, strategy/industry tracks, and inside industry tracks, all packed, all intense. There were parties—large, lavish events, and more selective, programmer-only soirees at odd San Francisco museums. Press announcements flowed as abundantly as slide handouts. Bouncer-like attendants guarded the pressroom doors. This was serious stuff, and there was lots of it. The place was pulsing.

There was a hint of this even before I arrived. I spent the flight next to a fellow attendee who opened his laptop and showed me the future of college science teaching. Applets, Java applets. Functional. Better than C. They were converting from C. These applets went beyond the mouse-driven molecules I had seen nine months before; they served a purpose; they had proven effective in classroom beta tests. The content was the "killer app," not the technology. But the technology decision made the content easier to develop, faster to deploy, and, well, it worked.

At the conference the daily keynote sessions set the stage. The myth of Java's creation was restated. James Gosling got up and talked about Java in phones, Java in doorknobs, and Java turning him into a predatory spider in *The Economist.* Alan Baratz, the new president of JavaSoft, talked about the JavaOS, Java chips, and the Java platform being used in anything "that feels, smells, walks, or talks like it has a processor"—PC desktops, workstations, servers, telephones, pagers, embedded controllers. Bill Joy was teleconferenced in from Colorado with his take on the Java revolution. The host, John Gage, gave out everyone's e-mail address, including Scott McNeally's, Sun's chairman and CEO. Gage *solicited* e-mails. It was a new world, measured in network time, seven times faster than chronological time and accelerating.

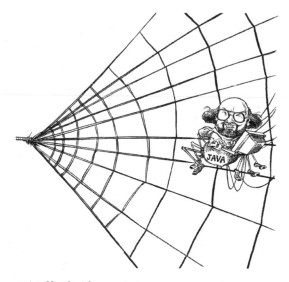

©1995 The Economist. Used with permission. www.economist.com.

Figure 1-2. James Gosling of Sun Microsystems led the Java development effort. The language is the foundation for a more dynamic, interactive, and useful World Wide Web—and a lot more. This cartoon, with Gosling as Java Web weaver, was in an October 1995 editorial in The Economist.

There was a contest for the best Java application, winners to get several hundred thousand dollars worth of Sun hardware. The buzz intensified for the award ceremony. Creative applications of Java were shown on a large screen and the winners swept across the long stage, murmuring thanks, while the packed hall sighed and exclaimed over what the winners had created. Half of the winners were from outside the United States, reinforcing the network power theme. More than half of the winning applications were plausible business applications that one would want to take home, put on one's machine, and say to competitors, "Well, there!"

At some of the keynote sessions were video clips of early case studies of Java success stories. Jack D. Hidary, President and CEO of the New York-based Earthweb, in one video clip said something that resonated: "Java will change the way we create, distribute, and pay for information." This was up my alley, this is why I had come: to build new marketing skills, to build new communication skills, to move business information in a new and interesting way, network-centric, media rich, cost-effective, and viable.

There were break-out sessions proving Java's viability in all kinds of industries, companies, and applications. Many of these applications and applets were pre-launch and beta demonstrations, but robust enough for presentation purposes and functional enough so they could be talked about. They could be cleaned up and deployed afterwards. They were there as Trojan horses: get Java inside the programmers' heads, give people ideas as to what Java can really do. The language's tools and the language itself were maturing quickly; real-world applications would fuel that maturing process, and the process would fuel the applications.

The summer following the conference was productive. New Java businesses were created. New applications were deployed. The story of this new language penetrated the business media, the general media, and the imagination of several hundred thousand programmers, all networked in a way impossible a decade earlier, even 30 months earlier.

In April 1997, there were over 10,000 attendees at the second JavaOne conference. New tools and new business applications were introduced. Advances in Java's speed and security were announced, along with the Java Electric Commerce Framework—and a Java Wallet that would slip into your virtual pocket. Impressive science applications were demonstrated, including a new Java-powered system for getting real-time and historical telemetry data from the Hubble space telescope to researchers worldwide. Sun,

Netscape, Microsoft, IBM, Marimba, Lucent, Mitsubishi, Oracle, Corel, Silicon Graphics, Hewlett-Packard, and others all had major Java announcements during the JavaOne Conference.

VISIONARIES AND PIONEERS

So, as an innovative marketing or information technology person, do you tell those senior executives about technology, about the means to the end? Do you mention Java?

Absolutely. Tell them Java is the language of the Internet—and their intranet. Tell them Java can significantly cut IT costs, cut print costs, deliver software, sit in your phone (eventually). Tell them it can work on any computer platform and in any browser worth a browse. Tell them it can work outside a browser and it can create personalized channels to customers. Tell them it is going to fundamentally change how we work on-line. Tell them it is under-hyped, like the Internet, and it is time to build in-house or virtual-house expertise in understanding, working with and developing applications based on Java. Tell them this particular tool can do things for their business that could not have been easily done before, or done at all. Tell them Java is the future of the Internet, and time is running. Tell them IBM, Oracle, Lotus, Microsoft, and a hundred other software companies are lining up behind Java. Tell them it makes the network computer (sometimes called the "thin client") possible, that it underlies the market-leading Netscape browsers and servers. Tell them it is a language that has arrived at the perfect confluence of network ascendancy, business need, and computer power. Tell them it is the Shakespeare of computer languages: It does legacies. It does multimedia. It does little applets. And does them all well. Tell them programmers with object-oriented programming skills can learn it quickly and that Web designers with the right tools can use it without any programming knowledge. Tell them it works on their molecular biologist's Mac and their finance cruncher's Pentium. Tell them if they don't like it you have the e-mail address of every senior executive at Sun and JavaSoft.

Then draw a network cloud.

Well, forget the cloud. Tell them these business stories:

Reuters built Java-powered applications into its Reuters Web, an extranet built for the fast-paced, high-volume trading room. Security was a major prerequisite. With Java, Reuters realized significant gains in development and deployment time, with the overall effect of reducing their time to market.

CSX developed and deployed to hundreds of their customers a customer-service commerce application based on Java. The application saved the company months of development time and millions of dollars in development costs, while improving customer service. Customers love it; they can order a railroad car, track their shipment, contact their CSX representative, review their account, and more. The application is deployed in the United States and is being licensed for deployment in Europe.

The *Nando Times* was the first daily newspaper on the Web, and the first to incorporate Java as part of its dynamic tool set. Java was used initially to animate the front page and later for advertising. The *Nando Times* recently introduced an instantaneous news watcher application, powered by Java.

HotWired, the interactive media arm of Wired Ventures, used Java as a navigational aid for its multifaceted and multidimensional Web sites. As a business tool, the language has enabled Hotwired to enter new markets more quickly, and expand the reach of its innovative content with chat applications and the Wired desktop.

Physicians from the National Jewish Medical and Research Center and scientists from the Los Alamos National Laboratories used Java for their TeleMed application. TeleMed consolidates patient data from a variety of sources over time and makes it easily accessible to physicians and distant consultants over networks. This has quality and cost benefits for the treatment of chronic patients, and offers tremendous potential for rural telemedicine.

F. Hoffmann-La Roche used Java to publish its regulatory-mandated and worker-protecting chemical safety data sheets to several hundred locations and a heterogeneous IT infrastructure using Java. This simplified distribution considerably and cut printing and administrative costs while increasing worker access to safety information.

National Semiconductor used a Java-powered parametric search engine to get device design information to their customers faster. Print costs went way down. Customer satisfaction went up. Information is more available, targeted and complete.

The @Home Network is delivering local Internet content to its high-speed cable customers using Java and Javascript, and gearing up to deliver software upgrades on-line. Java is a key part of their technology infrastructure.

Virtual Vineyards and Sun Microsystems teamed up to do a live, real-time, on-line wine auction with video, audio, and interactive bidding and registering. The auction helped raise money for charity, and it demonstrates the multimedia and interactive power of this young programming language.

The electronic commerce potential of Java is demonstrated by the HOME Account Network case. This firm has a complete package of tools for on-line consumer financial services and contributed to the development of the Java Wallet.

Corel has put an office suite on-line with Java, a functional, practical package that makes the most ubiquitous business tools—word processing, spreadsheets, presentations—ride on a network. You do not have to put a lot of fat on your hard drive or 400 bells and whistles you never use; just the tools you need. Updates and infrequently used functions—including the bells and whistles—can be pulled down as required. This is a new way of working.

Marimba is also in the "new business tool" category. Its products enable businesses to build new channels to customers—helping innovative companies like Trilogy deliver software and software upgrades on-line, enabling companies like EntertainNet to deliver a new type of on-demand entertainment and companies like CBS SportsLine to offer personalized, up-to-the minute sports information to its customers. Excite has a "channel of channels" powered by Marimba technology. The key breakthrough of Marimba: automatically delivered up-to-date software and data within companies and across the Internet.

Finally, Mitsubishi is putting Java in silicon chips with the aim of bringing exciting Java-enabled applications to the consumer-embedded electronics market.

These cases are from different industries, markets and types of companies, and they highlight different applications of Java. The health care, financial, pharmaceutical, semiconductor, media, transportation and consumer goods industries are represented.

There are companies who have applied Java to their businesses, and companies who provide Java-powered business tools. There are some recurring themes in the business cases: shortened development time, faster deployment, graphic and visual power, customer satisfaction, competitive gains. Some of the applications are very new and early: Marimba personal broadcast networks and the @Home cable network, for example. Some are more traditional business functions such as information distribution and searching where Java adds value. Several of the cases are cross-linked: HotWired, @Home and Corel have Marimba-powered channels. Reuters and HotWired have teamed up for a venture.

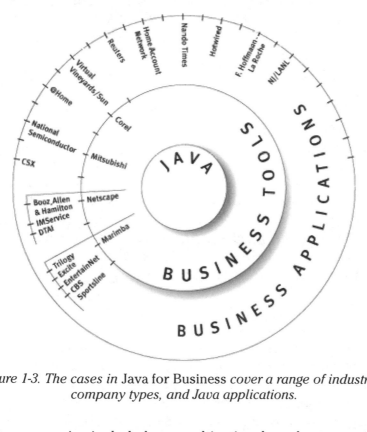

Figure 1-3. The cases in Java for Business *cover a range of industries, company types, and Java applications.*

The companies include large multinationals and new start-ups, and U.S.-, Europe-, and Japanese-headquartered firms. Early adopters all, and all with the optimism, resourcefulness, and risk-taking that characterizes early adopters.

COMPLEXITY AND REVERBERATION

Being first has its advantages: you set the rules, benefits accrue. My company, Millipore, was first in its particular industry on the Internet. This had its benefits; nearly half of our traffic comes from hyperlinking, according to an on-line survey we conducted, a level of connectivity achieved by having been on the Web for almost three years.

Complexity theory notes that systems—financial, chemical, biological—carry vestiges of the first entity to enter the system. Being first is risky, but if things click, it carries significant benefits. Netscape: first out with a commercially viable browser. Microsoft: first out with an operating system for the IBM PC. The Internet accelerates the pace of complex systems; the effects of being early to market are magnified.

Java has paid off for the early adopters in this book in money saved, lessons learned, customers won over. In a few cases, Java is their business. The lessons go beyond Java. For Reuters, early adoption is causing a rethinking of the entire software development process. CSX's commerce application has opened up the Internet to some of its customers who never had the rationale or impetus to go on-line. There was a recurring theme of using business partnerships and alliances in just about every case study in the book; speed-to-market, knowledge and marketing value were gained. National Semiconductor and F. Hoffmann-La Roche both had alliances with Java specialty firms. Netscape offered a vehicle for third-party developers to post Java-based intranet and extranet applications. Physicians from the National Jewish Medical and Research Center worked with computer scientists from Los Alamos National Laboratory to create a Java-powered TeleMed application.

Everyone, particularly these early adopters, is in a continuous learning and continuous improvement mode. In addition, early adopters gain knowledge and skills that lead to further gains. John Andrews and Marshall Gibbs from CSX make the point that in a networked world they have at most a 30-day head start on their competition.

The message is this: start using Java, start accruing the benefits to your business. The language is reverberating in the marketplace. Your information technology vendors are ramping up; Java programmers are at a premium.

The "reverberation" is partly accidental and partly engineered. Sun Microsystems had this computer language code-named Oak in development for interactive television, a languishing project, and suddenly the Internet exploded. There was an strong market need for a well-designed network-centric language with innate security features. Concurrently Sun has a brilliant marketing effort with the right positioning, the network-beta distribution model, and the right name, Java, not D or D++. This combination of events created market reverberation. Everyone talking about this new language. Everyone wanting to learn it. All those two hundred or so technical books on Java. Sold-out developer conferences. Four hundred thousand Java developers working with Java. Tool vendors. Fifty thousand people attending a JavaDay in Tokyo. One hundred thousand Web sites with Java. People starting new businesses based on the Java platform. A $100 million Java venture fund. Computer sciences majors itching to learn it and over 100 universities teaching Java programming.

And at least in California, limo drivers who discuss it with you, as I discovered on a long and engaging ride from San Jose to San Francisco Airport.

Java was well positioned, well named, well executed. It came at the confluence of customer need, Internet ascendancy, technical innovation, and smart marketing. Built for network computing, the language has benefited from riding on the network. It has put a new tool in the hands of programmers as well as nonprogrammers.

JILL THE PILL

Occasionally, it is useful to see how the search engines are doing in finding material on your company on the entire Web. Type in your company name and see who has linked to you. I did that once for my company and found a site called "Jill the Pill," the home page of a woman who worked at Millipore, a recent hire, an engineer, Web-savvy. Jill Boski worked in our microelectronics training department. She had an idea for a gas-filter selection guide, and went ahead and created it, first in Visual Basic, then in Java. As an undergraduate she had some programming background, C, C++, but was not an active programmer. In her off hours she created a functional Java applet that quickly and interactively drills down through a set of variables to arrive at the right product to purify the right gas at a particular volume and flow rate. It was a clever and quickly developed Java applet.

Jose Lizardo is a graphic designer who does multimedia programs, annual reports, and Web sites. As we moved our Web site from dead to dynamic, we experimented with Shockwave, frames and Java, successfully. Jose suggested using a Java scrolling news applet, an applet publicly available off the Web. We put this applet within a graphic window, and put the code with the scrolling news in a Lotus Notes database. As news develops, we simply cut and paste a line of text in the scrolling news. Clicking on the news headline gets you to more information.

These are both very useful, quickly developed, and quickly deployed applications using Java. They were created by people who are not full-time programmers, but were looking to solve an immediate business need.

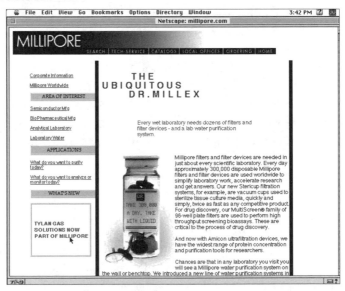

© 1997 Millpore Corporation. Used with permission. All rights reserved.

Figure 1-4. Java is a useful tool for creating interactive Web applications: product selection guides, chemical compatibility guides, and scrolling news updates. Millipore has used Java and/or JavaScript for all of these applications.

Our catalog database vendor, Stibo Datagraphics, has developed Java-powered product selection guides and filter compatibility guides.

The utility of these applications for our business is visible. They are targeted for our Web site and communication purposes. That a designer, an engineer, and an IT vendor are experimenting or working with Java demonstrated to me its penetration of traditional and nontraditional markets. This language is easy to apply to business. You can develop on any platform (Jose on a Mac; Jill on a PC; Stibo on a UNIX workstation) and see the application on any platform.

Ammiel Kamon at Netscape talks about the whole Internet as a clipboard for Java. There is a high degree of reusability of Java code. The language of the network is fueled by the network. This has rapidly accelerated Java adoption and Java knowledge. The technology has diffused much more quickly than computer languages in the past, thanks to the network. It has diffused faster than C, faster than Windows API.

But it is a computer language; it is not something that everyone can do. It is more complicated than HTML coding and on a par with C or C++ in terms of skills needed to program well. There are, however, new tools making it easier to program, and tools that may make it as easy to create workable Java applets as it is now to create animated multimedia programs.

And you do have that large clipboard to work with.

COLD WATER

Is Java ready for prime-time business use? There have been major concerns about speed and security. One of the fundamental advantages of the language—cross-platform development—has been challenged. There have been a lack of programming tools, a lack of programming expertise, and a lack of precedents for business applications. There are, as always, competing technologies and alternative visions.

The speed issue is real. Waiting for a large applet to download can be as frustrating as working with an old 2X CD-ROM drive. Java as a language is not yet as fast as C++, its nearest equivalent. Speed equivalency is expected, however, in 1997, and some experts predict that Java will eventually be even faster than C or C++ in the coming years. Successive versions of Java are faster than previous versions. For the demands of business applications, the CSX and Reuters case studies are useful models; Java has met their speed threshold for end users. Improvements in the language's speed will only further the gains of CSX and Reuters and other early business adopters using Java. There are other aspects of speed that tip in Java's favor: speed of application development is significantly accelerated with Java. New delivery systems, like Marimba's Castanets, can speed up the delivery of very large and robust Java applications as opposed to small, browser-linked Java applets.

The security issue is also real. Hostile and malicious Java applets have been created in Internet security think tanks. There have been reports of very mature Web sites blocking all Java applets from getting inside their firewalls. In response to these challenges, successive versions of Java have added security enhancements. Netscape and Microsoft, with their Java-enabled browsers, are addressing security issues. Firewall software companies are addressing security issues as well, taking steps to block malicious applets with their products.

Is Java secure enough for business applications? A qualified yes. There have been theoretical challenges, and there have been very practical responses to those challenges. Java is fundamentally more secure than other computer languages like C or C++. The language has what can be described as a sandbox security model; only Java applications can get into and run in this sandbox. They cannot get out and interfere with other parts of the computer hard drive. There will be new challenges and new responses, so any endorsement has to be qualified. Java, however, has met the security requirements of several early business adopters. The financial trading (Reuters), electronic commerce (CSX) and banking (HOME Account Network) case studies in this book, as one might expect, are very attentive to security issues. There are a number of security references on-line, noted in the Java Business Resources appendix. Based on its fundamental security model and the continuous and rapid flow of tests and improvements, I expect Java will play a major role in the coming wave of electronic commerce.

The lack of tools and expertise has been problematic for Java. In just about every business application in this book, the companies were using Java for the first time and learning and doing simultaneously. There were few tools available during this development period. Recently, however, a number of tools have been introduced that greatly simplify the creation of Java programs. Symantic Visual Cafe, a visual development tool, was introduced late in 1996 and has received awards from *PC Magazine, Byte, Comdex,* and other publications and organizations. There are a number of other tools now available and more are expected; lack of tools is no longer a problem.

The cross-platform benefit of Java has been challenged. Several of the cases in this book note that Java—at the time of their business application development—was not available for the older Windows 3.1 platform or embedded in all Internet browsers. The 3.1 issue has been resolved, and Java is enabled in the latest versions of the two leading browser programs. These were simply timing issues. More serious is the nightmare of dueling Java programming classes and standards. JavaSoft has embarked on a 100 Percent Pure Java initiative intended to sustain and promote the cross-platform integrity of Java. Key licensees of the language have signed on to the program.

Java has also been faulted for the speed of some of its mathematical calculations and the fact that it was faster on some microprocessors than on others. This issue is being addressed, and should be short-lived.

I do not mean to minimize technical concerns and shortfalls. The language, however, is developing rapidly and is a moving target. Java applications are in the plans of most corporate IT departments and most major software companies. Successive versions and beta releases of Java have addressed customer concerns; the network distribution of these versions accelerates the speed of feedback and improvement. The language has been deployed successfully in tens of millions of browsers, tens of thousands of applets, in microprocessors, and it is starting to be deployed in a number of mission-critical business applications.

Several of the cases in this book are mission critical. The contributing authors point out Java's past shortcomings and the pains and risks of being early adopters. They remain very enthusiastic about what it can do and has done for their business applications.

WHY JAVA FOR BUSINESS?

The speed and ease of development is one reason why Java is good for business. You cut your development time and you cut your costs. You program for multiple platforms once and you avoid re-working and recoding proprietary solutions. You reuse bits of Java programming and avoid redundant coding. In terms of development, Java also has a feature called "automatic garbage collection," which saves a considerable amount of time in programming. Unnecessary code, called garbage, is automatically collected and discarded. Developers have told me that programming in Java is five to ten times as productive as programming in other languages; the cases in this book back up this claim. This in itself is a great business reason to start using Java.

The ubiquity of Java is appealing in several dimensions. First, you have a cross-platform capability that reduces development time and makes applications built with Java highly portable. Second, you have ubiquity across types of computing; Java runs on network computers, client PCs, workstations, servers, and mainframe computers. It connects these different elements within a business environment. It also can connect to the existing hardware and software infrastructure. This makes it appealing. You get a paradigm shift without rewriting all of your legacy applications and getting a paradigm-sized invoice.

Ubiquity has another dimension: with Java ported to consumer devices, phones, pagers—anything that uses a microprocessor—there is the potential to integrate those items in a broader definition of a business network.

The speed of development is a persistent theme in the case studies in this book. The cross-platform benefits are also consistent. There is a bias in these cases toward the visible, customer-focused business applications, and the graphical, interactive benefits of Java are apparent. Patient medical records, train cars, organization charts, sales literature, product selection guides: these are interactive, attractive, easy-to-update, and easy-to-use network tools, all powered by Java.

So, why Java for business?

Customer Impact. Java enables dynamic network content with animation, interaction, and links to transactional databases. Java functionality is built into all the leading browsers. Java is also used for stand-alone applications and personalized broadcast networks. Quicker, higher-impact marketing on networks is possible using Java.

Cost-effectiveness. Faster development and faster deployment of computer applications saves money and time. Five times as productive? Ten times as productive? The innate characteristics of the language, the elimination of the need for cross-platform redundant development, and the reusability of publicly available code all contribute to the cost-effectiveness of Java. As noted in the cases in the following chapters, Java network applets and applications can replace some traditional communication and marketing activities. The real payoff is in the connectivity among different computer platforms and languages that Java offers within a business. Java can lower the cost of computing within a company.

Growth. The Internet has opened up a new marketing channel and the intranet has opened up a new means of collaborating and communicating within a company. Java can help drive growth in these relatively new areas. For entrepreneurs and Web heads, Java offers a new platform for building a business.

JAVA WORKSHEET

This book is focused on early-adopter business case studies of Java. It consciously pursued a mix of industries, companies, and Java applications to give you some idea of what you can do with Java. There are some wonderful resources on-line that will give you more creative raw material and some of these are noted in the appendix.

The book answers many questions of the business person, marketer, or communicator interested in how to apply this new language to their business. What was the rationale for using Java? What were the results? How is this relevant to me and my business? Most of the cases focus on front-end and back-end customer applications that run over a network. The Mitsubishi case is different. It

focuses on embedding Java in a DRAM-enabled RISC microprocessor. If you use microprocessors in the products you manufacture,
think about the implications of the Mitsubishi case. Think of Java in
pagers, telephones, doorknobs. There are some technical concepts
the contributing authors have simply and clearly described that
may prove useful to marketers and communicators.

For the programmer or Web designer, there is some technical
information; the network topologies and the time to develop the
applet or application may be of most interest. But the business aspects of the cases may prove helpful, something to convince those
people in the business cubicles that your Java idea has precedence,
is worth pursuing, and has enabled other companies to cut costs
and drive growth.

Chances are very high that your business is using Java in one
form or another now, particularly since it underlies browsers, is
used in so many Web sites, and is endorsed and developed by all
the leading computer hardware and software companies. A more
proactive stance, however, for those of us on the outer ring of applying new technology, is called for. What can you do? Focus on the
business problems and customer issues noted in the case studies in
this book. They may resonate with your own industry and company. In addition, consider these steps:

1. Build IT skills in Java for your business. Get your MIS people to
   a Java training session. Your IT vendors all have Java initiatives: the vendors doing databases, EDI, groupware, office
   suites, middleware, multimedia. They all are building Java expertise. You need some expertise in-house. This will take time,
   but start now.

2. Build or buy a business-oriented Java applet for your Web site.
   Make it something focused on your business: a product-selec-
   tion guide, an animated site map, a flow diagram. See how it
   works. Find out how customers like it. Then move on to more
   complex Java applets and applications.

3. Seriously look at the new category of "personal broadcast networks." The Marimba case provides some examples of what
   these networks are and what they can do. Thousands of net-

works will be created over the next 12 months. Consider a competitive head start.

Marketing, communications, and business have changed with the ascendancy of the Internet and the growth of intranets. You need to know how to use new information technology tools to more effectively market and communicate and brand to customers and colleagues who are increasingly busy. There is also more competition. Having strong digital-literacy skills in marketing and communications is a business advantage. Harnessing the power of relational databases can free passive marketing dollars spent on unnecessary printing and production for active lead-generating and customer-support activities. Knowing how to use multimedia effectively can shorten the sales cycle, accelerate training, and motivate colleagues.

Roles are shifting inside corporations. Information technology is becoming a larger part of everyone's job. Content and information technology are more closely intertwined. Separate them and very little happens.

The Web has opened up a whole new area for being effective or ineffective in business marketing. Marimba's personalized channels are a real marketing breakthrough and open up a new way of working with customers, but you have to know about them to use them. Java is a breakthrough, but this elegant, revolutionary language is only as good as its applications and the business strategy behind the applications.

Table 1-1. The case studies refer to Java applets, applications, servlets, beans, and computing platforms, as well as JavaScript.

Java	Java is a computer programming language developed by Sun Microsystems. The language was designed for network use and has two key benefits for business applications: portability across computing platforms, and built-in security.

(continued)

Table 1-1. (continued)

Java applets	An applet is a Java application that works within a Web browser. For example, a scrolling news ticker can be Java-powered. Applets can be interactive, graphic and connected to back-end databases. No browser plug-ins are needed for Java applets.
Java servlet	A servlet is a Java applet that works on a server. Java works on both the client and server side of a network.
Java applications	A Java application is a stand-alone Java program that works on a PC, server, mainframe, and/or device. For example, the Corel Office for Java is a stand-alone Java application.
JavaBeans	JavaBeans is a tool for developers to facilitate the creation of Java applets and applications. JavaBeans is a developer tool that simplifies the creation and assembly of Java components, called Beans. The assembled components form Java applets or applications, as well as connections to non-Java applications.
JavaScript	JavaScript is a tool for nonprogrammers to script Java applets into Web pages. It is a scripting language developed by Netscape and Sun Microsystems.

(continued)

Table 1-1. (continued)

Java computing platform	Java is more than a computing language. It underlies smart cards, consumer electronic devices, and a new type of network computer. It is used in PCs, workstations, servers and mainframes, and, from another perspective, it is used in front-end interfaces, middleware and back-end databases. It is a platform for network computing in the broadest sense.

RELIGIOUS WARS

I was cautioned, as I moved from pure content creation to the new mix of content powered by information technology, that people feel strongly about their computer platforms and languages. They are passionate, even religious about these things. There is warfare. There are heretics and orthodox and MIS departments split into camps. Make a mistake and your hard drive will be tied to a SCSI and zapped. Given the pace of development, the uncertainty of change, and the investment risk, this is not surprising. Users are demanding more and becoming more knowledgeable. Things are changing very quickly.

It is not just passion within an organization. There are competing technologies and views in the industry. There are competing actions. Putting software like an office suite on a network is much different than shrink-wrapping a CD. Delivering and updating software on-line has major implications for how networks are managed and how software is priced. Network computer or PC, or both? Thin client or fat client? Pay-per-use? Pay-per-applet?

As business people, we can focus on the job at hand and leave the standards to the standard bodies and the pure Java to Sun. The language and support for Java have matured very quickly. It is clear that the Java computing platform offers the best solution to the new challenge of conducting business on a network. Our focus: Is Java suited for our particular application? Has someone else done something like it? How can we get it done?

Metcalf's law points out that the value of a network increases exponentially with the number of users connected to a network. That value curve holds and conceivably is accelerated, for the computer language designed for a network, Java. Java is the Shakespeare of computer languages, with its ability to work legacy tragedies and applet comedies and everything in-between. It is the Jazz of computer languages, allowing programmers to put various pieces of reusable code in new compositions. It is more of a Jeffersonian than Hamiltonian language—open to the unwashed masses, reducing barriers to entry for start-ups, accelerating market advantages to industry leaders. Laws and metaphors aside, Java is an impressive business tool. It is the language of the network; businesses increasingly compete on the network; Java has utility and benefits for business today, as the following cases show.

END NOTES

1 George Gilder, "The Coming Software Shift," *Forbes ASAP,* August, 1995.

CHAPTER 2

MARIMBA: BUILDING THE NEW CUSTOMER CHANNEL

Kim Polese, CEO, Marimba

There is a new way of working with customers on the Internet: personal broadcast networks, or PBNs. Marimba, a start-up software company, has created PBN tools that enable businesses to set up their own customer networks. These networks can be used to attract customers with multimedia events and programming. They can provide up-to-date, self-installing software and data to customers—and get feedback and preferences from customers in return. Marimba's Java-based business tools are deployed in hundreds of organizations. Its "Tuners" have been downloaded onto tens of thousands of PCs. Alliances with companies like Netscape, IBM, Oracle, Intel, Sun, Lotus, Apple, Macromedia and Corel are extending the reach of Marimba technology and may make it the de facto *standard for distribution of software and content over networks. Using Java as its initial platform accelerated Marimba's time to market and enabled it to provide immediate updating, security, efficiency, scalability and multimedia advantages to PBNs.*

Marimba is a start-up software company founded by four members of Sun Microsystems' original Java development team: Kim Polese (CEO), Arthur van Hoff (CTO), Jonathan

Payne (senior engineer), and Sami Shaio (senior engineer). The company publicly launched in May 1996 and announced its first products, Castanet and Bongo in October 1996. Marimba was one of the first beneficiaries of the $100 million Java Fund, backed by the venture capital firm Kleiner, Perkins, Caufield and Byers.

One truism about a start-up: it is risky to raise the ire of all the five-hundred-pound gorillas on the West Coast. Start-up ideas are themselves risky; chances are, with more than sixty million individuals networked worldwide, that a great idea has its precedents, replicators, and echoes.

But Marimba is the only company initially using Java as its primary technology platform for personal broadcast and software distribution networks. Its products complement those of Netscape, Microsoft and Pointcast, and do different things. What sets Marimba apart from other client/server distribution approaches is the nonproprietary, open, secure, network-centric attributes of Java—and a head start. We have solved the problem of distributing and maintaining software and data over the Internet and over intranets. Marimba is not a content provider; it provides tools to content providers.

Marimba's Castanet today delivers Java applications and content over networks, but in the future will also deliver other kinds of software and content,—anything, really, that can be digitized. Although Marimba's initial focus is on channels coded in Java, Marimba's technology is not language-based; it is file-based. You can think of a channel as a folder of files that is replicated from a central broadcast point (a Transmitter) to a PC (specifically a "Tuner" on the PC).

Marimba has alliances with leading Internet technology vendors, corporate customers, publishers, media companies, consulting firms and international software distributors. This is a conscious strategy to increase the reach and business utility of Marimba technology. Tool companies like Borland, Symantec, Macromedia, Lotus, RandomNoise and FutureTense are incorporating Marimba technology in their developer tools, which makes it easier for businesses to create and deploy PBNs for their customers. Businesses have the freedom to choose the tools that work best for them and to publish their creations as Castanet channels with the click of a button.

PBNs based on Marimba technology enable businesses to do new and different things. Companies are using Castanet to strengthen customer relationships, deliver new products and services, and lower operating costs. Lehman Brothers is using Castanet to explore new ways of delivering financial information and services to its customers. Bellcore is improving its own internal systems as well as its customers' experiences using Castanet. Bentana Technologies, Inc., an Aetna-funded company, is using Castanet for its electronic commerce platform.

Business productivity tools are also being distributed and maintained with Castanet. Corel Corporation is using Marimba's Castanet to distribute its new Corel Office for Java. Successive beta versions of this software are updated on the fly through a running channel on a user's PC. This is an extremely efficient way to get the latest software updates automatically to thousands of Corel program users. Customers simply double-click on the icon and they always get the latest version of the application. Similarly, Trilogy Development Group, an innovative vendor of software for front-office re-engineering, makes updates to its Selling Chain software suite over a Castanet channel. This method of software distribution and updating has implications both for the software industry and for the management and version-control of software within a business.

Castanet channels are also used to deliver news and information. EntertainNet, a Hollywood-based company, is using a Castanet channel to deliver Internet programming that users can watch when convenient, and that can be used to provide viewer feedback. Excite has created a channel of channels, which previews channels for users. CBS SportsLine has created a sports channel with instant updating of scores, personalized for the user. BulletProof is using Castanet to carry WallStreet Web, a channel that lets individuals track, graph and analyze their stock performance. Intel, in partnership with Marimba, Macromedia and PBS, has created an "infinite CD" for PBS. This leverages the storage capability of CDs with Castanet's ability to continually update content from a PBS channel.

HotWired, @Home, the Children's Television Workshop, MGM Interactive, CMP, CNNfn, Corel Systems, IBM, Sony, and Ericsson are some of the other companies and institutions that have implemented or evaluated a Marimba PBN, or channel. In Marimba's "channel of the week" we have featured a radio station (streaming audio without plug-ins), business productivity tools, and various games and Java resource centers. Netscape recently announced it will integrate the Castanet Tuner into its set of technologies called Netcaster.

Marimba's Castanet has proven valuable as an efficient, effective way to directly distribute software and information. It has implications for all kinds of businesses in how they work with their customers and how they administer their information technology.

THE NEW CUSTOMER CHANNEL

Web technologies have changed the way we communicate and are having a fundamental impact on the way businesses interact with their customers, suppliers, and with their own employees. The simplicity of the point and click interaction, the ubiquity of Web information, and rapid advances in searching and filtering tools all contribute to the rapid growth and connectivity of a wired world.

A business channel strengthens that connectivity. It strengthens the connection between a business and its customer. It personalizes that connection. It creates a two-way path along which information and applications flow. A customer does not have to remember to go and get information he or she needs; it comes to him or her automatically. Similarly, software can be updated automatically. Feedback on how information is used can be beamed back to the channel provider and used to personalize the channel each subscriber gets.

Consider a sports channel delivering information on a regular basis to customers around the world. Any one customer would turn on his or her channel and see the latest scores, interviews, and programs. While he or she is watching the channel, the latest updates are sent in the background. Channel use is tracked and programming altered based on that feedback. When disconnected from the network, a customer would have the last updated program, which could be viewed if desired.

Assume you have a Castanet Tuner installed on your PC and a new feature is built into the Tuner. The tuner itself is a Castanet

Channel so the update is transmitted automatically and transparently to your computer. The Tuner is updated the next time you are connected to the Internet.

This is different from the "pull" model of HTML browsing. Customers do not have to go out and find and download the information. This is also different than the "push" broadcast tools that continuously stream generic news and other information to a client's desk top. A more apt description of Castanet PBNs is "smart application management." Software and data is delivered and maintained in a highly efficient manner. Customers select the channel and the frequency of updating.

Castanet networks are particularly useful for business. They conserve bandwidth, work across multiple platforms, reside inside or outside a customer's browser, and can be used for internal and external business applications.

There are benefits on both sides of the transmission. Customers have instant access to channels, and they "click and play." The channels are tightly integrated with the desktop and work like desktop applications - and they can work whether or not the customer is connected to the network. (Updates, of course, require connection). Large, media-rich applications are possible, thanks to the approach. The application is downloaded once, and then only the files that need updating are downloaded later; this is called differential updating. There are automatic, transparent-to-the-customer updates of content and coding. The customer also may have a new experience every day, every hour or every ten minute's on a business's channel, which is an inducement for a customer to return.

On the server side there is a dramatically reduced server load since the application is only downloaded once to each customer. Detailed usage monitoring is possible and server-side plug-ins extend the capability of channels to personalize content. Automatic distribution of software and data is possible, which significantly cuts distribution costs and simplifies version control.

©1997 Marimba, Inc. Used with permission. All rights reserved.

Figure 2-1. Schematic of a Castanet a network. A Transmitter at a company sends a channel of information to Tuners inside or outside the company. Tuners on PCs would be able to tune to different channels, receive the information or software, and send back feedback on usage, needs, or results.

WHY CHANNEL?

Creating a customer channel is a new way for businesses to compete. Channels can attract users and win customers. They can cut development costs and cut network administration costs.

Attracting users is a challenge in the increasingly cluttered marketspace. Content on the Web is exponentially increasing. Hosts are exponentially increasing. Competitors are chasing each other on-line. Businesses can attract users by providing personalized, content-rich channels to existing customers and potential customers. They have the tools to create powerful on-line marketing events and education programs that are not bandwidth-challenged. All of a customer's electronic interactions with a business can be consolidated, offering time savings and convenience to the customer. Having a direct, two-way channel on each customer's desktop is a means of strengthening and defending a brand.

The channel idea also serves the business need of cutting development costs. For coding new software, the two-way channel offers a means of adding or deleting features for software based on customer use. Bugs can be fixed instantly, and software can be seen as streaming like content. This reduces the time to market, and reduces development costs. The software example is most clear, but this development cost reduction can be envisioned for other businesses as well, such as publishing firms amending and revising their streaming content, or drug companies screening new drug compounds.

Channels have a very practical application within an enterprise. They can simplify network administration by automating software distribution and eliminating tracking of software versions. With a Marimba network, applications can be delivered independent of the platform, a major advantage in a heterogeneous, distributed organization. There are also some technical features of Marimba channels that reduce and eliminate bottlenecks on networks, both inside and outside an organization. The Marimba approach channels large, interactive Java applications, opening the way for robust Java applications (as opposed to applets) to thrive. You get the rich, multimedia content of CDs without the copying and distribution problems. And you get the ability to constantly update information and applications.

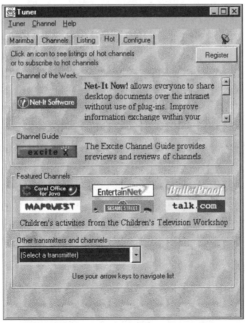

Figure 2-2. The Tuner on a customer's PC has a hot list
of channels that the customer could subscribe to. Multiple channels
can be run simultaneously.

CASTANET SYSTEM

There are three basic components to a Castanet system: Channels, Tuners, and Transmitters. Channels are programs and data/content files stored and updated on servers and mirrored and executed on the user's PC. Transmitters transmit these programs and files through the Internet or an intranet network to Tuners installed on user's PC. Tuners and Transmitters work together to automatically keep the channel files on the user's PC consistent with channel updates made on the Transmitter server.

The Castanet system also includes two other components of interest to business: Repeaters which make scaling-up to thousands and millions of users cost-effective and easy, and Proxies which reduce channel traffic across a corporate firewall.

The television broadcast metaphor is useful. Content is transmitted from a central location. Customers tune-in to channels. To carry it further, the Castanet system puts an automatic, pre-programmed VCR and an automatic Neilson family evaluation box on every customer's desktop.

You can do a lot with a channel. You can provide news to your customers that is updated weekly, daily, hourly, or as often as every minute. You can release software products in auto-installing increments, starting with a rudimentary beta and following up with incremental improvements and bug fixes. You can deliver product training with virtual laboratories, multimedia presentations, and interactive tests. You can connect a customer with his or her order status, financial history, salesperson contacts, and fellow-customer community. You can create on-line special events with the multimedia impact of CD-ROMs over a skinny 28.8 modem bandwidth.

A channel works like a traditional application on a user's desktop. Since the channel software is mirrored, rather than cached, on the user's disk, it operates just like a conventional application. It is as fast and as reliable. The channel works whether or not the user is connected to the network at any given time. Try that with your television setChannels are really a new class of software for doing new kinds of things with the Internet and intranets. Marimba's differential updating of channels is unique. For example, assume you have 40 MB channel and a small piece of a 1 MB image file is changed. Just that small piece is updated. This simplifies and speeds up the updating process and reduces network traffic.

Users obtain channels by subscribing to them with a browser or a Tuner. They go to the Gamelan directory, for example, which is a leading Java applet, application and channel resource on the Web. They click on a channel of interest, and follow the subscription instructions. Users start and interact with channels like they do applications on their desktop. A channel can be launched from the desktop by double-clicking right on the channel symbol or name put right on their desktop, or from a menu or Tuner.

A channel also has the ability to store and communicate feedback data, such as user preferences and patterns of usage.

BEAM ME UP

A company would specify the updating schedule for each channel: one channel might direct the Tuner to check for updates once a month, another might schedule updates every ten minutes. Independent of any programmed schedule, a user can direct the Tuner to update a channel at any time, or to cancel a channel.

The updating process can take place while a channel is "on" or "off." If the channel is off, the Tuner installs the new files in the right channel directory, and they are available the next time the channel is tuned on. If the channel is "on," the updating can take place right away, which might be useful for displaying news stories as they arrive, or it can be deferred until after the channel quits. Alternatively, a notification of an update can be sent immediately, and the client or customer can decide when to update.

Consider a company with a catalog with several thousand products that is routinely updated. If a new product or product application is added to the database, the catalog channel would be updated. If a client or customer is looking at the catalog at that particular moment a notice can be sent: "New product just added to the database. Restart?" Alternatively the transmitting company can just specify that the update will wait for restarting or the channel is updated immediately.

A Tuner not only receives, updates and cancels channels, it is a channel. To get the latest Tuner improvements, a button on the

Tuner triggers the Tuner to update itself. The Tuner, written in Java, is small, making it applicable for a network computer and even, conceivably, devices such as personal digital assistants and cellular phones.

Transmitters, on the other hand, reside within a company or within an Internet service provider or other third-party. They can operate as stand-alone servers, or can be extensions to HTTP servers. Multiple channels can reside on one Transmitter, and one channel can be distributed by multiple Transmitters. The Transmitters do more than simply broadcast a business channel. They transmit and receive data and preferences. Server-side plug-ins act on the transmitted preferences. For example, a channel can maintain a file of the user's language. For a Japanese customer, the channel would send that preference to the Transmitter, and the Transmitter plug-in would return Japanese language materials. Another example: the Transmitter plug-in could be used to record the impressions or click- throughs of banner advertising.

Interestingly enough, impressions and preferences can be recorded whether or not a user is on-line. Assume a user opens up his or her channel on a plane trip across the country. The next time the user is on-line the banner advertising impressions and preference logs are uploaded to the subscribed channels.

The creative use of channels, Transmitters, and Tuners enables effective one-to-one marketing. New ways of interacting with and delivering content to customers are possible.

There are two other key components of a Castanet network: Repeaters and Proxies. Repeaters periodically poll Transmitters for updates and in turn serve channels to Tuners Repeaters are used to simplify scale-up, to provide redundancy and robustness to a PBN, and to geographically distribute content. They make content available locally so that all requests to not have to be served by the main Transmitter; this reduces network traffic loads and bandwidth requirements. Repeaters are essentially self-updating Transmitters that can be sited wherever the Internet reaches. One Transmitter can serve hundreds of repeaters, offering a high scale-up potential. The scale-up aspect is important for a growing business; channels can serve hundreds, thousands, even millions of users. Repeaters facilitate the geographic distribution of data and information, and require no administrative work. They are transparent both to the business channel creator and the customer.

The redundancy aspect is helpful. Say one repeater goes down; this does not impact the delivery of information or data since the data or information can be re-routed.

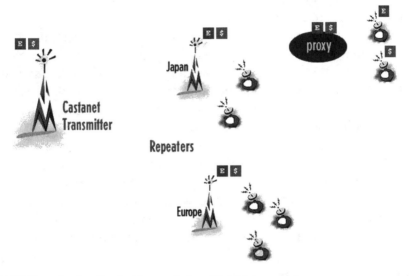

©1997 Marimba, Inc. Used with permission. All rights reserved.

Figure 2-3. Castanet Repeaters simplify the scale-up and distribution of channels, and reduce the barriers to entry for small and medium-sized businesses. Castanet proxies protect corporate security and minimize channel traffic.

Castanet proxies run on corporate firewall machines, much like HTTP proxies used for Web sites. Castanet proxies are designed to minimize the load on corporate firewall machines and maximize security. For example, assume there are 300 subscribers inside a research institute to a protein database channel. Assume the protein database channel automatically provides a summary of all the new additions to major protein databases around the world. With the Castanet proxy, the updates to the protein channel are cached outside the firewall and passed through once rather than 300 times. This reduces the load on a firewall and is a more secure approach.

DELIVERING SOFTWARE APPLICATIONS AND UPDATES: TRILOGY

Distributing software and software updates over the Internet and over intranets accelerates and lowers the costs of deployment. Trilogy, an Austin, Texas, software company, uses Marimba's Castanet and Bongo products to achieve these benefits, both for themselves and their end customers.

Trilogy has innovated in the area of front-office re-engineering. The company has created software products that automate the front-end of a business and build an automated sales process from initial customer contact and product introduction to billing transactions and sale completion. Their enterprise-wide software is called "Selling Chain™" Chrysler Corporation, for example, uses Selling Chain to allow car buyers at 6,000 dealer kiosks to choose standard and nonstandard options for a particular car. The system reaches into the back-office database to get the cost of any custom configurations—and to see if the configurations are even possible. Trilogy's customers include a who's who of high technology and innovative consumer business companies including Sequent Computer Systems, Hitachi, Data General, Boeing, Silicon Graphics, the Custom Foot, and hundreds of others.

Selling Chain's Internet application suite, SC Web™, was written entirely in Java. In terms of development time and cost, the Java version achieved savings of 60 to 70 percent compared to the prior C++ version of Selling Chain. Using Castanet and Bongo products, Trilogy expects the same if not more savings in deployment costs. However, the key payoff for distribution is not for Trilogy distributing Selling Chain applications to their customers, but for their customers' distribution of customized Selling Chain solutions to *their* customers. Castanet and Bongo products become part of the selling chain; they make it move faster and simpler.

The Trilogy Channel delivers Selling Chain software and updates to Trilogy customers. All distribution and updating is transparent, that is, the software and software updates self-install in the background without any work on the part of the user. The distribution and updating is also bandwidth-conservative; differential updating means that only new or changed files are replaced. Even the customer's Tuner gets updated with a single click.

To enable customers to customize Selling Chain applications, Trilogy developed Selling Chain component libraries for Bongo. This allows Trilogy users to easily and quickly customize the end-user interface for Selling Chain applications to suit their own individual business needs. The same application can be deployed on a desktop computer, on the Web, or on a network computer, and can be distributed and updated via a local area network (LAN), wide area network (WAN), or Internet network.

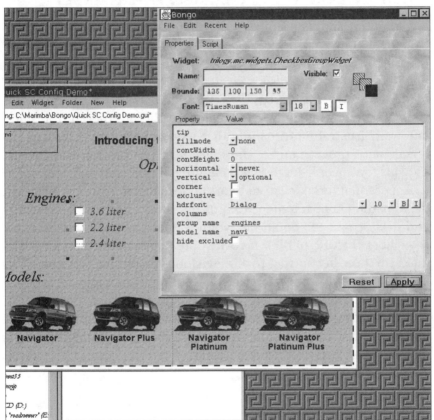

Figure 2-4. Changing the end-user graphical interface on a Selling Chain application is simple with the Bongo development tool—Java programming without being a Java programmer.

This software distribution model can be used for all types of software and is relevant to both intranet and Internet applications. Soft-

ware can be electronically shrink-wrapped by a software manufacturer and distributed over the Internet. This reduces the cost of
physical copying, packaging, and distribution, and it also simplifies
the addition of new features and upgrades. Across a WAN or LAN, a
network administrator can update users to a new browser or software application quickly and easily.

A NEW ENTERTAINMENT CHANNEL: ENTERTAINNET

EntertainNet, Inc., is a Hollywood-based start-up with seed funding
from idealab! that produces and distributes entertainment on the
Internet. Browser technology has its limitations for this type of application. In its market research, EntertainNet found that consumers had trouble finding Web sites and then returning to the
sites. There are bottleneck problems on the Internet and a "click
and wait" frustration threshold that would limit the success of entertainment programming. There are also problems with browser
plug-ins that people have to go out and get themselves.

A personal broadcast network approach was appealing. By
downloading entertainment to a user's hard drive, the bandwidth
and delay problems could be avoided. Viewers would not have to
remember the URL of their favorite entertainment page; they could
just turn it on. In contrast to a television-type broadcast network, a
PBN would enable EntertainNet to send programming it knew the
viewer wanted.

EntertainNet selected Marimba technology to implement its PBN
because it provided three key features EntertainNet saw as essential for a post-Web broadcast network.

CONTENT STORAGE AND DISTRIBUTION

Unlike television or the Web, Marimba's Castanet is a broadcast
mechanism much like voice mail or e-mail. With television, you
have to sit in front of your set while a show is being broadcast. With
Castanet, the show is copied onto your hard drive. This allows you
to watch the show when you want, instead of when the broadcaster
wants you to. Having the entire show stored on your computer also
means that, unlike Web browsing, you do not wait between mouse

clicks. In a way, Castanet technology trades expensive bandwidth for inexpensive disk space so the user perceives high effective throughput. Castanet's scalability also allows EntertainNet to easily expand its content distribution capacity to meet the demands of a growing audience. Castanet's Transmitters have the ability to transmit content to repeaters as well as Tuners. Repeaters can transmit content to Tuners or other repeaters. As its audience grows, EntertainNet simply adds more repeaters, allowing EntertainNet to comfortably supply content to several million viewers across the Internet.

VERSION CONTROL

Providing users with both up-to-date information and serialized stories is very important to EntertainNet's vision of entertainment distribution. Castanet lets EntertainNet accomplish both of these goals. Through Marimba's differential updating technology, EntertainNet continuously provides viewers with the latest information while consuming the smallest amount of bandwidth possible. EntertainNet also delivers serialized content by using the plug-in feature of Castanet servers. Plug-ins allow EntertainNet to modify the information sent to an individual based on that individual's channel history. By dynamically modifying what is sent to the viewer, one day's broadcast of a show can deliver different episodes of the same series to each user subscribing to that channel. (Worth reiterating: These plug-ins are "server plug-ins" that sit on the broadcaster's end of the transmission instead of the viewer's end.)

VIEWER FEEDBACK AND CONTENT FILTERING

EntertainNet believes that users should be allowed to shape and influence content by providing feedback about their viewing experience. Castanet has a back channel which allows Tuners to transmit viewer feedback to Transmitters. When a Tuner connects to a Transmitter to download a show, it also uploads information. This information is then transferred to EntertainNet's customized plug-ins, which analyze the feedback and respond by changing the type of information sent in the next broadcast. This allows EntertainNet to customize and personalize the content delivered to its audience so that each subscriber watches exactly what he or she wants to see. There can be customization even within a channel: adults seeing one version of a program and children another, for example.

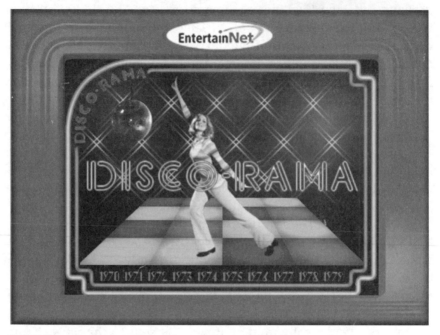

@1997, EntertainNet, Inc. Used with permission. All rights reserved.

Figure 2-5. Discorama is a 1970s retrospective that first appeared on the EntertainNet channel in December 1996. Other programs are expected to premier on EntertainNet throughout 1997.

DISCORAMA

In December 1996, EntertainNet premiered *Discorama,* a 1970s retrospective, on its network. Discorama is written by Alan Glueckman, a 20-year Hollywood veteran with TV and film credits as well as CD-ROM and Web credits. It stars Holly Martin Riddle as

Marmalade, a vivacious hostess who guides the viewer through all the music, film, sports, fashion and culture of the '70s that you wanted to forget.

The same production and distribution technologies used by EntertainNet could be used to produce content for corporate intranets. Product training, competitive analysis, and staff development programs could be created with daily or weekly updates to an entire company using a network similar to EntertainNet. For companies with an existing LAN or WAN, the cost of distributing customized (and entertaining) business information would be fairly small. The same system could provide daily updates to employees without desktop PCs through PC kiosks.

CREATING CHANNEL COMMUNITIES: EXCITE, INC.

One of the earliest adopters of Marimba technology was Excite, Inc., which created an Excite Channel Guide. This channel offers descriptions, reviews, and multimedia previews of all publicly available channels; users can browse, search through a directory, or use Excite's search engine to find a channel of interest. For the end user, this is a valuable service, particularly with the expected exponential growth in channels. Users gets a robust preview before they take the time to download a channel.

This is valuable to the channel provider as well: the video and audio, Java-animated preview of their site is an accurate representation of the channel's content, which helps ensure the right audience.

The Excite Channel Guide demonstrates the multimedia power possible with a Castanet system. The voice welcoming you and guiding you through the channel is that of Barbara Feldon, Agent 99 in the series *Get Smart*. The animated, interactive previews are created in Java with Dimension X's Liquid Motion.

As of March 9, 1997 there were 25 channels in the Excite Channel Guide. The infrastructure to handle this initial launch included two Castanet Transmitters. As traffic builds, infrastructure is quick and easy to add. In terms of development, it took a team of six programmers and designers seven weeks to design, produce, and broadcast a very media-rich, interactive channel. The Excite Channel Guide is currently updated once a day, a schedule that will be accelerated as the number of channels grows.

Other businesses might use this "channel of channels" approach. It is a good model for creating a community of channels that have the same targeted audience and the next evolutionary step of the industry-specific or niche-specific jumping-off point.

©1997, Excite, Inc. Used with permission. All rights reserved.

Figure 2-6. Excite, Inc., has created a "channel of channels," a great example of the multimedia, interactive content possible with a Castanet system. It also is a useful resource for keeping up with the rapid growth of channels over the coming months.

DELIVERING CONTINUOUS NEWS: CBS SPORTSLINE

SportsLine USA has created a channel demonstrating the effective use of Castanet technology for news updates. CBS SportsLine's new Instant ScoreCenter provides automatic instant updates on sports scores for virtually every major sports league and team, both the college and professional ranks. This includes scores, statistics and schedules from NFL, NBA, Major League Baseball, NHL, NCAA basketball and football, and many minor league sports.

Along with the cost-effective nature of the technology, a real benefit was the rapid deployment of an existing applet that allowed CBS SportsLine to create the Instant ScoreCenter quickly and easily. A Castanet Transmitter was the only infrastructure CBS SportsLine needed to create this unique channel.

CBS SportsLine's Instant ScoreCenter also allows customization and user control over the content. The user can not only pick the

games and leagues to follow, but the scores come in instantaneously without a browser, saving time and memory. The Score-
Center also gives the user the ability to view up-to-the-minute team
schedules, scores and statistics all on the desktop.

©1997 CBS Sportsline. Used with permission. All rights reserved.

*Figure 2-7. A customizable score center posts the latest sports scores
throughout the United States. Turn the channel on and see the latest
scores, as well as archived statistics and schedules.*

The SportsLine model is applicable to other news events, as well
as to corporate data and information on a business's intranet.

MARIMBA FOR BUSINESS

There are things you can do with your customers using personal
broadcast networks that were previously difficult or impossible.
You can achieve one-to-one marketing with personalized news and
connectivity to selected corporate databases. You can deliver rich,

multimedia events to communities of customers in a cost-effective, bandwidth-sensitive way. You can send software over the network, update software over the network, and get feedback on usage of selected software features. There are any number of other applications, specific to a specific business and its customer base.

The cases cited above demonstrate some of the capabilities of this "new customer channel." Channels exist for a number of case studies in this book. The Corel Office for Java is a great example of the use of a channel to deliver commonly used software quickly and easily, update that software, and accelerate the time to market. HotWired has talk.com, a channel for community discussion. @Home has prototyped use of Castanet technology for delivering headlines and news tickers to its cable modem network users. There are hundreds of channels in development or operation.

In building a channel to customers, there are some philosophical, practical and cost considerations. A fundamental question: make or buy? Build your own network or become a subset of another network? Building your own network requires an infrastructure of hardware and software and people. It requires content providers. It requires a strategic overview of all of your electronic connection points and potential electronic connection points to customers. Being a subset of another network eliminates some of the infrastructure and human resource requirements. The content is still needed, however, as well as the strategic overview.

Castanet and Bongo are infrastructure tools, and are being used within corporations as well as by Internet service providers and third-party channelers. There are control and customization and integration advantages in becoming your own personal broadcaster that have to be weighed against the cost and organizational readiness for setting up your own network. A rule of thumb: if you run your own Web site you have the skills and infrastructure fundamentals needed to run your own personal broadcast network. Users have found that managing a channel is easier than managing a web site. Starting to develop the expertise and feedback now, ahead of your competition, would be advantageous.

Another fundamental question: open or proprietary network? Proprietary networks require a particular set of tools, computer platforms and processes. Marimba's bias is for open personal broadcast networks, personal broadcast networks you can set up on your own and feed to any customer on any platform. You are not locked in to any one language or any one way of producing content. The open approach is faster to implement, accessible to more customers, and more cost-effective in the long run and short run.

There are a number of practical considerations in setting up a personal broadcast network with customers and/or with employees.

Security. PBNs have to protect corporate assets and sustain the firewall. Castanet proxies are used to minimize traffic across the firewall enhancing security.

On the client side, Castanet channels store data in a special directory on the client disk. The directory approach ensures that versions of news or software do not get mixed up. This directory or file space is called a sandbox separate from the other areas on the user's hard drive. It cannot access the rest of your Mac system or Windows folder, or the root access in your UNIX box.

Company Network Utilization. Talk about rich, 3-D, video and audio content constantly streaming over your LAN or WAN, and chances are your network communications people will want to string up your information-hungry executives with old Ethernet. There have been corporate bans on some push communication tools. Marimba's approach husbands bandwidth, and is the least network demanding of any Personal Broadcast Network streaming news or applications. A Marimba network also enables your network administrators to more easily update and deliver new software over the network, a major cost-saving and headache reducing application when they have to do this for hundreds or thousands of client applications.

Customer Network Utilization. Your company's network is one you can control and influence; your customer's network is one you cannot control. By minimizing the bandwidth requirements, and by providing secure content, you maximize your customer's company network and make it easier for your customer to interact with your channel. PBNs should also reduce traffic on the Internet as a whole since they will be delivering and channeling content to subscribers who are not out looking for it individually and redundantly. The Castanet repeater and proxy model better ensures the scalability and delivery of the right information to the right person than current

Web technologies.

Database Connectivity. Delivering free news or entertainment over a PBN may not require database connectivity; paying for that content would. A robust PBN should have some means of easily connecting to a corporate financial database, applications knowledge base, or groupware system. Marimba's PBN approach has database connectivity.

Nomadic Workers. Can your salespeople connect efficiently to your intranet PBN? The differential updating process offers advantages. Before a trip, connect to the net and update your channels, including your expense reporter channel . Disconnect and depart. Enter expenses as you accrue them; the expense reporter can save them on disk. Reconnect again when you return, and the expense reporter transfers the stored expense items to the corporate database. If you have a network connection on the road, update your product price list channel, or the order entry channel at any time.

Channeling Tools. Easy-to-use tools and systems are needed to create content and update content for a channel. Bongo was created as a tool to simplify building channel content for Marimba's Castanet. Macromedia's Shockwave also can be used to create channel content, as well as Java tools, like Symantec's Visual Cafe, Liquid Motion, FutureTense, and Java Workshop. In a world of streaming content, you need simple and smart ways to deliver that content.

Scaling Up. How can you efficiently get your PBN delivered to hundreds, thousands, hundreds of thousands, or millions of people? How many servers? At what cost? How easy is it for customers to get and set up the application they need to view the PBN? The repeater approach taken by Marimba is one that makes it relatively easy to scale up, and relatively easy to update and have that update quickly propagated. Channel content is available locally, increasing access speed and reducing network traffic. Instead of one large computer distributing data a network of repeaters provides support and redundancy.

By designing a PBN with local and remote repeaters, channel providers can quickly scale up their capacity, provide fast response worldwide, and update once and have the update cascade throughout the system.

Security, network utilization, database connectivity, channel content tools, scaling-up - all of these are important issues in designing and implementing a PBN for a business.

Creating a Marimba Personal Broadcast Network makes implicit sense in terms of generating revenue and cutting costs. Getting a continuous stream of useful information and interaction to customers and potential customers is a means of generating revenue. Personalizing that stream is revenue enhancing. Costs can be saved in development time, in market research, in Internet time (assuming the push delivery of valued, timely information as opposed to pulling that information). Network administration costs can be significantly reduced by updating software over a network.

There are infrastructure and development costs associated with setting up a PBN as well as hardware, software and human resource considerations

©1996 Netscape Communications Corporation. Used with permission. All rights reserved. This image may not reprinted or copied without the express written permission of Netscape.

Figure 2-8. Castanet technology is being integrated with the recently announced Netscape Netcaster component of the Netscape Communicator. This will make it easier for millions of Netscape Web client users to subscribe to Castanet software and content channels.

Content providers will be challenged; this is a new media. The dead web of text and marketing brochures will be finally eclipsed; the dynamic web of personalization, interaction, rich multimedia, continuous updates, and continually fresh content will just be beginning. In this new environment. digital marketing skills are as critical as the technical tools that systems such as Castanet provide. A business applying both can realize a competitive advantage.

MARIMBA'S FUTURE

In eleven months, Marimba has incorporated, coded, beta tested and introduced a new set of business tools offering significant advantages for one-to-one marketing, event marketing, software development, and network administration. Innovative technology is important; the speed of its diffusion and utilization is also important in a market moving at Web speed. Partnerships, alliances, and one-to-one relationships with its customers, along with its unique technology, are ways in which Marimba will succeed. Marimba has alliances with leading Internet technology vendors such as IBM, Oracle and Netscape. Its technology is being incorporated in developer tools from companies like Borland and Symantec. A Certified Consultants program with organizations such as Poppe Tyson and CKS helps support the corporate content side of PBNs.

The integration of Castanet technology in Netscape's recently announced Netscape Netcaster component of the Netscape Communicator is an important step for Marimba. It makes Castanet software and content channels available to the fifty million or so users of Netscape browsers; it puts software distribution functionality within the Netscape browser, simplifying network life for the 80 percent of Fortune 500 companies that have Netscape-powered intranets. It will allow intranet managers to more easily deploy software through their company. It will also reduce version-control problems and reduce network traffic because of Castanet's highly efficient use of bandwidth.

Bundling the Castanet Tuners with the Apple MacOS Runtime for Java is also beneficial; it makes the technology more accessible to a key multimedia and Web-savvy group of people.

For businesses, Marimba technology offers tools for effective one-to-one marketing. Personalized news networks can run through Marimba; software upgrades can flow; preferences and click-throughs can be tracked. Tuners can sit in browsers, and browsers can flow through Tuners.

That is not to say that competition will fade away. PBNs are the next big thing. Marimba does have a Java head start, both with its expertise with Java and with the first release of its Castanet system. Java has enabled Marimba to deliver PBN tools that are secure, scalable, cross platform, and robust. It has enabled Marimba to develop its products quickly, due, in part, to the network-centric design of this language, along with the expertise of its coders.

The benefits are reciprocal. Marimba boosts Java's utility; it eliminates the bandwidth problem for large Java applications; it fulfills the promise of Java for transparent software delivery.

Networks will never be the same.

CHAPTER 3

REUTERS: USING JAVA IN THE TRADING ROOM

*Dave Weller, Technology Manager and
Glenn Wasserman, Reuters Ltd.*

Reuters is a multinational information firm. It provides the financial markets with news, real-time prices, and analytical and trading products. It provides publishers, broadcasters, and on-line services with multimedia news. And it provides briefing products for industry specialists and corporate executives. For the financial markets, the products Reuters delivers have high security, volume, and speed requirements. The new Reuters Web—an extranet—is targeted at financial markets. Several applications within the Reuters Web have been developed with Java. During development, there were early start-up issues with the successive beta versions of Java, and there were issues with browser and Java virtual machine incompatibilities. Major advantages were realized, however, in development and deployment time and additional Java applications are being developed for the Reuters Web. For Reuters, Java has led to a new model of application development and deployment, with the overall effect of significantly reducing time to market.

Reuters is a leading international news and financial information services company. Our customers watch news and prices on more than 362,000 terminals in 161 countries. In this context, a terminal typically represents a person who uses financial information either as part of a trading function or in related activities such as settlement or research.

In 1996 Reuters had a total revenue of £2.9 billion with an operating profit of £641 million. We are currently ranked in the top 20 companies of the Financial Times Stock Exchange (FTSE) by market capitalization.

We characterize our product offering into information, transaction, and media products, all of which are network and information technology-intensive.

Reuters information products, the most recent being the new 3000 range of trading room information management systems, consolidate real-time data from 267 different exchanges and markets and 4,800 contributors. This data is normalized and then broadcast to the 362,000 screens that Reuters supports. A price change from any of these sources is delivered to a screen anywhere in the world often in less than one second. The data covers currencies, stocks, bonds, futures, options, and other financial instruments. In total, the network supporting these products carries more than two million different instruments, and at certain times of the day sees update rates exceeding 1500 per second. In a typical day the network handles over 25 million transactions and this number is steadily increasing.

The data is delivered either to Reuters Terminals, which include sophisticated Windows-based interfaces for the display and manipulation of the data, or to Reuters or other third-party information management systems via datafeeds. In addition to real-time prices and news, there is also a wealth of historic news, time series, and background data.

Reuters transaction products allow traders to deal, from their keyboards, in foreign exchange, futures, options, and securities markets. The Reuters Dealing 2000-1 information management system allows dealers to contact one another and negotiate and conclude trades in foreign exchange for spot currencies. Once a trade has been completed, a trade ticket is automatically produced. Each trader on Dealing 2000-1 can hold up to four simultaneous conversations with other traders.

Dealing 2000-2, launched in 1992, is an electronic matching system that goes one step further than Dealing 2000-1, allowing traders to see the best buy or sell price that is currently available for a currency pair. This automatic, anonymous service matches bid and offer orders using a central computer. The prices a trader sees depend upon the credit worthiness of both counterparts to the transaction. In 1995 Dealing 2000-2 achieved its latest target of 20,000 matches a day. The foreign exchange market as a whole handles $1.2 trillion a day and some of our clients say they trade up to 80 percent of their spot transactions on Reuters systems.

Reuters has an electronic brokerage system for equities that is run by its subsidiary Instinet.

Reuters media products reflect the journalistic tradition in Reuters harking back to its formation in 1850 by Baron Julius von Reuter. Most people recognize the name when it appears in the byline or dateline of newspaper articles. To provide the latest news, Reuters now has nearly two thousand journalists worldwide. Reuters TV is the largest television news agency in the world and supplies news to CNN, NBC, and the BBC, among others. Reuters TV news is seen by over two billion people a day.

In addition to more traditional media products, Reuters is also active in new media. On the Internet, Reuters provides news to six of the top ten sites as measured by advertising revenue. The company also has investments in Yahoo!, Infoseek, and a number of other Internet companies.

WHAT IS THE REUTERS WEB?

The products Reuters delivers are technically complex. Traditionally, in order to meet the stringent performance characteristics that our customers expect, the networks supporting these products have been developed using proprietary technology. The network infrastructure is highly optimized to deliver relatively small amounts of data at very high speed around the world. This is ideal for prices and textual data, but is completely unsuitable for richer forms of information, such as graphics pictures, audio, and video.

The Reuters Web, based on standard Internet technologies and protocols, is an extension of the Reuters global private network. It is an example of what has been termed an extranet and is used to deliver additional services to complement the existing range of information products. The desktop container for these services is a browser. The diagram below shows a stylized view of the Reuters Web. A session server is used to connect the Reuters side of the network to a network at a client site. This main function of the session server is to map IP (internet protocols) addresses between the two network domains. HPSN is the High Performance Shared Network forming the backbone of the Reuters Web, based on frame relay technology. HPSN is to the Reuters Web what the Internet is to the World Wide Web.

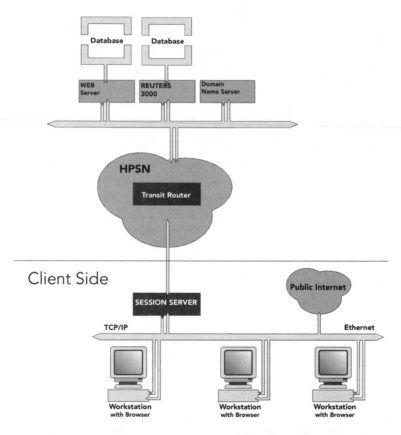

Figure 3-1. Reuters Web is a private extranet that offers more speed, security, and reliability than the public Internet, characteristics demanded by financial traders making thousands of nearly instantaneous transactions.

In North America about a third of all trading rooms already have direct access to the public Internet. This is bound to increase steadily, as will the growth outside of the States. So why would anyone want to also have access to Reuters Web? There are two main reasons: technical and commercial. The technical advantages of an extranet arise from the fact that it is managed as a whole network. This means that it is more secure, more reliable, and more trustworthy than the public Internet. From a commercial perspective, products delivered through Reuters Web can be interoperated seamlessly and quickly with those delivered through traditional methods.

WHY JAVA?

The sorts of services that are already available on the Reuters Web include scanned and converted copies of company annual reports, and market commentaries containing graphics and pictures, as well as localized information services. Additional services will take advantage of the fact that the Reuters Web offers traders in different locations the ability to communicate with each other in a secure way. Java applets embedded in browsers will provide facilities for electronic trading and targeted notifications of new content. The promise of Java, for a company like Reuters, is multidimensional. There are a number of reasons, both business oriented and technical, why we decided to review its worth.

Reuters was first alerted to Java primarily through our close relationship with Sun, particularly in the trading room side of our business. By far the most popular platform for our Triarch data distribution system is Sun. In 1995 Reuters represented over one hundred million dollars worth of business for Sun, not just through Reuter's use of Sun products but also through our clients' use. It was therefore not surprising that Reuters was invited to send some of our developers along to the official launch of Java in New York in September 1995.

At this stage the use of Internet technology was beginning to become widespread throughout Reuters, particularly by the technical and development groups. However, at that point there was not an obvious way in which something as sophisticated as a Reuters display application like the Reuters Terminal (a C/C++ Windows-based real-time financial workstation) could be recreated using plain HTML. The key feature of our products is that prices and news are delivered in real time. When you think that a news story such as an interest rate change can move the market, a beat of just a few seconds on a rival vendor makes millions of dollars worth of difference to our customers. It was hard to see how a browser could provide an equivalent environment for the real-time delivery of news and price information.

With the launch of Java, however, and the promise of dynamic Web pages instead of static HTML, the notion of using a browser as a means of displaying stock prices and news became much more realistic. Some of the very early demos of Java were based around simple stock tickers running across the top of a page.

At this point, Reuters started to investigate Java in a fairly serious way, both from an intellectual and architectural perspective, and also by embarking on a number of prototyping activities. Fairly quickly there were many different applets that could connect to our datafeeds or the open interfaces to our terminal products and display market data.

REDUCED TIME TO MARKET

At an architectural level the use of Java appeared to hold out a number of promises that could lead to significant reductions in time to market. These included instantaneous product deployment and improved development productivity. The development productivity gains would come from cross-platform development, a language optimized for the network, and integrated support for internationalization. Another factor that would lead to significant reductions in time to market: customer demand.

The rest of this section goes into these perceived benefits in more detail. The following section reviews our development experience to date to see how these perceived benefits actually stacked up with reality.

A simplistic life cycle for the creation of a new product has three phases: inception, development, deployment. The elapsed time from the start of the inception phase, where the ideas of the product are first formulated, through the development stage, when the product is built, through to the deployment stage, where the product is delivered to customers, is the time to market. Typically, we expect each of these phases to be roughly the same duration; a reduction in any of these phases reduces the overall time to market.

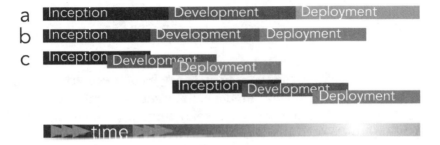

Figure 3-2. Java has the potential to reduce each stage of software application development, from inception to development to deployment. The major advantages are in the last two stages.

Inception. The inception phase tends to be much less technically oriented and much more focused on marketing activities; hence, it is not so amenable to technical fixes. However, the use of Java for rapid prototyping is one way in which the later stages of the inception phase can be accelerated, and it also provides a much cleaner handover into development. With more traditional Windows development, for example, the use of Visual Basic prototypes is fairly widespread, but all of the prototypes tend to be discarded once development starts. By prototyping in the same environment as the development will be done, there is far more scope for building on what has already been achieved, especially if an iterative development approach is being taken.

Development. Another way that time to market can be improved is by reducing the time it takes to build the product. The potential for Java as a language rather than Java as an environment to speed up the development process is what is important here. And there are many features of the Java language that could result in significant improvements in developer productivity.

LANGUAGE FEATURES

Although Java is in many ways a descendant of C++, it differs from this and other conventional languages in many ways. The features of the Java language that are of particular importance are:

- Simplification

- Robustness

- Multithreading

Long before Java was caught up in the hype of the Internet, it was just another programming language. Its origins in Sun date back to a project called Green that was a research initiative into set top and consumer devices. James Gosling, the inventor of Java, then called it Oak. Oak was a backlash against languages like C++ that were becoming increasingly complex. This was especially so in the case of C++, as it was basically a series of extensions to turn an existing procedural language into an object-oriented one.

To demonstrate the contrast between Java and C++, Arthur Van Hoff used to begin his presentations on Java by working his way through a standard C++ language reference book, erasing all of the constructs that were no longer present in Java. Given that the standard Java language reference book itself now runs to many hundreds of pages, it might seem that the goal of simplification has been lost. However, it is still the case that Java is a much simpler language than C++ and this is one of its big advantages.

For any organization with a significant investment in development staff there will be a cost saving. Programmers are able to learn Java more quickly and are also able to become proficient in less time. With a steady stream of new developers joining an organization, the ability to get them productive as quickly as possible is very important.

The bane of any programmer's life has got to be documentation. Clearly Java was designed by a programmer, because one of the things that it makes very easy is the ability to automatically generate documentation from the comments in the source code. This is not guaranteed to result in *good* documentation, but the fact that it is produced at the same time as the program rather than as an afterthought reduces the burden.

In a trading-room environment, robust software is absolutely essential. When deals worth millions of dollars can be executed with a single key stroke, any problem with the software has the potential to be catastrophic. An application such as the Reuters Terminal—a highly sophisticated Windows-based display of market data—is left running sometimes for weeks or months on end while it receives a constant stream of updates from our data delivery network and also responds to the commands of the trader. At the busiest times of the trading day, a Reuters Terminal could be receiving, processing, and displaying hundreds of new price movements and news stories per second. Not surprisingly, within Reuters a lot of effort is spent qualifying and assuring our software products to ensure that they can meet the rigors of the typical trading room.

There are a number of features of the Java language that improve the robustness of programs. For example, Java does not expose pointers to the programmer. In conventional languages such as C and C++, objects that are dynamically allocated are turned into *pointer variables*. Not only do pointers allow bugs that can cause memory locations to be accidentally overwritten, but it is up to the programmer to ensure that any such dynamically allocated objects are carefully managed and properly de-allocated when no longer needed. When these objects are not properly de-allocated, programs fall prey to so-called *memory leaks*. Such programs can eventually exhaust system resources and cause instabilities either to themselves or to the entire system in which they are run. By eliminating pointers, Java completely avoids this problem, thereby eliminating some of the most common problems of software development. At the same time, Java still allows programmers the full flexibility to dynamically allocate objects; it simply takes away many of the risks that typically accompany pointer-based languages.

One of the other features of the Reuters Terminal is that it supports many different tasks running at the same time. The user can divide the application up into different screens, or panes. One pane may display summary information for all of the stocks that make up the FTSE 100, another might have a graph of the prices for one particular stock, another will show news headlines, and yet another will show details of all of the different options for a stock—all updating in real time. The ability to run several processes concurrently, known as multithreading, is therefore very important. The Java language directly supports multithreading. While multithreading facilities are also available to other programming languages, the fact that the language itself supports the concept means that, in certain cases, it is easier to implement multithreading correctly. For example, in Java a method within an object can be made thread-safe simply by adding one keyword to the definition of the method.

PLATFORM INDEPENDENCE

The Java byte code that is generated when an applet is compiled is platform independent. The byte code is interpreted by the Java virtual machine running within the browser to generate platform-specific instructions. This means that an applet can be developed once yet theoretically run anywhere.

As has already been mentioned, Reuters display products are delivered on both Windows and UNIX workstations. The systems that manipulate and deliver the data run on a variety of operating systems and platforms. Quite often, though, the same component has to be delivered on multiple platforms with an enormous amount of development time spent porting code rather than adding functionality. The use of Java should reduce the development time by avoiding the need to port code.

INTERNATIONALIZATION

A key feature of our customer base is that it is global. In order for us to compete effectively in marketplaces where the native language is not English (or even American), we have to be able to offer local language versions of our products. This is especially so in the Asian and Eastern European markets where support for character sets such as Kanji, Korean, and Cyrillic are demanded. With conventional software development on Windows and UNIX, the costs to internationalize our products, both in terms of the text making up the user interface as well as the actual data that the user interface displays, are high. For us, one of the great advantages of Java is that the basic character set is Unicode.

Unicode is an industry-standard character set that encompasses all of the world's scripts. The Unicode Consortium, of which Reuters is a very active member, consists of many leading software companies. The conference in September 1996 was focused on the Internet and featured keynote speakers from Microsoft, Netscape, and Sun. The use of Unicode in Java will help us to produce localized products and services much more cost effectively.

Deployment. Reuters supports a worldwide terminal population of over 362,000. These are primarily Windows-based PCs but a significant number are UNIX workstations. Each terminal is running a large amount of software, from Reuters, other suppliers (for example, Microsoft Excel), and their own custom-built applications. One of the biggest problems we face is updating our software on those workstations when we release new products and new features. In some cases we do have the capability of downloading software over the data-delivery network, but often a site visit is required by an engineer, which is expensive.

With Java, the byte code is downloaded from the Web server and interpreted on the workstation when the applet is launched on a Web page. It does not need to be installed on the workstation. As soon as an applet is ex-development, it can be installed on a Reuters Web server and made available to all of the Reuters Web users. Furthermore, each time that applet is retrieved by a user, the user will get the most recent version of the code. This means that new products can be introduced instantaneously and changes to existing products can be made on the fly.

Java encourages a modular approach to development as opposed to creating large, monolithic applications. If an application is going to be installed onto a workstation, all of the functionality must be contained within the software package at the time of installation. However, the possibility of dynamic downloading means that little if any actual software needs to be installed. Application functionality is downloaded if and when it is needed. A well-designed application framework means that it is easy to add new or unforeseen functionality when customer requirements demand it.

In reality, the process of deploying a new product or changing an existing product is not as simple as just installing the software. There are a whole variety of activities associated with the way the product is marketed, sold, and administered, as well as issues related to user training that are not as amenable to a quick technical fix. It is also worth remembering that users and the people responsible for supporting them like to be able to control the introduction of new products (particularly within the financial marketplace where huge sums of money can be at risk on a daily basis). However, it is still the case that the physical process of installing the software adds a significant overhead to this overall deployment and any reduction in this does affect the total time it takes to bring a product to market.

The three phases of the life cycle have been considered as consecutive phases. Another way of reducing time to market is by starting one phase before the preceding phase is complete, and also by running multiple streams in parallel. Some of these ideas will be discussed in the section below on Tornado Projects.

CUSTOMER DEMAND

Another reason for considering Java is customer demand. There is quite a marked difference in attitude to Java in our various marketplaces. Not surprisingly, the most interest is in the United States, where the exposure that Java and the Internet receive in the press means that many of our customers want to hear the Reuters Internet story. More often than not, our customers are constantly trying to leverage new technologies to gain competitive advantage, just like Reuters. Although technology in and of itself is not what Reuters sells, our customers want to be assured that we are moving in a direction that will be compatible with their own technical strategy.

JAVA ON THE REUTERS WEB

We have a number of Java projects in various stages of development and deployment. The expected benefits of using Java have indeed accrued. Initial customer response to the prototype Java applications and applets has been very positive.

NEWSWEB

Reuters is perhaps best known as a news agency, although that area accounts for a relatively small percentage of annual revenue. It is real-time news that underpins many of our information products because of the effect that a single story can have on the financial markets. On an average day Reuters generates many thousands of news headlines and alerts delivered to traders' workstations. Each of these headlines are tagged with one or more topic codes to indicate what subject the headlines relate to. Traders then make requests to see all of the headlines for a given topic or combination of topics.

© 1997 Reuters Ltd. Reproduced with permission.

Figure 3-3. NewsWeb is one of Reuters's first Java applications. The application demonstrates the ability to connect Java to a database, and is also a good example of the advantages of Java's use of Unicode, which simplifies the delivery of two-byte languages such as Japanese.

NewsWeb is a fully functional prototype developed to investigate the delivery of real-time news within a browser, to test new ways of navigating and searching through Reuters news. The prototype consists of a scrolling news headline applet that can be invoked either from a tree control for headlines related to a specific topic or via a sophisticated search interface that allows different topics to be combined together with Boolean operators (AND, OR, NOT) as well as free text. In all cases, the actual codes are hidden behind a textual description. Clicking on any headline will retrieve the underlying story. The story text is then formatted into HTML by the Java applet and displayed in a separate browser window.

From a technical perspective, a Java object request broker (ORB) is used to handle the communication between the applets and a Reuters news feed on a remote server. The ORB on the server is Sun's NEO product, while the Java ORBlet in the browser is Joe. Every time the Reuters feed delivers a new headline, the ORB is used to send it to any applet that has expressed an interest in the topic code associated with the headline. There could be many different applets and many different workstations all looking at the same news topics. Each one would receive the new headline.

Figure 3-3 shows the headline applet and a story, generated by the applet, being displayed in a separate browser window. One thing to notice is that some of the headlines and the story itself are in Japanese. This is possible because the news feed delivers data using Unicode. Also notice that the references to different companies in the story are hyperlinks. Clicking on the hyperlink will display the current stock price for that company.

From inception to development to prototype deployment, the Reuters NewsWeb took four months, significantly faster than similar types of projects done in the past. The early customer feedback has been universally positive.

DEALING WORLD MAP

Delivering large amounts of financial data as a raw feed of bits and bytes is a highly complex business. But for the raw data to be useful it has to be displayed in a form that makes it easily understood—especially as it is constantly changing. The display of financial data can take many forms, from a screen of stock prices to a highly sophisticated three-dimensional visualization. Somewhere between these two lies the Dealing World Map applet.

The Dealing World Map, shown below, is a two-dimensional visualization of the World's spot currency market. Each line on the map connects two participants in an active conversation on the Dealing 2000-1 network. A conversation between two dealers ultimately results in a trade being executed. The applet actually shows one in every 100 conversations, first in yellow and then fading through orange and red before disappearing from the screen after a few seconds. New dots and lines constantly pop up on the map as new conversations are started.

This applet gives a fascinating insight into the dynamism of the global foreign exchange market. The concentration of dots moves around the world as the markets in different countries become more or less active during their trading day. The density of the dots and lines reflects the amount of activity in the market at any one time. Interestingly, it is always possible to see some active traders in all parts of the world, whatever the time of day.

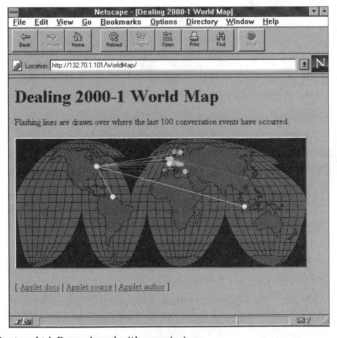

© 1997 Reuters Ltd. Reproduced with permission.

Figure 3-4. The Dealing World Map is a quick visual tool to see where the action is on worldwide currency transactions. This is a useful tool for a currency trader to always have in the corner of his or her screen.

REUTERS WEB TRADING

Many Reuters clients trade with each other, and Reuters has already had considerable success with foreign exchange trading systems (the Dealing network) and the execution of equity trades through its subsidiary Instinet. There are other opportunities to apply electronic trading, and the development of the Reuters Web Trading applet is a first step in providing an electronic trade facility for the fixed income market.

Reuters Web Trading allows market makers to advertise executable prices to their clients on the buy side of the market. Using the Reuters Web Trading applet, the client can route buy or sell orders to the market maker simply by clicking on the relevant instrument.

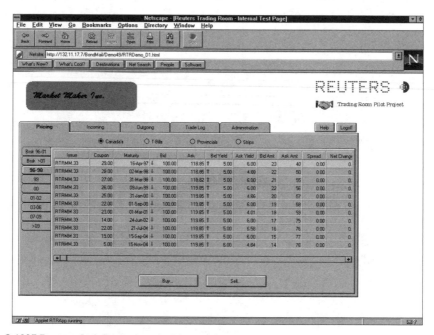

© 1997 Reuters Ltd. Reproduced with permission.

Figure 3-5. Reuters Web Trading is a Java-powered applet that enables a client to buy or sell orders from a market maker, with rapid execution and confirmation.

The trade is completed with acceptance or rejection from the market maker trader or, if the trader does not respond to the order within a specified time, the deal is timed out. A record of the trading activity is logged at both the market maker and client sites to provide the users with a consolidated record. This information can be transferred into back office or portfolio management systems.

Reuters Web Trading provides fast trade execution and confirmation, and has the potential to increase trade volume and sales productivity for the market maker. Branding, advertising, and on-line subscription facilities will also bring the market maker visibility and customer loyalty.

The first operational release of the Reuters Web Trading application was developed in and deployed at pilot sites in less than six months.

LESSONS LEARNED

In the mid-1980s Reuters was one of the first companies to ship a product on Windows 1. This was the Reuters Terminal, which has since become the industry's best in class display application for financial data, quickly replacing the previous generation of green screens. At the time this was quite an ambitious approach, Windows was a very new technology and very immature. There were also many objections raised concerning security and customer acceptance. This all seems quite ironic in hindsight, given that about 80 percent of customers now use Windows PCs to view our data.

For some of the Reuters veterans from the early Windows days, the world of Java seems like a bit of a time warp. Many of the problems that Java developers face today are similar to those problems faced a decade ago: immature technology, crude development environments, lack of technical support. There are some differences and some new problems, however, and we will discuss those in more detail. But what is also different is the rate of change and the speed with which Java is maturing. Without being unduly conservative, it took about a decade for Windows as a technology to be considered mature. The reality of Web years—the notion that just like a dog year represents seven human years, so a Web year represents seven calendar years—means that it will take Java dramatically less time to reach the same level.

BETA ON BETA SYNDROME

While the rapid evolution of this technology is a boon in terms of how quickly some of its deficiencies will be addressed, it is also problematical.

Today, developers are faced with using beta versions of the Java Development Kit, with beta versions of a Web browser, with beta versions of add-on Java class libraries from third parties, with beta versions of integrated java development environments, etc.

This beta on beta on beta effect is a direct result of the enormous amount of industry effort associated with the rapid evolution of Java and associated technologies. However, when trying to develop robust, high-quality, production systems, this beta on beta syndrome adds significant complication. When a problem arises, it is not trivial to determine what software is causing the problem, let alone to create a work-around that avoids the problem. It also becomes much more difficult to plan product release because of the dependence on so many third-party pieces of technology that have not yet been formally released in their current form.

Nevertheless, this beta on beta syndrome is a reality likely to continue for as long as the Internet revolution continues at this rapid pace. Development and product groups will therefore have to evolve strategies for dealing with this problem if they are to be successful in delivering products using these technologies.

BROWSER AND VIRTUAL MACHINE INCOMPATIBILITY

The ability to "write once, run anywhere" is one of the most important features of Java. Our experience to date suggests that the reality of this aim is still a little way off, as one of our biggest problems is compatibility across different browsers and different virtual machines. This is especially so for the user interface components of Java associated with the AWT, Abstract Window Toolkit. What might work in the applet viewer will behave differently in HotJava or Netscape Navigator or Internet Explorer. The subtle interdependencies between the versions of the virtual machine and the JDK, and the implementations on different platforms and browsers has caused us many problems.

The browser wars of the last year, fueled by Microsoft's desire to get into the Internet game, has resulted in each of the main browser vendors having a different Java virtual machine, each one claiming to be an improvement on its rivals and hence the best in class. In some way this is reminiscent of the database wars, where each new release of a relational database from Oracle, Sybase, Informix, or Ingres claimed to outperform the others. But again, Internet years come into play, with the release cycle for browsers being far shorter than for relational databases.

The existence of multiple Java virtual machines is not in and of itself a problem. Indeed, the rapid improvements in performance are a direct result of competition between vendors. The Java licensing agreement that Sun has put in place also recognizes that there will be different implementations. The problem is that, while the licensing agreement requires conformance, there is no comprehensive set of tests to guarantee it.

The impact of this on a development group means either spending additional effort during the testing phases or only supporting a limited subset of the myriad combinations of browsers, versions of browsers, and operating systems. This choice has to be driven by the environment in which the applets are to be deployed. If the target environment is the public Internet then there is little option but to support as many combinations as possible, unless market research suggests that you can focus on a limited subset. In the case of the Reuters Web, though, we have a little more control over the browser and operating system that will be used.

Looking ahead, the next major release of Java is JDK 1.1. Indeed, as this chapter is being written, the first beta version has been made available on the JavaSoft Web site and our developers are recompiling their applets to test them out. On a positive note, the 2,000 conformance tests that were defined for JDK 1.0 have been extended to over 5,000 for JDK 1.1. It remains to be seen if this will reduce the inconsistencies that exist today.

DESKTOP INTEGRATION IS HARD

Like many other organizations, Reuters has significant investment in existing desktop components. One of the main challenges is integrating this existing code base with new Java components in a browser framework. Many of our existing components represent complex delivery infrastructures and functionality, and there is no business justification for rewriting these for the sake of using a new technology. Further, it is often difficult to provide interesting functionality without access to native platform-specific resources such as the file system.

In some ways the desire to integrate these components into a Java/browser environment is in direct conflict with some of the goals of Java, especially portability and security. By definition, the existing components are platform-specific, whereas the new Java components will not be. From a security perspective, one of the strengths of Java is the robust security model integrated both as part of the language and as part of the environment. Under the control of the Java Security Manager, local access to the file system, remote access to any host other than the source of the applet, and access to other executables on the local system are explicitly disallowed.

SECURITY

Perhaps the biggest concern over the use of Java, especially in a financial trading-room environment, is security. The worry that a malicious applet, carelessly introduced into the trading room, could corrupt or destroy data, effectively disable a trader's workstation, or expose the network to outside attack is a concern of many IT managers. In reality Java is, in many ways, more secure than conventional technologies. One of the best reviews of Java security is by researchers at Princeton University's Safe Internet Programming group[1], so we will not repeat what they have already said. Theory aside, the need for well-defined quality-assurance procedures does not go away with Java, even in the frenzy of a Tornado project as discussed below. This, combined with the ability to digitally sign applets in future releases of the JDK, should address most concerns.

"KILLER BENEFIT"—DEVELOPER PRODUCTIVITY

The previous section focused on some of the general issues associated with the adoption of a new technology, and some of the specific issues associated with the adoption of Java. Not surprisingly, it has not all been plain sailing. However, the expectation is that short-term costs are significantly outweighed by long-term gains. We have also seen a number of immediate benefits that revolve around improvements in developer productivity.

REUSE

In an organization such as Reuters, with development groups scattered throughout the world, the components for reuse can come from a number of different sources: internal development groups (as a by-product of their development); internal development groups specifically tasked with producing them; and external sources.

The first case tends to be quite informal and with Java is partly the by-product of these groups adopting a new technology. Because there are no recognized experts, most developers are more than happy to expose their coding efforts to the scrutiny of their peers. This is part of a mutual learning process. In a more traditional development environment, most programmers are reluctant to make source code available. In a Java environment a useful piece of code or a few classes can be easily posted on an internal Web site for others to take, possibly alter, and reuse. During the early days of Java in Reuters it was not unusual for a graphical component, for example, to be posted, retrieved by ten different people, and then modified by all of them. At one level, the fact that the code base quickly fragments is not a problem when it is being used in prototypes, but the provision of a standard code base needs to be addressed if the component is to be used in production quality systems. So, this leads on to the second source of components: an object technology center.

The second case is much more important and evidence of a much more mature development organization. Whereas the former case typically revolves around snippets of code, a few classes, or a GUI widget, in the case of an object technology center the components that are made available are larger and more important. Typically, these are components that represent the fundamental

problem domains of the organization and are the result of significant effort in object modeling and analysis as well as coding. They
would also be made available as a class library rather than as one
or two individual classes. In Reuters it is no surprise that class libraries for the delivery of real-time prices and news, sophisticated
graphing and charting, and specialized user interface controls are
just some examples.

The final source of Java code is the Internet, where there is already a wealth of very good quality Java code available. (There is
also a much greater volume of very bad code.) Some of this is from
regular vendors already established in the marketplace, but much
of it is produced by nonmainstream developers. This means that
you can quite often get source code for minimal cost, which would
have taken a lot of effort to produce in-house. Security is foremost
in our minds when we get code from the Internet. Much of the available code is cataloged at sites like Gamelan[2], now the official directory for Java.

In some ways this is similar to the market that exists for VBXs. A
VBX is a custom control that can be used to develop Visual Basic
applications. As well as the Microsoft-supplied VBXs, third-party
developed VBXs can be incorporated into the Visual Basic development environment to add functionality in a standard way. Many different companies provide specialized VBXs which are often distributed on the Internet.

In the case of both Java and VBX technology, it is the ease with
which components can be integrated that fosters a vibrant market
in reusable components. In the case of VBX, there is a well-defined
component model. In the case of Java, there is no component model
yet, but the advent of JavaBeans will change that. At the moment,
however, the ability to have interfaces (in the Java sense) that
clearly define the behavior of a component means that, at a technical level, it is relatively easy to integrate components from different
sources. With JavaBeans it will be possible to do that even more
easily with graphical editing tools and development environments.
Furthermore, the cross-platform nature of Java also makes integration that much easier, as it avoids the operating system and compiler dependencies of classes written in, say, C++.

TORNADO PROJECTS

If you ask developers what fosters reuse, they will tend to focus on communication; how can they reuse something if they don't know it is available? If you ask senior (development) managers what fosters reuse, they will tend to focus on organization and process; what forces a group to reuse? Who is responsible for supporting the component? Where these both come together is in a Tornado project.

Within Reuters, much of the justification for the adoption of Internet technology in general and Java in particular has been reduced time to market. "Web years"—the notion that just like a dog year represents seven Web years—is very popular. With that in mind a number of high profile projects were chosen that would be used to validate these claims. Senior management gave these projects what seemed to be totally unrealistic timescales. These became known as Tornado projects.

The idea of a tornado project is that, given the right conditions, significant reductions in development time can be achieved. A lot of these conditions—like focus, good design, senior management commitment— are nothing new. But what we have seen is that Java and Internet technology add an extra dimension, primarily in how developers, who are constantly challenged, approach problems and look for solutions.

Focus. The first prerequisite for a Tornado project is a very clear focus on what needs to be done. This doesn't necessarily mean a lengthy requirements specification, but it does mean that the developers have a clearly stated goal of what they must deliver. What is just as important is that this goal does not change as the project progresses. However, even though the goal remains constant, the way that the goal is achieved is open to interpretation, and both development and marketing have to approach problems in a flexible manner and be prepared to compromise on the way that the goal is achieved. Commitment from development and marketing staff also needs to be coupled with high-profile commitment and sponsorship from senior management.

Team Work. From an organizational perspective, Tornado projects in Reuters involve multiple teams. Typically, one team of developers builds the actual product and is located with product management and marketing. The other teams, from some of the many development groups around the world, act as feeders to the build team, providing many of the infrastructural components that the build team uses. All teams communicate on a regular basis; face-to-face for some initial brainstorming, but primarily by video and teleconference. The responsibilities of the teams are clearly defined and the Java interfaces for the different software components are also well specified at the start. In this way, most development is done in parallel with infrastructural components being released on a regular basis and then integrated by the build team to progressively add more product functionality.

Off the Shelf. Using off-the-shelf products and technology has to be one of the most frequently stated aims of any development project, but also one of the least achieved. However, with Tornado projects there is no option to "roll your own"; no one group can possibly develop everything itself and still expect to deliver in months. And if you don't deliver in months you might as well not bother, as somebody else will have beaten you to the marketplace. This means that some hard design decisions are made up front which, once agreed, are stuck to rigidly. In some cases the off-the-shelf component only satisfied 70 percent of the functionality required for an ideal solution, but this is exactly where compromises have to be made.

Culture. Perhaps one of the most noticeable features of projects undertaken with Internet technology is that a different culture pervades the development teams. What in the past might have been rejected as impossible is now looked at in a fresh light with more of a can-do approach. Internet technology seems to allow developers to approach what are sometimes old problems in a new way. It enables people to come up with a solution that works.

What we have seen in Reuters is that the development community is much more prepared to work cooperatively and borrow and share code with other teams. This echoes the point about using off-the-shelf components, the twist being that in many large organizations these components are often from other groups within the company rather than from external suppliers.

Often a new technology generates a lot of excitement within the development community, and this is certainly the case with Java.

Programmers are keen to apply their skills in a new area and approach Java with a lot of excitement. The image of the West Coast hacker is one that springs to mind—prepared to put in long hours but in a very productive way. It is also interesting that many less experienced developers, not necessarily with a computer science background, also jump onto the Java bandwagon and become productive in a very short time. We have found that the combination of enthusiasm and excitement, with mature managerial consideration and direction, is very powerful. It allows people to tackle sometimes quite old problems but in a new way. Things that might not have been possible before are now achievable.

Infrastructure and Architecture. Often Tornado projects are leveraging up-front investment in technical infrastructure. These projects are often only possible if work is already underway to implement the underlying infrastructure. The design decisions that are taken to ensure products are delivered quickly may sometimes appear inelegant. But they are taken in the context of a broader, more coherent, architectural framework.

Sometime infrastructure and architecture, especially when driven by technology, are hard to justify, that is, until a product comes along that could not happen without it. Then the argument about infrastructure changes from "Why are you doing it?" to "Why isn't it ready yet!"

One piece of infrastructure that significantly contributes to the productivity of the Internet developer is the browser itself. This provides a ready-made desktop environment with a set of fully integrated protocols. In the past this would either have to be developed or would only be available in a proprietary form.

MORE THAN A NEW COMPUTER LANGUAGE

As a new technology, Java is certainly impressive, with many features that commend it above what is currently seen as the mainstream. But the use of a new technology, in and of itself, is seldom going to result in significant changes to the efficiency of a development group or the ability to bring product to market more quickly. What we have found is that the combination of Java technology with what are best seen as cultural changes in the way we build and deploy products has made a difference. In this sense, Java has stimulated us to change our development process, with new products being developed in less time. It will be interesting to see if the notion of a development methodology specific to Java can be taken further.

END NOTES

1   *Java Security: From HotJava to Netscape and Beyond,* by D.
    Dean, E. Felten, and D. Wallach, 1996. Available at
    http://www.cs.princeton.edu/sip/pub/secure96.html

2   The Gamelan Web site is located at http://www.gamelan.com

CHAPTER 4

CSX: CUSTOMERS ON-TRACK

John Andrews, President, CSX Technology

Marshall Gibbs, Assistant Vice President, CSX Technology

CSX is an international transportation company offering a variety of rail, container-shipping, intermodal, trucking, barging, contract logistics, and related services worldwide. It was the first company to implement Java applications for electronic commerce. The application provides a complete on-line interface for customer self-service, enabling customers to check the location of their shipments, get updates, contact troubleshooters, be alerted to schedule and ETA changes, request price quotes and place orders, look at equipment specifications, manage fleets of equipment, and more. Response by customers has been enthusiastic, and the application demonstrates the graphical, cross-platform, and security features of Java. The application is now in operation with CSX's largest customers, and will be available to its entire customer base in 1997. Additionally, the product has been adopted by the Association of American Railroads (AAR) as the standard for the entire industry. The use of Java by CSX demonstrates Java's appeal as a rapid development tool, having taken 90 days to develop and less than $1 million in development costs, which is a substantial savings over conventional processes. Ongoing yearly labor and equipment support cost savings are expected in the $10 million dollar range, versus the costs of a more traditional approach.

*The CSX development process—the vision, partners, pilots, and roll-out—
is an impressive model for any information technology initiative. Java
has enabled CSX and the railroad industry to improve its customer service
while providing significant savings to customers and to CSX.*

In January 1996, CSX Corporation hosted some of its largest
shippers in Ponte Vedra, Florida, at its semiannual Shippers' Conference. This conference provides a forum for the senior management of CSX, including its chairman, to share key information
with the senior managers of the customers in attendance about
CSX's future direction. The meeting aims to ensure that the CSX
strategy is aligned to service its customers appropriately. Among
the items on this specific conference agenda was a briefing by John
Andrews, president of CSX Technology, on the current state of Electronic Data Interchange (EDI) and more broadly, Electronic Commerce at CSX.

Andrews and his team had spent the previous three weeks final-
izing a prototype of a seamless Electronic Commerce interface for
all of CSX Corporation and its customers, delivered over the Internet using World Wide Web technology. The reaction of the customers was immediate and virtually unanimous. They wanted it,
and they wanted it quickly. Energized by the overwhelming enthusiasm displayed by the shippers, Andrews' team launched an ambitious 90-day development of what would become known as TWSNet
(Transportation Work Station Net), one of the first and most expan-
sive uses of the Java programming language in a critical business
application.

CSX TRANSPORTATION

CSX was well suited to being a live lab to test the viability of Java.
The corporation is an end-to-end transportation company providing rail, barge, ocean-shipping, intermodal, and contract logistics
services in over 100 countries. The most critical need for improved
customer information exchange was on the corporation's railroad,
CSX Transportation (CSXT). CSXT is one of the largest railroads in
the United States, with a rail network covering 32,000 track miles in
20 states and a portion of Canada. It averages more than 15,000 car-

loads per day and more than 4.5 million carloads annually. CSX Technology provides IT services for CSX Transportation and the other CSX business units.

In mid-1995, CSX had in place an Electronic Commerce product called Mercury, deployed at about 2,000 of the company's largest customers. It was a DOS-based dial-up application, which gave the customer rudimentary data entry capability for a number of functions. It was a slow and unreliable application, but it had stood the test of time, largely because there had never been an alternative. However, CSXT's customers were recognizing a greater need to have more information about their shipments, and they wanted the information in real-time.

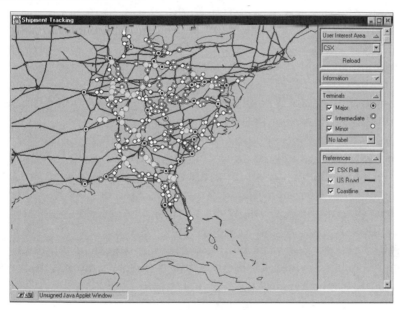

© 1997 CSX Corporation. Used with permission. All rights reserved.

Figure 4-1. CSX runs a freight operation throughout the southeast, middle Atlantic, and midwest sections of the United States and a portion of Canada. With the TSWNet system CSX developed, users can drill down on the train network to find their specific shipment.

THE SERVICE VISION

While CSX's customers were beginning to seek a better electronic solution, the company had already internally committed to reengineering its primitive Electronic Commerce platform. CSX envisioned a much greater role for Electronic Commerce, which it saw as a primary component for reaching its service vision of 100 percent shipper satisfaction, achieved primarily through on-time service delivery and comprehensive, current information about each customer's transportation needs. The company recognized that the information delivered to the customer is now considered to be part of the CSX transportation services offered and of high value to the customer. In fact, in many cases it is the logistics information that makes or breaks the customer's ability to succeed. Thus, CSX's service vision was to be not only a first-class provider of transportation services, but also to be the number-one provider of information and logistics information to the shipper's desktop.

With this in mind, CSX sought an electronic commerce solution that could seamlessly integrate with shippers' business processes to provide visibility into the supply-chain network to track shipments in real time, on-line customer service interaction, ordering and account balance information, and anything else necessary to facilitate the movement of goods.

CSX wanted to free customers from having to navigate among multiple systems and interfaces to conduct business with the corporation's business units. In addition, the company wanted all of this from a system that would have a small footprint, that is, take up relatively little space on the desktop, while being able to reach any customer, regardless of size, location, or operating system.

The solution had to be highly interactive and decision-point driven, not just allowing the customer to type information into forms. Finally, the solution had to have the highest level of uptime, the best response time, and complete security.

THE CHALLENGE

Traditionally, Electronic Commerce solutions in the rail industry had focused simply on transferring clerical work from the carrier's shop to the end-user shop, with the goal of increasing accuracy of the clerically entered data, reducing overall costs, and improving the accuracy and the service delivered to the customer.

It was abundantly clear to CSX that EDI provides an improvement over manual paper systems. The company calculated that paper commerce on the railroad is ten times more expensive than electronic commerce. For example, a bill of lading sent to the railroad electronically costs about 15 cents to process. A document sent on paper costs between $15 and $25 to process. On a railroad that processes 4.5 million carloads annually, the savings of electronic commerce are dramatic. Driven by these facts, CSXT was committed to increasing by four or five times the number of customers using electronic means to do business with the railroad.

The company's IT group quickly realized, however, that reaching this goal using its existing Mercury system would be cost prohibitive. CSXT figured that the cost of maintaining Mercury was almost $10 million annually, and this for only two thousand users. Mercury ran on only one operating system, and it required a proprietary dial-up system for the customer to communicate with CSXT. Both factors created considerable expense. The railroad frequently bought equipment for its customers and covered all of the telecommunications costs. Additionally, CSXT had to incur distribution costs for software. Diskettes were created and shipped to the customer, along with documentation. Every time the application changed, CSXT again had to cut diskettes—ten per copy of software—and ship them to each customer.

So when CSX's chairman asked John Andrews to report on the state of EDI at CSX, Andrews immediately saw the opportunity—in fact, the need—to reach for a next-generation electronic commerce solution. It would have to be a solution that could provide real decision-point information, allowing more efficient and effective management of shipments. Such information would allow customers to use real-time monitoring of the transportation network to actively manage their inventory on the rail cars en route to destinations, something that simply was not possible in the old environment. To reach this level, Andrews saw that the company was going to have to provide more than just static information, more than just forms for customers to fill out and transmit.

NEXT-GENERATION TECHNOLOGIES

With only three weeks to put together a prototype for the shippers' conference, Marshall Gibbs, heading the Advanced Technologies

Group and his team of CSX employees, proposed that the prototype take advantage of the Internet's World Wide Web-based technologies. If the team's proposal was accepted and developed, then the product could be delivered everywhere with minimal impact on the user's footprint and desktop and with maximum effect.

From a business perspective, the Internet represented an opportunity to develop a system that would be much less expensive than the Mercury system, which, with its legacy DOS code, was becoming cost-prohibitive to maintain. For example, going to the Internet would mean that much of the expense associated with cutting diskettes and mailing out upgrades and changes, along with documentation, would simply go away.

Just as important, customers could run the system on their existing desktop, regardless of what it was: Macintosh, OS2, Windows, UNIX. It did not matter to the Internet solution. Plus, World Wide Web browsers take up very little desktop space, and in nine cases out of ten, they would already be in place. No special connectivity would be necessary by customers with existing local area network (LAN) or modem connectivity. For these reasons, customers would be able to imbed the solution much deeper into their organizations, delivering the system's functionality wherever it was needed.

For example, the system could be on a traffic manager's desktop or on a loading dock platform, where a loading foreman could see all inbound and outbound traffic and use that information to schedule crews appropriately. More ambitious customers could use it to provide their end customers with visibility into inbound or outbound shipments, as the case might be. Clearly, functionality and economics favored an Internet solution.

With that decision made, the team recognized immediately that Java would be essential to the CSX mission, because it provided the required interactive capability on the desktop. The team intended to deliver real-time mapping in GIS-type information, as well as disclosing diagrammatic information of cars and their contents. All of these were things that could not, before Java, be delivered over the Internet without a proprietary system.

The team further concluded that it could best build a sensational new graphic user interface using HTML in combination with the new Java programming language. Pressed for time, the team quickly agreed to use Sun Microsystem's Java Development Kit—which was then still a beta version—for the Java code, while using Lotus Notes' beta Domino product to produce the HTML needed.

Everyone understood the risk in putting so much reliance on two very young beta technologies, but everyone had also seen what the Internet was becoming and recognized that these technologies would be the drivers to realize the vision. In essence, they were the only vehicles to take CSX where the team knew the company, and the Internet, had to go.

The team worked furiously in the days and hours leading up to the shippers' conference to debug the prototype so it would convey to the customers the ease and functionality such a system could deliver as part of their daily business routines. A failure would significantly impede the team's ability to rapidly pursue the corporation's vision of Electronic Commerce. Fortunately, the presentation was a tremendous success, and the virtually unanimous response from shippers was, "When can we have it?"

John Andrews's firm answer was a commitment to bring the first customers on-line in 90 days. Another difficult assignment had been handed the development team, but the group was eager to begin and confident the deadline could be met.

LEVERAGING EXISTING TALENT

Finding employees interested in participating was perhaps the easiest aspect of the entire development project. Like IT developers everywhere, CSX Technology employees are eager to be part of the revolution in computing technology happening all around them. They want to keep their skills current and sharp. The employees virtually lined up to be part of the Java/Internet/Electronic Commerce development team. Many were so energized by the project that they used personal time to hone skills and capabilities before approaching the team leadership to demonstrate their expertise in their efforts to become part of the team. The employees involved displayed great satisfaction at being a part of the development of a product which would have an immediate impact on customers and, unknown at the time, even an impact worldwide.

CSX Technology maintains a large mainframe complex in a central data center in Jacksonville, Florida, which also serves as headquarters of CSXT. Consequently, there was an excellent centralized mainframe shop with highly skilled mainframe developers and an entire systems administration for mainframe maintenance. But there was only a scattered implementation of mid-service or UNIX, and no Internet or intranet development existed in CSX at this time. In addition, when the project began, only a small cover team of graphical user interface (GUI) developers had experience in object-oriented computing, and they were working on other CSX products.

This lack of experience was quickly overcome, however, through a combination of outside vendors and the adaptability of the internal staff. As a pragmatic issue, the C++ programmers, who were good object-oriented developers, made the best Java coders. This was no surprise. It was also found that lessons learned in other fourth-generation language-type environments were quickly adopted by the Java development community. Visual development tools were the norm, which enabled a broader base of employees to participate in the development experience. For instance, Power Builder-skilled employees could pick up tools that were very familiar to them and create some of the Java interfaces very quickly.

Employees also were excited to find out that some of the basics did not change. Employees who worked on COBOL and CICS were excited to learn that they could be part of the Electronic Commerce revolution at CSX by delivering applications on the mainframe that would help feed the new technologies to the user desktop. They knew they could take advantage of their skills in the mainframe and administration environments, and then leverage Internet-based technologies to provide the solution to the customers.

At this point, everyone knew the team wanted an Internet solution that would use a combination of HTML and Java, and that a solid core of enthusiastic employees was ready. However, the fact remained that exactly one Sun system was part of the current operation and it was observing weather at the data center. In addition, much greater expertise in the budding technologies about to be embraced was badly needed. A development plan had to be created, and quickly.

THE PLAN

After assessing strengths and weaknesses, the team laid out a plan that included partnering with several best-in-class providers to achieve the solution. First, a list of the components to be put in place was developed, including security, servers, networking, Internet commerce servers, and content provision.

In each of these key areas, the team went to the marketplace and found strategic partners experienced with large-scale commercial implementations of these technologies, and who could work together to bring the CSX solution on-line rapidly.

BEST-IN-CLASS PROVIDERS

The first step was to go to the World Wide Web and find sample sites that offered the same kinds of capabilities to be included in the CSX solution. They were graphically rich, relatively complex, had forms, and supported Electronic Commerce. They also supported highly interactive Java and provided excellent response time and reliability. Consistently, the team found that the one vendor which put those systems in place was Sun. Consequently, Sun was invited to come to Jacksonville to literally copy into the CSX system the architecture implementation of one of the sites the team had seen on the Web.

Several additional vendors also were brought on board. Some provided Java talent and expertise on the World Wide Web site, and others lent expertise in Electronic Commerce sites, Java programming, security configuration, firewall configuration, server sizing and architecture. Once the partners were chosen, which was done over a ten-day period, the contracts were finalized and execution began.

From a content provider standpoint, the team planned to take advantage of remote development capabilities offered by the Internet. They divided up the proposed application and lined up a number of external development capabilities to work on these solutions. In doing so, a virtual development environment was created that was distributed on-line across the Internet.

PARALLEL DEVELOPMENT PROGRAM

When work began, the only mid-range server in production, as was noted previously, was a Sun workstation that monitored weather. Clearly, the team had much to do in the way of adding hardware in addition to developing the application. This challenge was answered by running a parallel development program, lining up the components, having the hardware, network architecture, and software installed and preconfigured, all while development had already begun at remote sites.

One team at CSX was able to oversee distributed software development, while another team focused on the physical implementation of the World Wide Web site. The software development team divided assignments across remote development locations using network connections to enforce strict software source code control and good software engineering principles, including designing, coding and testing, and incremental delivery.

The team used a virtual World Wide Web site that was a Web page with links to the remote sites, allowing them to constantly monitor and approve the development underway. In essence, the team could review code and output in real time and walk through the look, feel, and functionality of the sites, even though the work was being developed in six different states by upwards of 25 different professionals.

At the CSX data center, the physical implementation team was lining up security, network, hardware, and server software in a feverish attempt to get an entire site up and running in the very few remaining days. Standard hardware configurations were used that were already in use at other large commerce sites, dramatically shortening the specification time of the hardware.

Another aspect of the development project that permitted the team to meet the tight deadline was reuse. Existing legacy host systems were able to be leveraged by drilling into them through a TCP/IP connection. This created a front-end interface to customer systems that already existed with the new technology. It also gave greater capability to CSX customers in less time, as well as ensuring that the system was highly robust, because the legacy systems had been in place for some time.

This approach provided a new lease on life to the legacy mainframe systems. By establishing a fresh interface to an existing set of core systems, CSX gave itself another several years of use of systems it anticipated having to rewrite. The resulting savings will enable the company to focus on delivering new and better functionality to its customers.

SECURITY FIRST

Throughout the development process, security was a major concern. The team's approach was to: (1) ensure the integrity of CSX Corporation's technology assets by protecting them from any outside invasion; (2) strive to be unobtrusive to the end user; (3) provide a level of security and comfort to customers who needed assurance that their transactions were secure, encrypted, and out of the public eye; and (4) reassure shippers that their systems would not be compromised by CSX's software solution.

CSX had already made significant progress in security before this development project, but nevertheless brought in some additional experts in Internet security. Through a combination of firewall and encryption technologies—which at one point required the purchase of a munitions license from the State Department—the team was able to provide a very robust and complete multitiered firewall and security zone. This best-in-class Internet security solution has, as of this writing, never been penetrated by an outside party.

OBSTACLES AND SOLUTIONS

On the development team, the experienced development leaders knew that to be successful, adherence to the strictest software design standards would be paramount, especially in a new and exciting technology where there is a tendency to hack solutions. Knowing the remote development locations had to be controlled to ensure the highest-quality software, the team took the time to teach the remote users the best software engineering principles so that only good design would be coded; solutions were designed before they were coded; design reviews and walk-throughs were adhered to; scenario testing occurred; software source-code control was rigidly followed; defect-tracking mechanisms were in place at all the remote locations through a central source-code repository; and that rigorous remote-end integrated testing would be in place to ensure that, under the incredibly short time frames, the solutions delivered were the best they could be.

While the development team was furiously writing code and incrementally reviewing the work being done, the infrastructure team had begun to receive its hardware and to install systems. The "bleeding"-edge nature of the technologies involved became immediately apparent. Much of the team's time was consumed in matching up version levels of operating systems, system patches, software systems, server systems, and security systems.

Additionally, significantly more effort had to be put into revisiting the network topology than was originally estimated. This was caused by a combination of factors that included the complexity of very good firewall and security, as well as the capability to integrate multiple systems within CSX's network to provide security.

The development team had laid out for the architecture team the need to be able to access not only the World Wide Web servers and Oracle databases running in the mid-tier, but also to be able to run transactions on the host systems, to interface with the rail control system in a VAX environment, to interface with an RS6000-based system that manages carload inventories, and to have remote access to customer management systems. This posed a thorny network development problem, but with the help of a number of vendors, a solution was quickly reached that proved to be very robust and scalable, and has included nothing more than good network topology.

The infrastructure team ran into other stumbling blocks. While it tried to imitate a cookie-cutter approach taken from an existing commerce site, it discovered that no two commerce sites are exactly alike. Consequently, after hastily putting together the first of the crucial World Wide Web servers that were going to host TWSNet with the World Wide Web server software and the operating systems, the team encountered significant configuration difficulties.

It had to back off both system builds, replan them, and work closely with the engineers at the software companies providing the solutions to find the appropriate combination of patches and fixes that would enable these solutions to work properly. In the team's estimation, it was only through partnering with these strategic vendors that they were able to achieve such rapid resolution to these thorny compatibility issues.

The security implementation initially went extremely well in creating a secure firewall environment for the site. Configuration across the multiple back-end systems that had to be accessed became difficult, though, as they were on different networks and subnets. The security group provided a solution that met its objective to protect CSX assets, but was flexible enough, through a combination of different security zones, to allow the TWSNet site to function across multiple systems.

As the infrastructure team finally began to see the light of day with a functional World Wide Web site accessible from outside the company, yet secure, the development team was beginning to feel the pressure. With just 15 days remaining before the 90-day deadline, it still did not have a complete and running solution.

Most of the HTML on the site was being generated dynamically. In fact, there is no static HTML in CSX's site. The generator of the HTML was written entirely in Java and ran on the server. It was acquired through a third party, and CSX found few people who knew how to make it run. Consequently, the HTML was somewhat behind.

Also, the Java JDK was showing its youthful nature, and there were problems in creating the most important component of the initial delivery: the TWSNet map. Implementation bugs in the Java virtual machine then available on the Microsoft platform were causing drawing errors on the map. While write-once-run-anywhere is the promise of Java, it is up to the virtual machine implementers to make sure that vision is realized, and CSX was having trouble with Microsoft's early version of the Java Virtual Machine.

With ten days remaining, the benevolence of Sun's strategy of putting Java in the public domain became evident. Solutions to the Microsoft drawing problem came from a different third party, and were made publicly available on the Internet. These solved CSX's drawing errors.

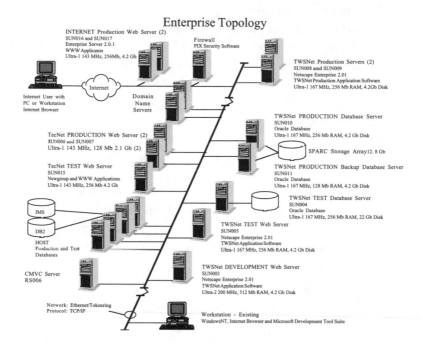

© 1997 CSX Corporation. Used with permission. All rights reserved.

Figure 4-2. The topology of the TWSNet: the infrastructure team created an architecture that was secure and allowed for expansion.

As if the team did not have enough to contend with in getting the infrastructure and software developed, at the eleventh hour the executive team decided to "improve" the look and feel of the artwork on the site. Graphic artists were hurriedly hired to create a completely new from-the-ground-up set of artwork to "jazz up" the TWSNet initial roll-out, which at this point was four days away.

Finally, on the Sunday before the system was to go live, the software was running and had passed tests, the site was running well, the artwork was in place. As of midnight on that Sunday, TWSNet was complete. On Monday morning, April 15, 1996, a meeting was held in Richmond, Virginia, CSX's corporate headquarters, to demonstrate TWSNet to CSX's chairman and the senior management team and to inform them that the first customer was being turned on at that moment.

FROM ZERO TO 30,000 IN 90 DAYS

With the intense development effort behind it, the team's next challenge was to resist the temptation to let down. If anything, the work intensity was only going to increase, as they now began rolling out the product to 16 pilot customers spread throughout CSX's geography and representing most of its business units. Efforts had to continue to expand, perfect, and refine the original application. One of the team's goals was to achieve a standard constant velocity of delivery, just as with every other product developed by CSX Technology.

Four more customers were turned up in the two weeks following April 15, and within one month of the launch date 30,000 hits per week to the TWSNet World Wide Web site were being experienced. The rapid roll-out pace continued throughout the summer and into the fall, and by December the system was being used by some 200 users at 16 companies and processing more than 660,000 transactions per week.

THE IMPLEMENTATION

Placing the system into CSX customers' shops required an educational effort as the customers went through a paradigm shift. Before TWSNet arrived, virtually none of the clerks who would use the system at customer sites had Internet access on their desktops, although the Internet was almost always available somewhere on the site. Typically, CSX first educated customers to use the browser before showing the users the product itself.

It was found that the end-user clerks were very quick learners. Usually only a relatively short time elapsed before they understood that no software would be installed on their desktop, now or ever. They understood that they would have a URL to access and an ID and a password. With that, the clerks had access to the latest and most effective shipment management system that CSX—or any company, for that matter—could offer.

Before users could access TWSNet, of course, their companies had to grant them access to the Internet. There are a number of schemes for doing that, and the team typically went through some learning experiences with that issue as well.

The team also found that security was another area requiring education. As mentioned previously, most of the pilot companies had Internet access, but had done little with it. (This, by the way, produced several instances in which IT officers thanked CSX for finally providing them with a major justification for giving their companies access to the Internet.) The team worked with several IT teams at the end-user sites to help them understand their firewall and configure it so they could do business on the Internet.

Yet another area to be addressed was the rate of acceptance of newer 32-bit operating systems, most notably Windows 95 and Windows NT. Many TWSNet users still run older 16-bit operating systems, and until very recently those operating systems could not run Java-enabled applications. Consequently, many TWSNet users upgraded their desktop to a newer operating system and newer capabilities.

After addressing these issues and receiving initial training, users were encouraged to continue to receive support through the CSXT customer service center and through TWSNet postings.

© 1997 CSX Corporation. Used with permission. All rights reserved.

Figure 4-3. Front page of TWSNet provides the quick and intuitive information customers want about their shipments.

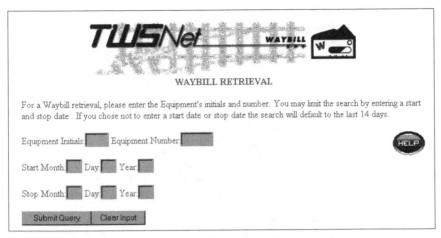

© 1997 CSX Corporation. Used with permission. All rights reserved.

Figure 4-4. Users enter their own queries for retrieving waybill information on-line. A directory of CSX contacts is also easily accessible from the top page of the TWSNet.

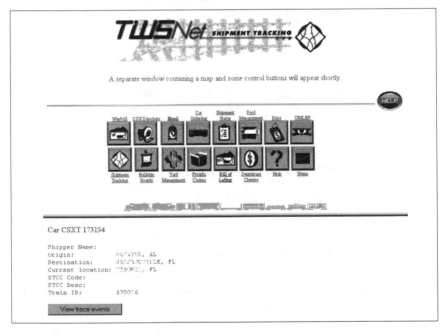

© 1997 CSX Corporation. Used with permission. All rights reserved.

Figure 4-5. Individual car rail shipments can be traced at a click of a button.

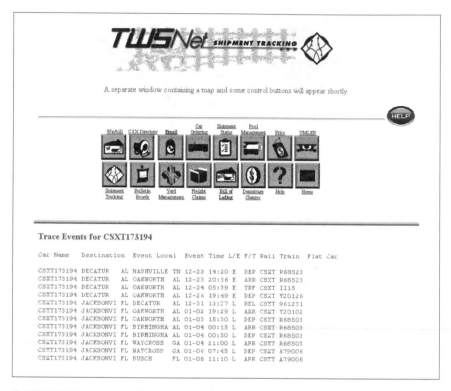

© 1997 CSX Corporation. Used with permission. All rights reserved.

Figure 4-6. The application lets the user track the progress of his or her shipment, simply and intuitively.

JAVATIZE THAT SITE!

Throughout the roll-out period, the CSX team continually improved the system. This was especially critical in the first weeks following the introduction, because the team knew that it had taken a few shortcuts in the overall implementation and went back to address those items. In addition, they were seeing growth and use far greater than expected. The infrastructure team began scaling up its area rapidly to handle the ever-increasing volume of activity it was experiencing.

The development team raced ahead implementing new functionality to address a number of capabilities they knew customers were eager to receive. Through extensive work with the pilot groups, new requirements were coming up faster than the developers could meet them. While this was happening, everyone was continuing to follow the original development plan of replacing all of the initial Mercury functions so as to vastly expand customers' access to information.

Initially, new functions were deployed as quickly as they came on-line. But, it became apparent that customers were overwhelmed by this strategy. They indicated they were finding it difficult to keep up with what was on the site, and, when new functions were there, how they worked.

As a result, the team agreed to bundle up and release the new functions once every six weeks. The team members found that this enabled them to advertise—through a highly visible "What's New" section of the home page—the functions about to be added, and then deliver and explain all of the new functionality in a single, comprehensive dose. The customers were very comfortable with this new approach and were very happy with the constant evolution of the system.

In five months after the site went live, more than a quarter million lines of code were added across more than 40 new functions. And it continues to evolve.

THE CUSTOMERS' RESPONSE

Virtually from the day TWSNet went live, customer response was overwhelmingly positive, notwithstanding a few concerns that will be discussed later. Customers' biggest complaint—if it could be considered that—was that they wanted more, more, more.

The pilot group, which consisted of major customers who represented almost one-third of CSXT's revenues, provided invaluable insight into the process, planning, and production of the content delivered over the system. The group proved to be very demanding, in that they quickly recognized the capabilities TWSNet could deliver—and the speed and integration it could achieve—and consequently they pushed for ever-increasing quantities and qualities of information to manage their businesses. They helped with everything from actually recommending new features and functions that were implemented to working on the delivery cycle.

The customers' input was valuable on items even as simple as colors. For example, Marshall Gibbs was previewing map capabilities with a customer, pointing out that the red dots indicated rail traffic in jeopardy; green dots were traffic successfully making its way to the final destination; light green lines were the rail track; and the blue lines were the Intermodal track. The customer stopped him after 15 minutes and said, "Marshall, I'm color blind. Can you please point those out to me on the screen?" As a result, TWSNet now uses symbols instead of colors in many areas of the application to avoid raising problems for people who have difficulty differentiating colors.

PILOT GROUP RESULTS

Perhaps the biggest testimony to the exceptional reception customers gave TWSNet was that usage figures far exceeded expectations. The overwhelming majority of inquiries on the site were based on the decision-type information delivered, such as location of shipments, alert status of shipments, and other information that the customers used to manage their business. Less used by the pilot group were the actual transaction mechanisms, such as the ability to order cars and shipments. This was primarily because the pilot group of customers were large Fortune 100 companies that typically transact much of their business with CSX via EDI.

As the customers in the pilot group came to understand the Internet delivery mechanism, they began to demand that all of their functionality be delivered this way. They understood that it can be anywhere they need it to be, to an unlimited number of users, any time of the day or night, and on any desktop—and in today's diverse electronic gadget market, the definition of a desktop is ever changing.

The customers commented that for the first time they felt as though they had good decision information and capability in tools being delivered to them by their carrier in a meaningful way in their environment. Interestingly, CSX found that customers of TWSNet, substantially more so than customers of the older Mercury system, call in to CSXT's Customer Service Center much more frequently to discuss service issues rather than system issues. The system is much easier to use, is much more intuitive, and provides a much higher grade of information; therefore, the customer spends more time having meaningful value-added conversations with customer service rather than asking, "Where's my rail car?"

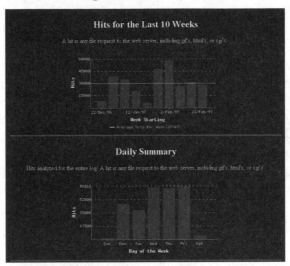

© 1997 CSX Corporation. Used with permission. All rights reserved.

Figure 4-7. The initial response to the system was very positive, measured qualitatively and quantitatively.

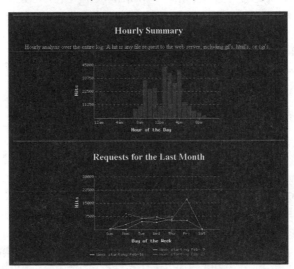

© 1997 CSX Corporation. Used with permission. All rights reserved.

Figure 4-8. Tracking usage over time for the first 150 customers assists in modeling the infrastructure for mass customer use.

Customers also commented that TWSNet's ease of use had allowed them to broaden the use of the tool beyond just a few specific targeted traffic managers in their enterprise. The demand for decision data through customer sites was far greater than estimated, based on previous models of usage of the older legacy systems.

As a result of the ease with which the solution could be delivered to multiple desktops at a user site, it was discovered that each site contained many more potential users than realized. All they needed was access, and now they had it. Customers were now comfortable giving capabilities for shipping, tracking and tracing, and inbound management to loading-dock personnel who are responsible for managing crews, and to inventory managers charged with making sure that enough goods are on hand to produce whatever the particular customer was in the business of producing. In some cases, customers even gave the capability to their ultimate end customer so that customer could see the overall supply chain, easily and intuitively.

Yet another significant benefit noted by customers was that TWSNet saved them time and expense in ways they had not initially anticipated. For example, they no longer had to administer a fairly complex proprietary system for monitoring their rail traffic. Now, they were able to use browser technology and simply type in a URL. In addition, they knew that the latest capabilities CSX had to offer would be delivered quickly and painlessly, without them ever again having to load a floppy disk into a disk drive.

PERFORMANCE OF THE PLATFORM AND TECHNOLOGIES

Some of the complaints heard from the pilot group were pretty much what the development team had expected. Occasionally during the day, especially first thing in the morning and in mid-afternoon, the Internet slows down, and customers felt that slowdown in the responsiveness of their systems. In addition, some of the larger Java applets took some time to download. The team was able to work through those issues, both with the companies that provide Internet service, as well as with the technology providers behind Java, to try to increase uptime and provide a higher degree of reliability to CSX customers.

Nevertheless, and even with extremely tight encrypting security, customers rarely complained about throughput or transaction time. Most customers were willing to accept the occasional sluggishness because they expected the problem to ease as telecommunications companies continue to increase bandwidth for the Internet. Like CSX, they anticipate that the problem will go away and their service will continue to improve.

Another area of concern was that customers in the pilot group, recognized fairly quickly that many of their desktop technologies were not up to the standard of the Internet technology being implemented. Specifically, many of the users still had older 386-class machines running 16-bit operating systems like Windows 3.1, where the Java environment was not yet available. By now, customers have progressed with their desktop upgrade plans, and vendors have made Java available on the 16-bit platforms.

As the pilot wound to a close in December, the CSX TWSNet team took some time to analyze the performance of the platforms and technologies it had implemented at the beginning of the year to host the new commerce site. They found that the servers were showing almost 100 percent availability, and that they were not in danger of being taxed in the near future in terms of capacity. It was also found that the servers were solid and had performed with the expected reliability over the course of the pilot.

An additional discovery, much to the team's dismay, was that the network and systems administration capabilities were not at a level which would ensure the continued ability to maintain the required level of uptime. Due to being a mainframe-centric shop, CSX was slow to accept and implement the technologies necessary to adequately manage this system in its shop. As a result, a new team was created to specifically manage the mid-range systems and to get solutions in place to make them 100 percent available, 100 percent of the time.

The UNIX platforms that support the TWSNet site were found to be very scalable and allowed the team to increase its capabilities on an as-needed basis. They allowed for effective planning for upgrades and ensuring an extremely high degree of reliability through a variety of fault-tolerant topologies.

An in-depth examination of the security solution revealed that, while it had been good at protecting CSX assets and providing a seamless interface for its customers, there were a number of opportunities to improve its overall performance and simplify its administration and ease of use, while also increasing flexibility. Thus, the security team set about implementing the latest technologies in firewall and security standards.

Furthermore, the development team analyzed the lines of code delivered, and function points and capabilities delivered over the Internet. It found that while there were some weaknesses in the current language, overall Java had paid off in a big way for CSX in the TWSNet effort. It had proven robust and reliable and complete as a language, never once hindering the team's ability to deliver the desired functionality, while performing almost always as advertised.

Even though the team noted an overall improvement in the maturity of Java tools during the pilot stage of the project, it knew that there was still a long way to go, particularly in areas such as the tools' ability to deliver first-class fit and finish in applications and to improve the development environment in the areas of debugging, code generation, and visual development.

A LOOK BACK: LESSONS LEARNED

The CSX development team's immersion in Web technology and the Java programming language enabled the group to come away with a clear understanding of three major aspects of the development effort:

1. *Planning, partnering, performing.* The first lesson in the Internet world is the oldest lesson in systems development: Nothing takes the place of sound software engineering.

   When getting ready to implement a solution in the Internet world, especially one involving technologies as new as the ones used in TWSNet, development teams cannot be misled by the claims of rapid development and instant solutions. This development still requires a high degree of planning and integration, perhaps even higher than earlier efforts.

   It also requires a degree of specialization in each of the component areas that almost mandates a partnering approach. That means going to the market and finding those companies that have substantial expertise, capability, and credibility in servers, security, networking, bandwidth, and content provision to help put together a complete solution.

At CSX Technology, it is believed that the strategy of identifying key business partners, planning what needed to be done, and then executing the plan paid off tremendously. It allowed the team to achieve very rapid systems development, in a robust way, with some very risky architectures and technologies.

Choosing business partners proved to be at least as important as choosing technologies. CSX Technology encourages any development team going down this path to find those partners who are leaders in their technical fields and who are committed to the ongoing implementation of these technologies.

Performance, of course, is the ultimate key. The CSX team owes a large part of its success to the wait-and-see attitude of its competitors who failed to embrace these technologies as ready for prime time. As a result, CSX was able to leave them behind in its quest to provide a high degree of Electronic Commerce.

2. *Bandwidth issues.* The team also relearned a lesson that has been recognized for a long time but was underscored when it tried to scale up the solution and make it larger and more capable. The lesson is that the network is the computer; bandwidth is king.

The team was able to successfully put together the site, handle all of the architecture and administrative tasks, and develop terrific content. They also knew it would run on the end-users' computers, but without bandwidth to deliver the solution, customers would get frustrated and walk away.

Targeting customers in the Fortune 100 initially who had LAN-based Internet access was key to the initial acceptance. Further, being very sensitive during the software engineering and design sessions to limits of bandwidth allowed the crafting of components that were smaller and tighter, and able to be transmitted easily over lower bandwidth Internet connections.

In addition, by recognizing that the network enables the ability to seamlessly pull together multiple disparate systems, the team had great success focusing on delivering seamless functionality on the front end by integrating systems that were already available on the back end.

3. *The reality lag.* The Internet world was built on hype, and continues to be hyped to this day. The responsible IT manager has to approach all of these technologies with experience and a skeptical eye, making sure to have a clear understanding of the reality of the technologies and not just the marketing literature.

Internet time is frequently mentioned by vendors in their product delivery cycles; and, no question, product delivery from development shops has never been faster than it is today. Capabilities, however, are frequently overblown in marketing literature, and underdelivered by software houses, potentially hampering an IT shop's ability to deliver promised functionality to its customers.

The reality lag refers to that period of time between marketing hype and truly robust solutions that can be used to deliver product. Typically, it is about three months. Planning for this makes delivery to the customer a much more painless proposition.

Many CSX customers had—and have—concerns about this technology, which they regard as new and unproven. One of the ways to overcome this concern is to understand the history of the Internet, the role it plays in national security, and its acceptance by the nation's major telecommunications companies as a significant business opportunity.

CSX customers were also often concerned about the doomsday scenarios painted in the trade journals regarding the impending demise of the Internet due to clogging by individual users and by companies. However, CSX saw no reason to be concerned, for the aforementioned reasons. Too many parties have too much of a vested interest to allow the Internet to falter and fail. We believe telecommunications companies in the immediate and near future will dramatically increase the capabilities of the Internet.

A LOOK AHEAD: THE FUTURE OF TWSNET

The outlook for CSX Technology in Electronic Commerce is extremely strong as a result of the TWSNet effort. In 1997, CSX expects to enroll an additional 5,000 users in the TWSNet system, many of them smaller shippers.

Although the pilot group consisted of major customers who realized tremendous benefits from the capabilities of the new systems, smaller CSX customers are likely to realize every bit as much benefit, if not more. CSX expects the majority of the end-user base will be smaller three- and four-person shops that need to move goods but do not have the extensive IT resources of a Fortune 100 company.

In many ways, these are the customers TWSNet is directed toward. Because of the system's ubiquitous capabilities, smaller users are able to reap the benefits that previously could be captured only by very large IT organizations. The smaller users get access to real-time data on their terms, when they need it, and they have significant EDI capabilities that they otherwise would not get. They also get an outstanding GUI and substantially improved customer service.

Because they are large in number, these customers also represent a significant portion of the CSX's paper-processing costs. As a group, they are more likely to be paper-based, which costs the company significantly more in terms of processing orders and inquiries. TWSNet will be able to remedy much of that situation.

Beyond the boundaries of the CSX network of shippers, the company has been successful in introducing TWSNet and the World Wide Web-based approach to the entire rail industry via the Association of American Railroads.

Supported and encouraged by the pilot customers, TWSNet was unanimously chosen by members of the Association of American Railroads for implementation as the single rail industry solution for Electronic Commerce. As a result, the system is expected to be on-line throughout the industry in the third quarter of 1997. The AAR expects the industry-wide roll-out will generate an additional 20,000 users of the TWSNet electronic commerce solution by that time.

As CSX looks forward, it expects to maintain its competitive advantage by always leading the transportation industry with tools, systems, and capabilities delivered to the user via the Internet and TWSNet.

It is actively advancing the globalization of TWSNet, placing it in the worldwide theater and providing the same real-time capabilities to users in far-flung and remote locations around the world. TWS-Net will be rolled out across all of the CSX operating entities, in addition to CSXT, including Sea-Land, a leading U.S. container-shipping company; American Commercial Lines, the nation's largest inland barge company; CSX Intermodal, the nation's only full-service, coast-to-coast intermodal transportation company; and Customized Transportation Inc., a provider of contract logistics services, including distribution, warehousing, processing and assembly, and just-in-time delivery.

TWSNet had already been resold by CSX to one of the company's strategic business partners in Europe—Deutsche Bahn AG, the German railroad, to become its premier customer-service offering on the continent. From this basis, TWSNet is positioned to become the de facto Electronic Commerce standard for rail transportation in all of Europe.

The next step for CSX towards its service goal for its customers involves evolving TWSNet into a set of publicly available APIs that remote systems can access to interact with CSX systems in a real-time basis. This will create a third-party market for logistics software and further integrate CSX into shippers' transportation needs.

CSX is working closely with a number of standards bodies to try to develop and standardize these APIs across the transportation industry. The company will market TWSNet as one of the service offerings capable of using these APIs to give users visibility in the supply chain.

It is an indisputable truth of the Internet that even the best companies can never be more than 30 days ahead of their competition. At CSX, the focus is to continue to provide quantum leaps in its approach to interacting with customers to maintain that 30-day lead over the rest of the transportation industry, and Java is at the core of the CSX mission.

CHAPTER 5

NANDO TIMES: FAST FORWARD TO NEWS

James Calloway, General Manager, Nando.net

Nando.net is a McClatchy New Media Company located in Raleigh, North Carolina. Its Nando Times *was the first daily newspaper published on the World Wide Web, and this daily was up before the PC version of Mosaic browser made the Web available to so many computer users. The* Nando Times *was also a very early adopter of Java, incorporating it into its front page months before Java was available in the industry-leading Netscape browser. Java was used initially as a means of animating the front page, a useful function for the busy reader. It later was used for advertising and was recently used to power an interactive "news watcher." A Java-based chat application is currently under evaluation. Early adoption had its downside; successive alpha and beta versions of Java required reprogramming. There were also some early performance-speed issues. Java was and is just one tool in the dynamic tool set that Nando uses for its on-line news site. There are, however, some very clear benefits of using Java in terms of platform independence and interactivity, and its use is projected to increase in the Web's first on-line daily, both on the reader side and the editorial side.*

By most accounts, Nando.net was the first effort by a daily newspaper to publish on the World Wide Web. The name "Nando" was derived from that of its parent publication, *The News & Observer* of Raleigh, North Carolina, known locally as the *N and O*. From its beginning on the Web at www.nando.net in March 1994, however, Nando.net sought to establish an identity as a Web publication rather than simply as a newspaper transferred to an electronic medium.

THE JOYS AND SORROWS OF BEING AN EARLY ADOPTER

Nando as an organization began in October 1993 when the *News & Observer*'s executive editor, Frank Daniels III, hired George Schlukbier away from McClatchy Newspapers Inc., with the mission of aggressively exploring opportunities in the so-called new media. Nando began in a mode of "try everything until something works." This philosophy led the operation to experiment with a community bulletin board, local Internet access, and CD-ROM products. Nando experienced a number of false starts and discovered its share of dead ends, but at a time when most newspapers were looking for alliances with on-line services like America OnLine, Prodigy, and Delphi, the Nando team chose the Internet as its most promising medium.

A willingness to experiment, tempered by an evaluation process that will be explained in detail below, led Nando to develop a Web strategy before Mosaic, the leading browser of the time, was available for PCs. That strategy resulted in *The Nando Times,* a news product created expressly for the Web. Back then, most Web sites were static, one-time "look at me" efforts. Recognizing that any Web site would soon languish if it did not change on a regular basis, the creators of *The Nando Times* designed it to be continually updated with news throughout the day.

Likewise, the philosophy of experimentation resulted in early adoption of Java. *The Nando Times* converted to a Java-based front page in May 1995, on the day that the sale of the News & Observer Publishing Company to McClatchy Newspapers Inc. was announced. This was only a month after Sun Microsystems released its own HotJava browser and several months before Netscape had released its first Java-enabled browser.

Being an early adopter has its joys and sorrows. It is a good way to attract attention, and in the publishing business, attracting attention can be assigned a dollar value. The use of Java was one of several early innovations that enabled the News & Observer to establish *The Nando Times* as a nationally and internationally recognized brand name in a new medium, something that would be extremely difficult for a medium-market daily newspaper to accomplish now. Although *The Nando Times* originated at a regional newspaper, it now serves a national market, and the News & Observer has since created a related but separate site (www.nando.net/nao) to serve its local market.

There was a downside, however. When Netscape released its Java-enabled browser, it used a different Java. At the time, *The Nando Times* was using the alpha version of Java that had been released by Sun Microsystems, the version supported by the HotJava browser. Netscape started with the newer, incompatible beta version. With the release of Netscape's Java-enabled browser, *Nando* had to rewrite its Java front page to conform to the Netscape version, and for months there were two versions of it: one written in the Sun alpha and another written in the Netscape beta. This was a minor nuisance, but it is a good example of the risks associated with the early stages of any new technology.

No technology is without risk even in its mature stages. The trick is to find the right balance of risk to benefit for a particular industry and business model within that industry. In the case of *Nando,* the initial flurry of experimentation with Java was followed by a long period of low activity, partly because of Java itself and partly because of external factors. By the time this appears in print, Java will have become more prominent at *Nando*. The reason for both changes can be found in the nature of the emerging business of Web publishing and in *Nando's* strategy for succeeding in it, which has been sharpened by the drive to develop a solid, long-term business plan under the leadership of its current president and publisher, Christian Hendricks.

JAVA AND THE BUSINESS OF WEB PUBLISHING

One of the most misunderstood aspects of Web publishing is the nature of the market. The confusion is understandable for practitioners who come to the Web from older mass media, like broadcast or newspapers, where readership or audience is measured in households. The assumption follows that Web publishers will find their market in the same place, in homes, albeit homes equipped with computers and modems. At our current stage of development, that assumption turns out to be incorrect. Figure 5-1, the chart of a typical week at Nando.net shows that the accesses, or hits, follow a clear pattern. During weekday evenings and daytime over the weekend, the accesses are relatively flat. The daytime hours during the workweek are a different story, showing easily twice to three times the activity of the evening hours.

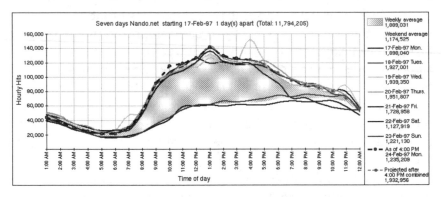

Figure 5-1. Monitoring usage patterns helps businesses decide whether to gear their technological sophistication to high-bandwidth or low-bandwidth users. Based on the patterns of its audience, The Nando Times *aims high.*

The implication is that the bulk of the users are people at work, people who have the ability to browse the Web from their desks at the click of a mouse button. These users typically work for companies with dedicated, often high-speed connections to the Internet. Their usage patterns track neatly with the lunch hour in the four most populous U.S. time zones. These users differ in several ways from those who access the Web from home, even though in some cases they might be the same people, and the differences have a substantial impact on how a publisher approaches Java.

The first significant difference is that bandwidth, which is to say the speed of the users' connection to the Net, is not as big a concern. This audience is not shackled by 28.8 kbps modems. That leaves the publisher more leeway to use ambitious Java applets that might be impractical for home users, especially users with older modems running at speeds of 14.4 or even 9.6. The temptation to win on design becomes powerful for the publisher, and Java is becoming an increasingly important design tool.

Another difference, one that can be inferred from anecdotal evidence, is that the office worker has limited time to browse the Web. The worker's boss might prefer that he or she not browse at all. Therefore, the publisher's use of Java needs to be efficient and oriented toward making the published material easier to use. Applets that waste time or that attract undue attention through the use of sound or animation should be avoided.

That is not to say the home user can be ignored. The need for efficient applets still applies. Ironically, at home, where limited bandwidth constrains the publisher's ambitions, the flashier applets have a better chance of succeeding. If packaged as toys or goodies, a Java chat client perhaps, or a virtual baseball game animated in Java, such applets will be sought for their own sake, even if they take a while to download. With that exception in mind, the publisher otherwise needs to avoid applets that could become barriers to navigation. An animation that always runs off the home page, for example, may alienate users even over high-speed connections.

Nando.net has dealt with this dichotomy by making its original Java applets optional. The old alpha version of Java was capable of running invisibly off the same Web page as the non-Java version. When a HotJava user accessed the top page of *The Nando Times,* he or she would see alternating photos and ticker-like streaming headlines. The Mosaic or Netscape user would see an ordinary, static Web page. For the beta version embraced by Netscape, *Nando* chose to provide a separate page. In the next few months, *Nando* intends to remerge the Java and non-Java pages, making the difference transparent to the user; *Nando* will sense the browser type and offer the appropriate page. *Nando* also is considering offering different editions based on the time of day, more graphically laden, Java-enabled pages during the workday and streamlined, text-dominant pages during the evening and on weekends.

JAVA AND THE EXTERNAL DESIGN OF *THE NANDO TIMES*

There are four areas of *The Nando Times* and its related publications (the *SportServer* and the Web sites of McClatchy newspapers like *The Sacramento Bee* and the *News & Observer*) that are ripe for Java or further use of Java: the top page, the inside pages, advertising, and what we call toys.

Figure 5-2. The top page of The Nando Times *has had a Java-powered version since May 1995.*

The top page of *The Nando Times,* at www.nando.net, is already available in a Java form, although the design is the same that was introduced in May 1995. In Internet years, that makes it pretty old. It takes about three and a half minutes to download at 28.8 kbps. The four photos in the upper right cycle through a selection of 16 images, which is the major source of the slowness, but the efficiency of the

Java code, which is by now somewhat dated, also contributes. One of the redesign goals of an evening edition of the page would be to reduce that to less than 30 seconds for a 28.8 kbps connection.

The most important existing element of the page is the headline ticker right beneath the pictures. It may appear deceptively simple and is barely visible in the illustration, but it increases the amount of content visible in the very limited screen area available to most people's browsers. To use an expression favored by Hendricks, it serves to "bubble up the content," that is, to alert the reader to stories in other parts of the server. *The Nando Times* is a site that is dense with information and in a constant state of flux. The back-end engine that builds the site adds and deletes news stories every six minutes. Over the course of a day, hundreds of stories are cycled through *The Nando Times* by its editors. Alerting the casual reader to the presence of stories that may be of interest becomes a major challenge.

INSIDE PAGES

Inside pages will lend themselves to similar but simpler treatment. Java can be used to make the navigation tools more interesting, and a news ticker may prove useful even on inside pages. Because of their sheer quantity and the tendency of readers to work through several pages in a session, the need for efficiency is especially great on the inside pages.

ADVERTISING

Advertising is a trickier issue. Like many Web publications, *The Nando Times* is supported by banner advertising, graphical links that steer some of *Nando*'s readers to the advertisers' Web site. An example of a banner ad can be seen in *The Nando Times* page illustrated. The ad appears below the headline ticker and promotes *Barron's Online,* the electronic version of *Barron's,* the business journal. That particular banner is animated and so isn't fully visible in the illustration. It begins with the phrase "Have Wall Street for Lunch" and dissolves into the *Barron's* logo. Users who click on the banner are taken to the *Barron's Online* site.

Nando has carried only one advertising banner that used Java, an early experiment by AT&T. The appeal of Java for an advertiser is obvious: its ability to create an interactive experience for the reader increases the reader's involvement in the ad itself. However, if the applet used by the ad is not tightly written, it risks alienating the reader. The AT&T ad had the usual problems of early Java efforts: slowness and finicky behavior. Since then, interactivity in ad banners has been limited to animated GIFs, a form of moving image (as in the *Barron's* ad) that doesn't require Java, and even those have been controversial.

The design of ad banners is driven largely by advertising agencies, and Java can be expected to resurface in the banners as the agencies continue to push the envelope trying to get readers' attention. Unlike some sites, which put restrictions on banner animation and file size, *Nando* maintains an open policy on agency experiments, but is quick to counsel the advertiser when the banner's interactive ambitions do more harm than good.

TOYS

Finally, there is the category of toys. A toy is any object on the Web site created simply for the enjoyment or utility of using it. These include the Cyrano Server, at www.nando.net/toys/ cyrano.html, which is a text generation script devoted to coining humorous love letters for the romantically impaired, as well as a number of video game-like creations at www.nando.net/toys/. Up to now, Java has not been the environment of choice for developing these toys, but that is beginning to change for reasons discussed below. At present, the most promising Java-based toy at *Nando* is one developed by a third party, Earthweb Chat. It is quick-loading and fairly robust, and is a good example of how far Java has come, both as a programming environment and as a serious alternative as a user interface. Like most chat clients, it enables users to converse by written messages in real time, a concept that goes back to the early days of on-line services. The beauty of creating the client in Java is that no special software or plug-ins are required on the user's end. The user simply connects to the chat server with an ordinary Java-enabled Web browser such as Netscape Navigator or Microsoft Internet Explorer.

In creating a toy, a Web publisher such as *Nando* has to keep in mind the requirements of auditable access tracking. In order for any content of the Web site to be of value to the publisher, it has to be of value to a potential advertiser, and for that the ability to track the number and nature of the accesses becomes essential. The advertiser wants to know how often the content is seen and by what sorts of people. Web servers employ a standardized approach to tracking this kind of information, which while imperfect for needs of advertisers has been grudgingly accepted by the emerging Web advertising industry. The standardized access tracking also lends itself to third-party auditing by firms such as ABVS or I/Pro.

With a Java applet, it is possible to enable the reader to perform functions that are not tracked, much less audited. Even if the Java developer replicates the logging process employed by Web servers, potential advertisers may be suspicious of the results. So far, no method of third-party verification of those results is available. This limitation impedes implementing sophisticated Java applets at Web sites as much as any technical issue.

JAVA AND THE INTERNAL NEEDS OF *THE NANDO TIMES*

The potential for Java at *Nando* is not limited to what is publicly visible on the Web. As of this writing, Java is under serious scrutiny as a tool for supporting a number of internal operations.

At present, for example, the editors of *The Nando Times* work simultaneously on two systems. They select and edit stories on an antiquated newspaper system that uses proprietary terminals connected to a 15-year-old Tandem minicomputer. At each desk, Coyotes terminals sit next to a PC or a Macintosh, which the editors use to organize stories into pages on the Web. *Nando* is in the process of replacing this hybrid system with one based on an object-oriented database, one capable of handling video and audio with the same ease as text. The Coyote terminals will be gone, and the editors will work entirely from their PCs or Macintoshes. In this scenario, Java becomes a leading candidate for the language in which the editing tools will be written, because a carefully written Java application is immediately able to run on both PCs and Macintoshes without needing to laboriously port the application from one environment to the other.

Java also is under scrutiny at *Nando* for creating system and business administration applications. Here the advantage is mobility. The system administrator or advertising clerk needs only a PC with a Java-enabled browser and access to the Internet to monitor the network or place ads regardless of where he or she is.

A controlling factor for the choice of internal applications will be development speed. New tools such as Microsoft's Visual J++, Netscape's Internet Foundation Classes, and Marimba's Bongo hold the promise of putting Java in the same realm as other rapid-development environments such as Microsoft Visual Basic. If these tools live up to their potential, an additional question will be the age-old "buy versus build" issue. An organization the size of Nando.net will tend to buy whenever possible. The build option is reserved for strategic applications, such as the editorial system currently under development. Finally, there is the issue of the performance of Java-based software in a production environment, discussed in more detail in the section on Mission Pertinence.

PRINCIPLES FOR EVALUATING EMERGING TECHNOLOGY

A theme has pervaded the discussion so far. At this point at *Nando,* Java is useful but not essential. Or to put it in other terms, Java is of tactical importance to *Nando* but is not strategic. It is a weapon in the arsenal, but not the only weapon. As such, Java is subject to the same scrutiny that all emerging technology must withstand at *Nando.*

There are three principles that emerging technology must adhere to in order to be accepted at *Nando:* potential universality, openness, and mission pertinence. In spite of the peculiarities of the Web publishing business, these three principles can be applied by any business in its consideration of Java.

POTENTIAL UNIVERSALITY

Determining the potential universality of a new technology is difficult, bordering on guesswork, but it is an essential step. The more obvious penalties for reliance on also-ran technology can be identified in the cost of maintaining specialized equipment and finding or training specialized support staff. Less obvious but ultimately more fatal are the artificial restrictions that a narrowly accepted technology can place on a business. For every special advantage the obscure technology brings, there is likely to be a laundry list of disadvantages, simply because such a small part of the universe is devoting any effort to enhance it.

While some businesses may still have the luxury of relying upon obscure or narrowly accepted technology, the days when doing so remains possible are quickly passing. For the Web publishing business such a time never existed, and even for print publishing, which long has lived in a peculiar technological world of its own, those days are almost over. Universality is the technological equivalent of what accountants call GAAP: Generally Accepted Accounting Practices. It might be called GAT: Generally Accepted Technology.

The first test of universality is the easiest, the "who needs it" test. This is to some degree a test of technical merit, but also one of utility. If the new tool, language, etc., solves an existing business problem or enhances the potential of a core business operation, it immediately passes this test. The value of Java when it was first introduced was that it provided the ability to add intelligence to Web pages that otherwise would be static and of limited functionality. For a Web publisher that means increasing the chances of creating a compelling experience for the reader, and by extension, increasing the number of readers.

Technical merit alone is not the only determinant. Betamax was long considered the superior videocassette format to VHS, but woe to any business that made its business plan dependent on Betamax. The difference between success and failure results as much from marketing and packaging as from raw merit. As a result, a business has to pay attention to how a technology is being handled by its backers, as well as how powerful or innovative the concept is. Companies such as Netscape, Microsoft, and Sun understand this, which is why many of their products are provided at little or no cost or are bundled with commonly used products.

The early signs for Java were positive on the marketing test. Sun Microsystems very wisely released the language to the public domain. Had Sun attempted to make money by licensing the language directly to developers or invoking royalties on software written in

Java, the language would already be dead. Further ensuring its widespread use, Sun licensed Java technology to Netscape and subsequently to Microsoft for inclusion in their respective Web browsers. To a Web publisher such as *Nando,* for which the Web is the universe, that move guaranteed Java's universality.

Finally, to achieve universality a technology needs, for lack of a better word, glamour. It needs to attract enough interest to have a chance of spreading. Many new products and concepts have passed this test, Java included. Those ranks include such successes as the World Wide Web itself, and such disappointments as Personal Digital Assistants (remember those?). The verdict is still out on cable modems and the so-called network computer.

OPENNESS

The second principle is openness. It is akin to universality, in that universality is rarely achieved anymore without openness. However, openness by itself does not guarantee universality. Openness can be defined as some degree of platform independence, combined with an adherence to standards, a high level of interoperability and versatility. By encouraging Java support in Web browsers on all platforms, Sun ensured that Java would not be chained to any particular hardware platform or operating system. That remains one of Java's great strengths.

Sun achieved an adherence to standards for Java by enabling it to become the standard. This is an old trick for Sun, which did the same thing with its Network File System protocol. In this case, the question of openness intertwines with universality, since universality or something approaching universality is essential in creating a new standard.

Java meets the interoperability and versatility tests by conforming to concepts of object-oriented programming. What this means on the business side is that the language can easily be extended with what are called class libraries. These add new capabilities to the language that might not have been present before. A perfect example is the Internet Foundation Classes (IFC) that Netscape has developed. With IFC, a programmer can design a new Java user interface simply by dragging elements of the interface into place with an ordinary Web browser. This kind of enhanced functionality makes Java a serious candidate for the development of *Nando's* new editorial front end.

MISSION PERTINENCE

In exploring the third principle, mission pertinence, a business has to ask whether the new technology fits what the company is doing and how it does business. This part of the evaluation may seem straightforward and self-evident, but it requires a high level of open-mindedness. It often is easier to reject a technology because it would force changes in operating procedure or corporate culture, when in fact those are the very changes that would advance the business. Not an easy determination.

One operational concern at *Nando,* and one that is likely to be shared by almost any business, is whether it makes sense to embrace an entirely new programming language. The answer at *Nando* is a qualified yes. *Nando* had standardized on Perl for rapid development and on C and C++ for applications where speed and robustness are more important. As it turns out, a programmer adept at C++ can easily slip into Java. Both languages are object-oriented, and Java is the simpler of the two, although Java should not be mistaken as a language for beginners. The biggest obstacle is the absence of the powerful tools (symbolic debuggers, object repositories, visual editors, etc.) that professional programmers are used to. That deficiency is rapidly being addressed by products such as Microsoft's Visual J++, JavaSoft's JavaBeans, and Marimba's Bongo, but Java is still emerging as a mature programming environment.

Related to the language issue is Java's place in the computing environment as a whole. While most fully developed languages reside on top of the operating system, Java functions one level higher, on top of applications such as Web browsers. This contributes to Java's platform independence, in that all adjustments to the underlying hardware and operating system are handled by the browser. Unfortunately, this also creates a large performance penalty because a Java applet does not have direct access to the operating system. It must do everything through its host application.

The performance penalty plays out in two ways: It slows the display of the Web page even on fast connections, and it may result in total failure of the applet for readers who do not have computers powerful enough to process Java applets. There is some relief in store on both issues. The Just In Time compiler in version 3.0 of the Netscape Navigator browser has helped improve the speed of Java applets. The continual increase in desktop computing power is gradually making the failure of Java applets less common.

At *Nando* these performance hits decrease Java's appeal as a development environment for its newsroom tools. The performance concerns do not preclude the development of enhancements to the published product, but they do increase the need for care in applet design.

Java also has to compete with other tools that can accomplish similar tasks. Most of the toys in the *Nando* toy box, for example, are created in Macromedia's Shockwave. The advantage of Shockwave is that it doesn't require a high-end (read, highly paid) programmer, and the development time is much shorter than for a Java application. The disadvantage is that Shockwave applications cannot run without the supporting Shockwave plug-in, a special piece of software that must be added to the browser before the Shockwave application can run. For a Web publisher, a Java solution generally will be preferable to one that requires a plug-in, especially if the plug-in does not have the wide acceptance that Shockwave enjoys.

Ironically, another competitor for Java is JavaScript, the Java-like scripting language supported by the Netscape Navigator Web browser. JavaScript applets tend to be faster, because they are part of the Web page, but that also imposes a practical size-limit on them. Unlike Java, JavaScript is not object-oriented, another reason that it is not practical for large applets. Finally, JavaScript code is plainly visible to any reader who invokes the View Source option on the browser, whereas the Java code remains invisible to the reader. In a competitive Web publishing environment, that one fact can be decisive.

FORWARD TO JAVA

As with any business issue, the decision comes down to a comparison of cost to benefit. On the benefit side are cross-platform capa-

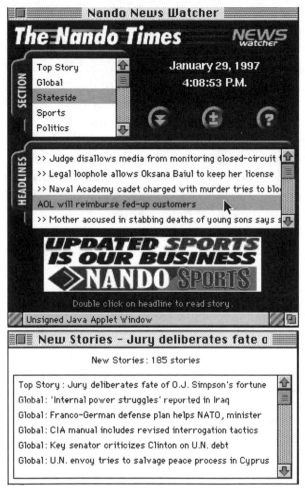

*Figure 5-3. The News Watcher™, a Java application shown above in pro-
totype, alerts users to news stories as they are posted to* The Nando
Times. *The main window (upper) lists the news sections and their stories. The story list is updated every six minutes. The alerter window
(lower) is optional and lists only the new stories as they come on-line.
The application was developed in Java so that readers would not have
to download and install a custom application.*

bility, increased interactivity for Web pages, and the power of a maturing object-oriented language. The costs include a need for increased bandwidth to support ever-larger applets, a need for more

computing power on the client end, and the inescapable reality that Java will be slower than more direct programming methods, at least for the near term.

So where does that leave Java at *The Nando Times?* As to whether Java will make a suitable user interface for the editors who work behind the scenes at *Nando,* we will definitely have some kind of Java tool for the editors. The only question is how much Java versus off-the-shelf software. For the end user and reader, *Nando's* front page and advertising is Javatized, and the News Watcher is live. A Java-based chat client is in evaluation. Use of Java on the front end and back end of *The Nando Times* is expected to increase as the language and its development tools mature.

CHAPTER 6

HOTWIRED: NEW TECHNOLOGIES, NEW MARKETS

Ed Anuff, Director of Product Management, HotWired

HotWired is the interactive media arm of Wired *Ventures, the publisher of* Wired *magazine. HotWired has a very innovative and useful Web site, as well as one of the top-rated search engines, HotBot. HotWired also runs the Wired daily news service (www.wired.com), a chat service (talk.com), and a number of targeted information Web sites such as Suck (www.suck.com), Dr. Weil (www.drweil.com) and Cocktail (www.cocktailtime.com). HotWired has used Java successfully to solve the problem of complex Web site navigation and build site traffic. Its chat service, Talk.com, was also built with Java and was one of the first applications that was entirely a "server-side" Java application. The Wired Desktop, a channel built using Marimba's Castanet technology, is being introduced early in 1997. HotWired's Java applications are widely deployed and can be viewed by anyone with Web access; their speed and utility are exemplary. Java has enabled HotWired to develop new interactive media faster, and compete more effectively in Web time.*

HotWired went live on the Web in October 1994. Since then, it has striven to demonstrate leadership both in publishing cutting-edge original content as well as using leading-edge interactive technologies. To accomplish this goal, the company created the HotWired Web site, at www.hotwired.com; the popular HotBot search engine, at www.hotbot.com; the Wired News daily news service, and the Talk.com chat service, as well as running a number of other popular Web sites such as Suck, at www.suck.com; Dr. Weil, at www.drweil.com; and Cocktail, at www.cocktailtime.com.

Although the Web site is closely linked with *Wired* magazine, HotWired's mission from the beginning has been to establish itself as a distinctive brand and voice on the web

For HotWired, the challenge in fulfilling this mission is to carefully walk the line between a traditional media organization and a technology company. Interactive media is the synthesis of media and technology. Over the last few years, we've seen many companies make the mistake of valuing one over the other, resulting in is either flat content sites better suited to a print format, or Shockwave-laden Web pages seldom revisited after the initial novelty wears off.

In this landscape, the Web producer has emerged as the figure who makes the decisions of content, technology, and interactivity critical to the success of a Web site project. The actual title varies from company to company, but whether it is producer, product manager, project manager, or publisher, the role is essential to ensure creative and financial success. This chapter gives some insight into the process and methodology used by Web producers in planning highly interactive Web projects, and the challenges faced in selecting and using new technologies, particularly Java.

A WEB REVENUE PRIMER

Before exploring how Java has affected the current and future directions of HotWired, we need to understand the dynamics of how a commercial Web site such as HotWired operates from a business standpoint. HotWired's business model is based primarily on ad revenue. When commercial Web sites first went live in 1994, the viability of advertising on the Web was untested and controversial. Over the next two years, the mechanics of ads on the Web were refined to allow better targeting, tracking, and reporting, and advertisers learned how to master the medium to get their ad messages across. By late 1996, the validity of the ad business model had been proven by the success of HotWired and other major commercial Web sites as they reported quarter after quarter of record revenues.

UNDERSTANDING THE AD REVENUE MODEL

Because ad revenue is essential to the success of content on the Web, it's important to explore the details of how advertising is implemented on the Web. The most common ad presence on a Web page is the classic ad banner. In practice, a number of different formats (shapes, sizes, animations, etc.) have arisen since HotWired introduced the first ad banner to the Web; however, the banner is still the predominant unit of Web advertising. An ad banner is a rectangular graphic, usually 476 by 56 pixels in size, displayed at either the top or bottom of a Web page.

©1996 Netscape Communications Corporation. Used with permission. All rights reserved. This image may not be replicated or copied without the expressed written permission of Netscape.

Figure 6-1. HotWired introduced the first ad banner to the Web. Web banner ads have become ubiquitous.

Two common measures used to describe the success of a Web site are number of page views per day, or numbers of ad impressions served a day. Each time an ad banner is displayed to a user, it is counted as an ad impression. For Web sites that have one ad banner per page, the number of ad impressions served per day is roughly equivalent to the number of page views a day.

In the early days, when the Web was at a purely investment stage, the number of page views per day was used to measure a site's potential financial success. As the ad market matured, Web sites became more successful in converting their page-view inventory into actual ad impressions, either by developing their own Web sales force, using sales reps, or joining sales syndicates.

Once a viable model emerged that linked traffic (page views/per day) to revenue (sold ad impressions/per day), the issue became how to maximize the revenue for the investment of creating the Web pages. For the small Web sites (which describes many of the original commercial Web sites in the early days), the basic business proposition was simple. Since overall traffic was more or less spread out over the basic number of pages, every page on the site was roughly equal in terms of the revenue return on the investment of creating the page. A classic example of this was the infamous Web site, Suck. Suck is an irreverent daily commentary on Web culture and the on-line industry. For a long time, the site consisted of a single page, updated daily with a new column. For a site like this, the overhead of creating the page is very easy to calculate, and the revenue becomes a function of traffic. To grow revenues, scale up the size of the audience.

EXPANSION, DISAGGREGATION, AND NAVIGATION

The issue of scalability is one of the central theoretical challenges of ad-supported sites. The more ambitious commercial Web ventures seek higher returns than the small, single-page sites, and in order to scale up their revenues, they must find other parameters that can be added to the revenue equation. The next such parameter is number of pages of the site. The more pages, the more surface area to display ad banners, and, logically, the more revenue. So the expansion path for most sites is to embark on content aggregation, either using in-house original content (HotWired, CInet, MSN) or repurposed content from print or other sources (Pathfinder, ZD-Net).

This led to the creation of the mega-sites. But economies of scale can break down, and sites find themselves in situations where their main pages get the majority of the traffic, while the deeper pages are seldom visited. The irony of this situation is that the deeper pages are often the costlier ones to produce, since they contain the rich original content, while the main pages consist of tables of contents.

When HotWired reached the stage in its growth where this became a factor, it realized that there were two key techniques that could be applied to ameliorate the situation. The first was disaggregation: instead of a single sprawling site, create a network of Web sites. The second was to study the issues of site navigation in order to ensure that users were aware of and could quickly navigate to any section of the site.

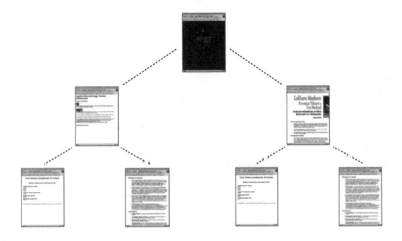

Figure 6-2. Typical content Web sites find an inverse relationship between site traffic and production costs.

SITE NAVIGATION: JAVA'S FIRST KILLER APP?

Java's first practical use on the Web was as a solution to the problem of complex Web site navigation. Java imagemap applets, which displayed an image and used mouse-clicks within that image to transport the user to a different Web page, had been available since the early days of Java. However, it wasn't until early 1996 that such applets started to see widespread usage on the Web. One of the early users of this technology was Suck, which used a Java applet to handle navigation when it made the transition from a single page to multipage Web site in April 1996. Similar approaches were used by HotWired's Packet, Pop, and WebMonkey sites.

These early uses of Java, while hardly the pinnacle of programming, were an important transition for using Java on commercial Web sites. Because Java was a new language, with a scarce labor market of capable programmers, most companies developed Java expertise through the self-education of their engineers. This was an often painstaking process, as the realities of the ultra-compressed product development cycles of the Web, called "Web time or Web years," conflicted with the learning curve of Java. Because a beginning Java programmer's first project, a navigation applet, could yield such a significant return in site traffic, it justified a continued investment in Java technologies for many Web companies.

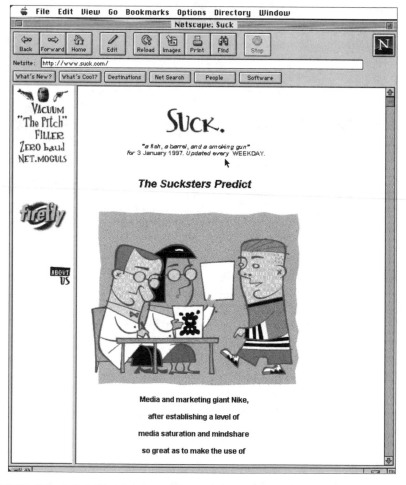

© 1997 HotWired, Inc. All rights reserved.

Figure 6-3. Suck is a witty, well-written, and jaded view of the on-line experience and its industry infrastructure. The Java navigation applet is in the left-hand column.

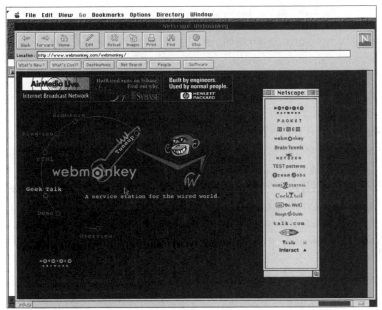

© 1997 HotWired, Inc. All rights reserved.

Figure 6-4. A floating navigation aid pops up on the HotWired site. It is easy to navigate to other parts of the site, no matter where you are. Every unseen page on your Web site costs you money.

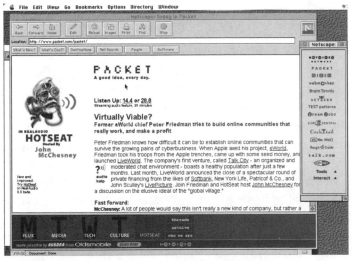

© 1997 HotWired, Inc. All rights reserved.

Figure 6-5. Note the continuity of the pop-up navigation window, initiated with Java. Packet provides useful content daily to the working digerati.

NEW MARKETS FOR HOTWIRED

With Java proven as a viable technology for Web development, it quickly became a central element of HotWired's product-development strategy. At the outset of 1996, the company identified several key objectives for the direction of its web efforts. As mentioned earlier, the process of changing to a network of sites rather than a supersite allowed us to greatly expand the scope of our offerings.

In addition to greater flexibility in the range and voice of our editorial sites, the network structure allowed us to add interactive and information-driven sites to the mix. Examples of this are Talk.com, HotWired's Java-based multiuser chat service, and HotBot, the company's search engine. These sites are characterized by a development process vastly different than the company's previous efforts in that they require a substantially greater technology investment in order to produce. The result is a development process more closely comparable to software or CD-ROM title development than traditional Web development.

In this section, we'll look at what this means for the product-development cycle, from concept and market analysis to deployment and distribution.

EVALUATING NEW MARKETS: TECHNOLOGY LANDSCAPE

One of the early steps of the HotWired product-development cycle is evaluating the technology mix for building the product. This is a fairly significant decision and while arriving at it is largely the responsibility of engineering and product development, it is very likely that many of the other departments will participate in the evaluation process. The choice of technology can determine the potential size of the audience, the length of the development cycle, and the overall project cost. Under the pressures of Web time, it becomes essential to have a core set of technologies that are dependably stable, cost-effective, and reusable.

Here, we'll focus primarily on client-side technologies, which means code that runs on the user's machines rather than on HotWired's central servers. The decision of whether to create a client-side or a server-side technology is the first step of the process. In general, unless a project requires a highly dynamic user interface, it probably should be developed using conventional Web HTML technologies. The difference in cost between client-side and server-side technology from a cost-benefit analysis will also help to answer the question. In general, an average client-side development project, even one created with Java, will prove to be significantly more expensive than a typical server-side project.

For most Web technology projects involving client-side execution, there are essentially three paths that a project can go. These are:

1. Build a stand-alone Internet application.

2. Build a browser plug-in.

3. Build a Java applet or application.

Stand-alone Internet Applications

The first option, building a stand-alone Internet application, has a couple of advantages and several severe disadvantages. The main advantage is that there are no technology constraints on the end product. For some applications, this might end up the best choice. This would typically be the path taken for the development of server software, for example. Good examples of client-side Internet applications would be Netscape Navigator or PointCast.

For HotWired, there are several severe disadvantages to developing stand-alone Internet applications that we intend for our users to run. First of all, compatibility becomes an issue when trying to support an application over multiple operating systems. In fact, just the challenge of handling customer support would be cost-prohibitive to most Web publishers.

A second major factor is that such development would be outside the mission and core competency of HotWired's engineering department, which means that to pursue such a project we would either need to recruit engineers with this experience or train our existing ones.

The last issue is that overall development time for this type of application would be too lengthy for us to competitively produce. For all of these reasons, the only type of stand-alone applications we develop are server applications, which only run on HotWired machines.

Browser Plug-ins

A second option for the development of client-side technology would be to either use or develop a browser plug-in. Most major browsers have a way for developers to write extensions to the browser that the user can download and plug in. Some examples of this are Macromedia's Shockwave and Adobe Acrobat.

There are a couple of issues for the use of plug-ins by content developers. First of all, Netscape's current approach for handling the download and installation of plug-ins is a time-consuming process not easily understood by new users, so sites that use plug-ins risk alienating users of Netscape's browser. Microsoft's ActiveX technology is more friendly from a user standpoint. However, plug-in development for either browser risks not being portable across operating systems. For these reasons, content developers have been slow to adopt plug-ins, although there is some indication that ActiveX-based plug-ins will be much more popular in 1997.

The development of plug-ins by content developers is rare for the same reasons that have made development of stand-alone Internet applications cost-prohibitive for content developers. Too expensive in time, money, and expertise, development of client-side Internet technology in native code is beyond the capabilities of most Web developers. Fortunately, Java has provided a technology path around these difficulties.

Java

Java has a number of benefits for content developers trying to develop client-side technologies under the constraints of Web time. Interestingly enough, despite the hype of Java as an Internet language, most of Java's strengths lie in the fact that it corrects many of the problems plaguing software development for the last ten years. In order to extract as much performance as possible from desktop personal computers, developers chose programming languages, such as C, that were perceived to allow them to write highly optimized code. Short-terms results encouraged this shift, and by the end of the 1980s, most new development was done in C. When the benefits of object-oriented programming started to become apparent, developers moved to C++, the object-oriented successor to C. Unfortunately, both C and C++ are notoriously difficult to debug, and software development cycles for many software companies started to extend to the point where 18-month projects were not uncommon, and products finally shipped with considerable bugs.

Java has the benefit of preserving much of the syntax of C, meaning that to a C or C++ programmer, it reads much the same, and most C programmers are able to learn the language very quickly. Java removes most of the features that were most commonly misused by programmers and instead provides new capabilities based on software objects, which are easier to use and to debug. Java-based software can be written and debugged in significantly less time.

The bottom line is that from the perspective of content developers, Java is the ideal choice for the reason that it makes software development in "Web time" economically possible.

For a manager responsible for product development, this is a significant enough reason to choose Java. However, from a marketing perspective, Java makes the most sense as well. Java applets are supported by every major browser on every computing platform. This means that the choice of Java will not limit the potential market for a Web site.

Of course, in practice, the benefits of Java can be tempered by several important caveats. First of all, the implementations of Java within specific browsers still have problems that can cause browser crashes, particularly on the Macintosh. It is expected that these problems will disappear over time but they are something to consider.

The second downside of Java is in developing or recruiting Java programming talent. While most C programmers are able to pick up the basics of the language fairly quickly, unless they've had some exposure to object-oriented development, it can take some time to for them become proficient with the language. Because of the newness of the language, most books and resources about the language discuss only the more straightforward aspects of Java development, which means that major Java projects risk getting stalled when a project goes into uncharted territory.

Lastly, as a new language, Java is still under development by Sun.

Java 1.02 is the predominant version of the language. However, Java 1.1 was released as an early beta to developers in late 1996 and there are some indications that 2.0 will be released sometime in 1997. The evolution of the language is good, in that it adds important new capabilities for developers, but it has the negative effect of paralyzing developers when faced with developing their own solutions or waiting for the next Java release.

In the software industry, when a new platform or enabling technology like Java is introduced, there is often tremendous uncertainty in the industry until a clear value chain emerges. It is often unclear which pieces of the puzzle will be supplied by which players. Does Sun maintain the value of their contribution by releasing new versions of Java, or by focusing on development tools? What does this mean for tool vendors? Near the end of the chain are content developers, who must carefully weigh their technology choices to create the best interactive experience for the users.

CASE STUDIES

To understand the practical considerations for Web publishers using Java, it's useful to examine two cases in closer detail. HotWired embarked on two major Java projects in 1996. The first was Talk.com, a multiuser chat service, which launched in October 1996. The second was Wired Desktop, a channel built using Marimba's Castanet technology and slated for introduction in early 1997.

TALK.COM

In evaluating the idea of launching an Internet chat service, we observed an important trend in the methods by which people connect to the Net. Many users are migrating from on-line services, such as AOL, to using flat-fee Internet Service Providers (ISPs) to connect to the Internet. In the recent Odyssey Homefront Survey, it was found that more households now reach the Net directly by ISP rather than through an on-line service.

This trend has important implications for the types of sites and services users are going to expect from the Web in the near future.

Two years ago, companies such as HotWired led the migration of content from on-line services to the Net. The Web now provides a more rich content experience than can be found on any of the on-line services. However, until recently, interactive services, such as multiuser communities, transactions, and fee-based databases, have been the exclusive province of the on-line services. The primary reason for this is that it is easier for these on-line services to construct a viable revenue model for their interactive services, since they are credit-card billed, and users are not asked to resend payment information for every purchase or transaction.

When users switch from an on-line service to an ISP, they often do so because they believe that they can get the same experience for a lower cost. From a content perspective, this is true. However, users will quickly find that services such as chat rooms are conspicuously absent.

In order to provide a chat service on the Net, a suitable revenue model must be adopted. The fee-based model is questionable. If users were amenable to it, they would likely keep their on-line service accounts. The best case scenario is to adopt an advertising approach based on the competencies already developed by the major content sites.

For our Talk.com service, we decided that an advertising-supported chat service would be the most compatible with users' expectations of the Net, and with HotWired's overall business model. It then became a task of deciding on the specific implementation. As a new service, we wanted to make it as easy as possible for current Web advertisers to participate in Talk.com. This meant choosing an ad banner as the main ad unit, so that advertisers could use their existing banner ads with the service. In order to make banners work outside of Web pages, we developed a time-based rotation, which showed the banner ads at 30-second intervals.

Product Requirements

Along with the decision to make the service ad-supported, we identified several other key requirements. Among these were the following:

- *A simple, familiar user interface.* We wanted to be able to provide users with an experience as similar as possible to that of the major on-line services.

- *The ability to run a well-managed service.* Although we did not intend to censor discussions the way that the on-line services do, we needed to ensure that malicious users were not able to disrupt the service for others.

- *The ability to tie content to the chat experience.* We believe that combining a live chat experience with content and commentary can provide a new type of interactive content experience. Services like AOL have demonstrated the viability of this with services such as The Motley Fools, and HotWired has made chat an integral part of its Packet (www.packet.com) Web site, with daily chats discussing topics and issues from the Packet site.

- *The ability to host special auditorium-style events.* Celebrity interviews, debates, panel discussions, and other special events are an important part of HotWired's content programming and are an essential way to build traffic for the service.

- *Scalable, cross-platform technology.* The service needed to be accessible for users surfing the Web via browsers, thin clients, information appliances, and any other way of accessing the Web that might be developed. More important, it needed to support very large numbers of simultaneous users.

Development

After identifying the basic product requirements, it became important to identify the technology path for the development of the product. At this point, let's examine the basics of how on-line chat works. At their simplest, chat services are basically implemented as client-server systems, where the user runs a chat client connected over the Net to a chat server. Other users also connect to the chat server. When a user types a message in a chat room, the text of the message is sent to the chat server, which then sends that text to all the other users in the chat room. The chat server basically keeps track of all the users connected to it, tracks which chat rooms they're in, and routes the appropriate text to the appropriate chat room. In practice, it gets a little more complicated when there are large numbers of users connected at the same time and the server needs to track multiple chat rooms. To handle the complexity, the work is often distributed over several servers.

In the case of Talk.com, the decision how to develop the service was not a simple one for a number of reasons. There are many chat technologies on the Net, ranging from the still-unproven 3-D avatar systems to IRC and MUD servers. The 3-D avatar systems give users an "avatar" that moves and chats in a virtual world; these can be icons, comic book caricatures, microorganisms—anything, really. IRC stands for "Internet Relay Chat," where a threaded chat technology. MUD means "Multiuser Dungeon," where basically a user plays a role in a virtual world. From a financial perspective, using an existing technology would be the most cost-effective approach in the short-term, but if the technology did not match up with our product requirements, it would hamper our ability to operate a successful service.

When we started the project, IRC servers (both commercial and public domain) were the main chat technology on the Net. Unfortunately, IRC has several shortcomings that make it a weak choice for a commercial service. Issues such as the security of the service, the ability to deliver advertisements, and event moderation are difficult to implement using IRC technology. Other commercial chat software had similar limitations as well as being unproven in a commercial context.

The approach finally selected was to build both the chat client and server in Java. Although HotWired was one of the first developers to build an entire server application in Java, we expect that server-side Java development will become more common as most Web servers are able to run Java servlets (Java applications that plug in to servers). By going with a custom-built approach, we are able to have full control of the feature set. Using Java for the entire system ensured that users on all platforms would be able to access the service.

Some of the key features that we were able to implement were:

- Self-filtered chat, which lets us avoid censoring chat discussions by allowing users to choose what users they wish to avoid.

- Instant private messages, which allow users to have one-to-one private discussions.

- Multiple user nicknames, so that users can assume different identities in chat rooms as well as protect their anonymity.

- Member-created chat rooms, so that users can create areas to congregate and discuss topics of their choosing.

- Live auditorium events with moderator controls that allow chat administrators to coordinate events and filter guest questions.

In addition, we were able to create a version of the Talk.com chat client usable via the Marimba tuner. By using Marimba technology, we were able to take advantage of its advanced user interface construction tools to create a more attractive and accessible user interface, as well as add features not possible in the original version of Talk.com

Roll-out

In launching the service, we found that while many users and press had some familiarity with Java, quite a bit of education needed to be done to explain the benefits of Java. In many ways, the project required us to market Java as much as we did the service itself. The challenge here is that the end goal is the promotion of your product, as opposed to having the story be too much about Java. This is a delicate balance, especially since it's often easier for users and press to view a Java-based product as part of the Java phenomenon, rather than paying attention to the specific features and benefits of the product. Marketers of Java-based products must avoid the temptation to allow Java to be the central part of the story. Sticking to the product story, as opposed to the underlying technology, is the essential course of action.

For HotWired, the central theme of the roll-out was that Talk.com represented the first time a major Web publisher had launched a full-featured chat service—for conversations, live events, debates, etc.—that is as easy to use as the paid alternatives, yet as freely accessible and open as the Internet.

WIRED DESKTOP

Properly speaking, the Wired Desktop is not a technology project. It is the umbrella term for HotWired's push media initiative. Combining HotWired's Wired News service with a multimedia screen saver, the Wired Desktop is designed to be deployable over Marimba Castanet, PointCast, Microsoft's Active Desktop, and other push media services. The technical implementation of each version depends on the specific platform. For example, the Wired Channel on PointCast, which launched in December 1996, is the first implementation of the Wired Desktop. In this section, we'll take a look at some of the issues regarding the design and development of such a product, and some of the steps taken to implement it as a channel using Marimba's Castanet system. At the time of this writing, many of the details of content programming are being finalized, and by the time you read this, you'll be able to see how these turned out. The purpose of this section is not to serve as a description of the actual product, since many of the details will change before launch, but will instead provide an overview of the critical considerations for planning a media project using Java and other interactive technologies.

Although this section explains some of the basics of channeling (the distribution of content, code, and data as channels over the Net) as implemented by companies like Marimba and PointCast, additional information can be found in Marimba's white paper, "Building the New Customer Channel," and is recommended reading.

Note: In this section, we use the term "programming" in several places in the broadcast media sense of the word. To avoid confusion, in most places in this chapter the process of writing code or developing technology is referred to as "software development."

Background

During 1996, three important developments changed the direction of content publishing over the Internet. First, push media emerged as a viable alternative to the current Web pull model for content distribution. At the same time, Java and new browser technologies have enabled a new level of expressiveness in the presentation of visual media. Lastly, growth of Internet-linked intranets have made it possible for content publishers to harness the capabilities of the intranet to deliver high-bandwidth content.

PUSH MEDIA PROGRAMMING

Push media refers to Internet broadcasting technologies that allow users to receive content via subscribed channels, which are updated in either real time, or at regular intervals. Push media technologically has much in common with both off-line browsers, like FreeLoader, or streaming media applications, like RealAudio. For the new media content producer, push media has a very different significance.

The Web until now has been a pull media, where users choose which information they wish to receive, the sequence in which they receive it, and the pace and timing of the experience. Because many Web producers came from a print media background, the limitations of pull media were often not immediately apparent. Most major Web sites were not that far evolved from traditional print magazines.

With the introduction of PointCast, Marimba, and similar technologies, it became apparent that content on the Internet could be delivered in a manner similar to television programming. Among the characteristics of push media programming are:

1. Content and information delivered to the user in the form of "program segments," multimedia presentations using animation and digital video to deliver a news report, advertisement, or story.

2. A classic television programming grid where program segments are scheduled for exact times and rotations.

3. Less viewer interaction than the Web or other forms of interactive media, although not as passive a medium as television.

These differences, when taken together, represent a fundamental shift in content development for the Internet. To understand why, you must start from the profile of current consumers of push media.

At the moment, most people who use push media software (tuners, etc.) do so at work, where they are on a company intranet connected to the Internet via a fast direct connection. This is an environment where conventional broadcast media such as television or even radio are inappropriate. Further, the time constraints of most people require that information be delivered fast and to the point, without requiring a huge investment in attention or participation to get the content they're interested in. For these reasons, the Web, which requires a tremendous investment in concentration and interaction, can prove a distraction as well. Publications for MIS managers and IT professionals caution managers about the risks to productivity when employees become "mouse potatoes" after spending inordinate amounts of time surfing the Web.

Typical push media programming consists of news headlines, weather reports, stock tickers, sports scores, as well as filtered industry-specific information. Delivered throughout the day, such information provides office workers with a lifeline to the real world as well as supplying crucial information essential to them professionally as well as of benefit to their company. When a company's competitor announces a new product, delivering that information enterprise-wide is of immense strategic value. For these reasons, the use of push media has spread through many corporations at a phenomenal rate.

Product Concept

The basic objective of the Wired Desktop is to provide the following two key elements to users of the service:

1. Push distribution of Wired News content.

2. Internet-based multimedia broadcast programming.

The third requirement is to be able to deploy the service over multiple distribution systems. The importance of this requirement will be detailed in the next section. The initial distribution systems chosen to support were:

1. Marimba Castanet

2. PointCast

3. Microsoft Active Desktop

Note: Although Marimba technology is used in system descriptions and examples, a version of the Wired Desktop already exists as a PointCast channel and other versions will ultimately be deployed on a broad set of distribution technologies.

For users, the Wired Desktop consists of a Marimba channel subscribed to using the Marimba Castanet tuner. The channel runs in either a full-screen kiosk mode (maximized window) or as a standard system window. This allows users to interact with the system in whichever way they feel more comfortable. The display consists of two views, an information layer, in which Wired News is displayed, and a media layer, which is used to display real-time animated programs.

At its simplest, the system consists of a pipeline, which starts with content creation and editing, databased content management, and through a transmitter infrastructure, pushes content to a large number of users on a regularly scheduled basis.

From this standpoint, the system is not unlike traditional Web production and serving. However, key aspects of this system enable us to deliver high-bandwidth content over a variety of distribution platforms, and to update this content at regular intervals throughout the day.

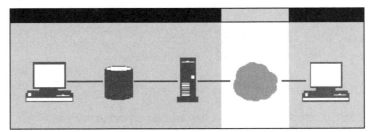

Figure 6-6. Diagram of Wired Desktop: the flow path is very similar to traditional Web publishing and serving.

PRODUCTION FOR MAXIMUM DISTRIBUTION

Wired Desktop is about distribution, both the distribution process of pushing content to the user instead of the traditional Web pull mechanism, as well as distribution through the variety of emerging push media distribution technologies and systems.

When we started the project, our first step was either to choose a distribution system, or to build our own. While it was obvious that the latter choice was outside the scope of the project, the selection of a single distribution technology proved difficult for a variety of reasons, ranging from the technical to the lack of a clear market-place leader among vendors of such technology. Companies like Marimba, Microsoft, PointCast, BackWeb, Arrive, and others are offering systems and services for push media distribution. We decided to support as many of these systems as we could. This challenge was not unlike that faced by CD-ROM producers, who faced the decision of how to produce their titles for Mac, Windows, DOS, CD-I, 3DO, Sega, etc. The classic multimedia title production process consists of the following stages:

Figure 6-7. The production process for the Wired Desktop is similar to that of a CD-ROM.

The challenge in this case was not just one of cross-platform development (stages 1 though 4), but multiple channels of distribution (stage 5).

To deal with these issues, we developed the concept of mass deployment, a system combining the following elements:

1. Media asset management through the use of database technology.

2. Cross-platform technologies, such as Java.

3. Deployment-neutral production process.

Media asset management refers to the ability to acquire, catalog, store, and reuse any media asset, whether textual, such as headlines or stories, or media formats, such as image of photos from Reuters, or in later versions, digitized video from televised news sources. This is made possible through the use of relational databases.

Cross-platform development is the key to dealing with the multiple platform nature of mass deployment. Ideally, we should be able to present a reasonably similar experience to Macintosh Marimba users and Windows Active Desktop users. The easiest way to accomplish this is through the use of cross-platform component development technologies, such as Sun's Java language, as well as component integration technology, such as ActiveX or JavaBeans.

The production model is the last and perhaps most important aspect of the mass deployment process. It consists of a media creation methodology that keeps the platform and system-specific media assets (images, text) in a deployment-neutral format until as late a stage as possible. This makes it possible to create multiple versions of the same images for the various supported platforms.

After media assets are approved, they are passed through an assembly-line production process that results in a system-specific media format optimized for the target platform. For example, images are optimized for file size and memory usage, before finally being stored in Web or Java-friendly GIF file formats.

PUSH MEDIA, BANDWIDTH, AND INTRANETS

For every content producer, bandwidth is one of the major considerations and constraints to the creation and delivery of compelling content over the net. A sound production methodology starts with the end in mind, meaning that every link of the chain from developer to consumer must be examined for weakness. In most cases, bandwidth is the weak link. To cost-effectively produce Net content, the realities of bandwidth must be considered in the first steps of the production process, so the audience is not limited by bandwidth considerations.

Push media as a viable market hinges on the ability to delivery very large quantities of multimedia data to users throughout the world. For most people developing push media content, the initial target market consists of users within intranets or corporate local area networks (LANs). This is an important decision because it allows us to take advantage of two key properties of intranets to efficiently deliver this content. These are broadband local data capacity and local proxy servers. The Wired Desktop uses distribution systems like Marimba Castanet and PointCast, which use these properties to facilitate the transmission of multimedia data over the Net. To understand how many of the perceived laws of bandwidth on the net have been seemingly suspended, it's useful to review the basics of Internet-linked intranets.

Intranet LANs are typically built on Ethernet, which allows the transmission of 10 Mbps, a speed far in excess of either modem or most T1, or direct, Internet connections. This is the (theoretical) speed that one machine of the intranet can transmit to another. The bottleneck for traditional Web content publishing is that all connections to and from machines within an intranet to machines on the Internet is limited by the speed of the intranet's Internet connection, which is usually a T1 (1.5 Mbps).

This means that if users within the intranet can avoid having to connect to machines on the outside Internet to access a publisher's content, they can retrieve data at a much faster rate. The basic idea is that closer content is faster to access than farther content. Despite many claims to the contrary, proximity still has some meaning on the Net.

The solution to this is through the use of proxy servers, such as PointCast IServer or Marimba's Castanet repeater, which maintain local copies of the data pulled in from an Internet Web server so that the next time an intranet user connects to that Web server, the proxy server can instead send the local copy rather than going back out through the Internet to get the data again.

When dealing with push media, the need for proxy servers becomes more significant. Because push media client software (PointCast, Marimba Tuner) connect to servers on intervals as short as every 15 minutes, the chance that a significant number of users within an intranet are connecting at the same time and swamping the intranet's Internet connection is a very likely possibility. Further, since push media is seldom user-tailored, all the users are essentially downloading the same data. By using proxy servers, this can be avoided by having the proxy server be the only machine that connects over the Internet, and all the clients instead connect to the proxy server. The proxy server stills connects to the push server every 15 minutes, but since it's the only machine making this connection, the bandwidth usage is reasonable. Simply put, for users within an intranet, HotWired content lives on the intranet's proxy server instead of on a HotWired server.

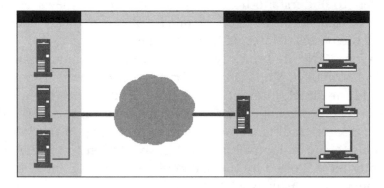

Figure 6-8. Basic overview of push media from HotWired servers to users within an intranet. Content data is pushed from left to right.

The proxy-served Intranet can be also looked at as a model for high-bandwidth delivery into the home via cable modem systems. Most of the major cable modem services intend to segment users in a similar model to that of the way intranets are organized. This can be seen by comparing the flowing diagram to the previous one:

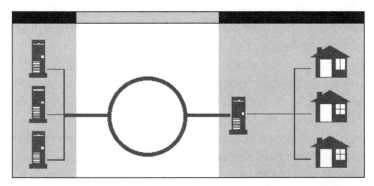

Figure 6-9. From a technical standpoint, the cable modem neighborhood and the corporate intranet are the same thing.

There is much speculation about the usability of push media services by modem users. Many of the assumptions of these systems are at odds with what we know about typical home computer use (bandwidth on demand, always on, etc.). As higher-bandwidth, dedicated connections, such as the @Home system, become available to home users, we expect that push media will become popular within that setting.

NEXT STEPS

Web publishers today strive to strike the balance between content and software development. For a relatively long time, Web producers had the option to focus simply on the issues of producing compelling content, safe in the fact that the Web reduced the number of choices for technology usage to issues such as which browser's version of HTML should they use, what type of Web server they should run, and how many T1s were needed to handle traffic. In the next year, many will look back at those days as the calm before the storm.

The shifting landscape of Internet technology is going to provide a number of new opportunities for Web sites, interactive Net services, and transactions. These opportunities will be pursued by the current Web publishers as well as entertainment software vendors who will bring their proven interactive media production discipline to the net, traditional print media companies with existing content they can reuse, broadcast media companies with their understanding of programming, on-line services looking for new relevancy in the Internet world, and many, many others who have until now sat on the sidelines. It's very likely that success will only come from understanding and combining the competencies of all of these players. The key to success will hinge on the ability to create compelling media products in Web time while harnessing the latest technologies, without falling victim to the "bleeding edge."

By the time you read this, Wired Desktop has already been deployed over PointCast and the Marimba version should be in public beta. The success of the project will depend on a range of factors including successful marketing roll-out, quality content programming, ample advertisers, and the competitive landscape. For product planners, however, important lessons and insights into the essential considerations for successful Web product development can be seen, including these basic ideas:

1. Start with the product concept, not the project technology.

2. Design a sustainable production process flexible enough to be adaptable to new opportunities.

3. Understand all the steps on the distribution value chain, and choose appropriate partners, systems, and technologies.

When taken together, these prescriptions will prepare the Web producer for the one reality of new media product development.

There is seldom a single safe technology path. The winners and losers won't be safely determined until the industry reaches maturity, at which point the opportunities will be restricted to the few large players. Use this uncertainty to your advantage. When presented with a choice of which browser to support, or which technology to embrace, choose all of the above. Design your product-development process, production methodology, and organizational planning to support and promote the development of multiple versions of products to reach the widest possible audience.

Since the time this was written, there have been a number of developments in the push media space. Microsoft and Netscape have update their browsers with push media capabilities and the adoption of these technologies by Internet users have motivated HotWired to expand their focus on channel content for these platforms. Some of the content examples used in this paper, such as POP, have been replaced with new content areas, and there have been numerous changes in the technical implementations of these examples. These developments reinforce the key point of the paper, which is to maintain flexibility and be prepared to adapt product plans to whatever directions the industry and the marketplace turn.

CHAPTER 7

NETSCAPE: JAVA FOR THE NETWORKED ENTERPRISE

Ammiel Kamon, Senior Product Manager,
Netscape Communications

Netscape changed the Internet with its technologies and products. It championed the use of these technologies within businesses, creating "intranets" that accelerate communication and access to information. These intranets can be extended to a businesses' customers and partners. To help businesses jump-start their own intranets, Netscape developed App-Foundry, an on-line resource with intranet applications, tools, and support. The third-party applications in AppFoundry are available for downloading, evaluating, and proving performance. They cover all areas within an enterprise—human resources, marketing, sales and distribution, information systems, and finance. Java, and to a greater degree, JavaScript, are used in many of these applications. The third-party developers found productivity gains using Java, although there were some limitations with early adoption. Use of Java for intranet applications is expected to increase dramatically as developer tools and the language mature.

To enroll for all 1997 benefits, I went to the Netscape intranet, clicked on human resources, and used our on-line benefits application to make selections and enroll. Paperless. Painless. Quick. And I had a confirmation back immediately. To upgrade my computer system, I went to our information service help site, picked a pre-configured system, and ordered it. To take vacation time I filled out a form on-line and a notice was sent to my boss. Before I left I checked the latest number of downloads of AppFoundry, the status of my top three projects, the order and lead pipeline for our Enterprise servers, and the publicity schedule for our new intranet tool set. I pulled down the "breaking down the walls" graphics, which I needed for this book. I alerted the Web team to the promised delivery of three new third-party applications to AppFoundry. I clicked on the Java resource and found out the status of the new set of class libraries I had been waiting for.

Netscape's intranet has enabled me, the teams I have been part of, and the company as a whole to be more successful. Information flow is accelerated; projects and products move faster; intercompany transactions are simplified and automated. Every major division or function has intranet content: human resources, legal, marketing, sales, information services, finance, facilities. A top-level spot is reserved for Java as well.

The human resource policies and benefits are on-line; no out-of-date binders. Hiring requests and job postings are available. In a fast-growing organization, these tools aid in the hiring process and new employee orientation. With all the new faces, the directory server on Netscape's intranet is used quite a bit. It retrieves names, numbers, e-mail addresses, and additional information. It does this through a Lightweight Directory Access Protocol, or LDAP. This protocol, supported by all major industry vendors, simplifies the maintenance and consistency of directories across multiple platforms and applications. Inside a company, this eliminates duplication of effort. Outside a company it will mean that finding a person on-line will become easier than finding them by phone in the United States with the ubiquitous 411 and 555-1212 telephone numbers.

We access the Netscape directory server either through an HTML interface or directly from within applications like an e-mail composition window. From within my browser I can also reach out to external directories to find developers and suppliers. Our industry relations group maintains the ONE Directory, composed of Netscape partners and solution providers. These are available to

Netscape employees as well as external solution seekers, such as customers or developers.

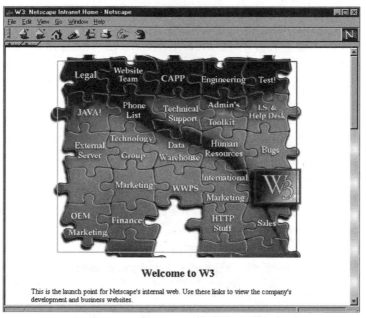

©1996 Netscape Communications Corporation. Used with permission. All Rights Reserved. This image may not be reprinted or copied without the express written permission of Netscape.

Figure 7-1. Netscape's intranet links all the major functions and divisions of the company and is key to the rapid pace of growth and innovation at Netscape. It also links to Netscape's partners, suppliers, and customers.

On the Netscape intranet, interested parties are quickly updated on the status of key projects. Every project has a project home page. Typical information includes the team members with mail links, project objectives, schedules, status reports, marketing specifications, engineering deliverables, test plans, presentations, related information, and early prototypes. Through the Collabra Server, the project home page is often linked to a project discussion group, open to project members or a broader community. Netscape Composer is used to author and publish on project home pages, where team members have authoring privileges.

Through our intranet, Netscape's data warehouse in accessible. Sales information, purchases from our home page, and marketing leads from programs such as Test Drive and In-Box direct are available through a myriad of reporting options. The results are accessible directly via Navigator or through e-mail delivery. Similarly, marketing leads are delivered to our telemarketing team.

Security, of course, is a concern. Security levels and access privileges are assigned and controlled. Few have the time, interest, and need to see absolutely everything on our intranet, but in general the information flow is remarkably open, enabling us to grow, innovate, and learn at a rapid pace.

The Java resource on our intranet, for example, includes a list of Java courses, links to Java utilities, general Java information, and access to source code for various Java programs. Product managers look for a Java solution or function for their particular need. The engineering development group can keep a central repository of its Java knowledge and progress. This is a great example of building and sustaining a core competency of our organization on-line.

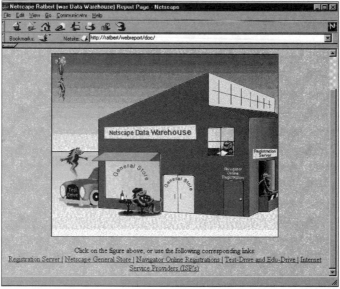

©1996 Netscape Communications Corporation. Used with permission. All Rights Reserved. This image may not be reprinted or copied without the express written permission of Netscape.

Figure 7-2. Netscape's internal data warehouse enables any employee with proper access privileges to view aspects of the business from a variety of data systems or information databases in real time. From the data warehouse, for example, a product manager can see how fast a new server is being sold through the Web site.

NETSCAPE'S INTRANET VISION

What makes the Web so compelling for its 60 million or so users is that it is intuitive, graphic, friendly, instantaneous (most of the time). It allows collaboration and messaging worldwide. Documents are easy to create and publish. There is seamless integration with databases and image banks. Software can be downloaded. Communities can be joined.

The same advantages hold when Internet technologies are deployed inside a company. An intranet is a Web inside a firewall. All employees become publishers and subscribers; everyone uses e-mail; groupware is used for projects and teamwork; people can find out about benefits, babies, bowling scores, and last quarter's sales results; colleagues have seamless access to archived news, financial databases, and human resource databases.

Training is accelerated, since Web technologies are so intuitive and easy, and most knowledge workers are now familiar with the World Wide Web. Development of applications is also accelerated, since external applications can be applied internally. For example, buy a search engine to simplify life for the customer visiting your site and a new employee can use the same search engine. Development is also accelerated since there are so many companies and people working with Web technologies; more solutions are available off the shelf or more likely off the Web.

One key advantage of a an intranet is that it allows easier and faster collaboration *outside* the firewall with suppliers, vendors, customers, and partners—the entire market infrastructure of a company. This is commonly referred to as an extranet. Open standards are what make this possible. It is one thing to decide on an internal proprietary system, quite another trying to get everyone else to use the same system. Proprietary systems are migrating to Web technologies to facilitate communication and collaboration. It is easy to see why: these technologies are easier to use, faster to develop, and simpler to deploy. And they keep improving.

INTRANET PAYBACK AND ROI

Wander down the corridors of some major corporations and you might come across one of those video conferencing rooms of the late '70s and early '80s. The room is full of expensive and dusty equipment: cameras hanging down over light stands; large screens, multiple screens, a fax machine in the corner.

Walk into an office and look at the large three-ring-binders on the bookshelf: the benefits book from five years ago, the long-range strategic plan of last year, the financial reports—sales, orders, shipments—from last quarter. Look at the stack of product catalogs.

Consider how you order products and services and track your department budget; the level of checks and balances, the end-of-quarter and end-of-year reconciliations.

Companies want to communicate and want to facilitate communication among their employees. They have used print, fax, phone, face-to-face, telephone, television, cassette tapes, videotapes, CDs. Central servers have been set up to allow access to financial databases and department budgets. Kiosks have been employed. Sales forces have laptops and PDAs.

All of this, even the first-generation proprietary groupware and the levels of red tape approval, was well-intended, functional, and valuable. It put information in the hands of employees, enabling them to do their job, figure out their benefits, and communicate and work with each other, while protecting privacy and financial data.

Intranets accelerate and expand that information and workflow, and they provide easy access to business applications. They cut steps out of the process, saving time and money. Take the ever-present benefits binder: put benefits on an intranet and you save all the print costs, you keep it up to date, and, if you are smart, you deploy an intranet application that links it directly to your human resource databases so that employees can access and change their own benefits options.

Another example: hiring new employees. You finally have that headcount authorization and hopes of working less than a zillion hours a week. You cooperate with human resources, post a job internally on a bulletin board or printed sheet, get nothing (no one wants to work with such a workaholic), and then you advertise and get a stack of external resumes to read, sort, evaluate, and pass on to a colleague for comment. An intranet job posting application would simplify the process. Post a job once on a database. The information can now appear on both internal and external pages. You can get applicant information electronically from both internal and external candidates; attach notes to the resumes and pass on to your colleagues; e-mail the job offer. A single application can be run for prospective employees and current employees, with different interfaces and information as appropriate. Everything flows, inside and outside.

This is not a revolutionary idea; in the past it has been proposed, done, and kludged together. Web technologies, however, make it easy. The applications exist and are working. A main reason these solutions actually work is that a company need not dictate the computing infrastructure of external entities with which they communicate. To access and run the application one need only have a standard Web browser.

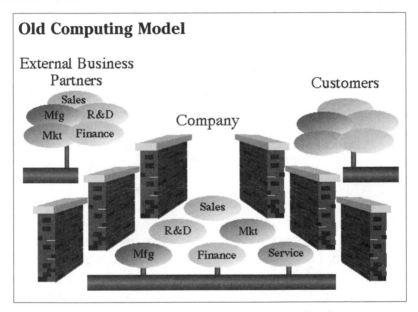

©1996 Netscape Communications Corporation. Used with permission. All Rights Reserved. This image may not be reprinted or copied without the express written permission of Netscape.

Figure 7-3. In the old computing model a disparate, segmented infrastructure and lack of communication standards hindered cross-functional work within a business as well as collaboration with external business partners and customers.

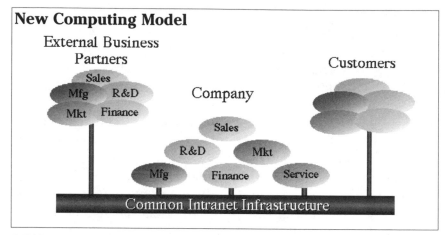

©1996 Netscape Communications Corporation. Used with permission. All Rights Reserved. This image may not be reprinted or copied without the express written permission of Netscape.

Figure 7-4. In the new computing model the adoption of open standards on the Internet and intranet facilitates cross-functional work inside a business, and breaks down the walls to customers and external business partners and suppliers. These open standards include HTML, LDAP, IIOP, Java, and JavaScript. Netscape sees its business as that of providing corporate information technology with this common Internet/intranet infrastructure through its broad range of network servers and the leading standards-based client.

The nature and type of applications being built and used in businesses is changing. In business, we are migrating from the financial, structured, and transactional to interactive, collaborative, and unstructured applications. Business functions that were rarely automated, areas such as human resources, marketing, and sales, are getting a lot of developer attention these days. Web-based technologies are key to automating these business functions, since they rely on communications, information exchange, and relationship building. Often, these business areas contribute 40 to 60 percent of a company's expenses and have seen no significant automation. The bottom-line implications are significant.

The simplicity and intuitiveness of the intranet is more than a "feel good." It offers significant financial advantages in terms of payback and return on investment. Intranet applications deliver service from any department, thereby empowering people throughout an organization. This gives organizations the tools they need to flatten structures, and free passive investments and time for active, business-generating investments and time. How long does that paper-chase purchase-order process take? How much does it cost? How much time do your managers waste in end-of-quarter reconciliations? Is there an opportunity to improve your forecasting?

There are revenue-generating as well as cost-cutting advantages of intranets. Booz, Allen & Hamilton, for example, has created an innovative knowledge-base that enables the consulting organization to fully leverage its consulting resources worldwide. Its 2,000 private-sector consultants collect and share their best thinking and expertise on its intranet, which they call Knowledge On-Line. Client need and consultant expertise are matched on this intranet. Global teams work together in global discussion groups. A knowledge repository enables consultants to do quick searches for best practices, frameworks, business intelligence, competitive data, comparative analysis, and business tools and techniques to help them solve client problems.

A detailed analysis by IDC on the payback of this intranet indicated a return on investment of 1,389 percent, a payback in 0.19 years, total three-year savings of $21 million and total three-year costs of $3.5 million.[1] Not a bad return, by any yardstick.

NETSCAPE AND JAVA-POWERED INTRANETS

Marc Andreessen was an early enthusiast and champion of Java. The characteristics of the language fit right in with the vision of Netscape products and technology: open, network-centric, dynamic, interactive, platform independent. In May 1995, Netscape became the first licensee of the Java programming language from Sun Microsystems, and Java was incorporated in the Netscape browser by June of that year. This made the benefits of Java available to 80 percent of the World Wide Web users using the Netscape Navigator, which in turn accelerated the diffusion and development of Java technology.

To further the use of Java for intranet and Internet applications, Netscape and Sun Microsystems developed and introduced JavaScript in 1995, a language to help nonprogrammers create applications by linking HTML and Java applets, and scripting their behavior. It is an open, cross-platform object-scripting language. The company is working closely with standards groups including the European Computer Manufacturing Association, Internet Engineering Task Force, World Wide Web Consortium, and other industry leaders to advance Java and JavaScript as standard development environments for intranet and Internet applications.

In the short time since their commercial introduction in early 1996, the new languages have seen rapid developer acceptance. There are several hundred thousand Java developers, and hundreds of thousands of Java- and JavaScript-enabled pages on the Internet today.

Java and JavaScript are the cornerstone technologies of what Netscape calls its Netscape Open Network Environment or Netscape ONE platform for developing Internet and intranet applications. Netscape ONE unifies into a single platform such open Internet standards as Hypertext Transmission Protocol (HTTP), Hypertext Markup Language, (HTML), Internet Inter-ORB Protocol (IIOP), Lightweight Directory Access Protocol (LDAP), Java, and JavaScript. The platform includes a tool chest of open, cross-platform technologies for creating rich, distributed applications.

Java and JavaScript are incorporated into Netscape's client and server products. With millions of browsers installed worldwide and the leading market share in Internet servers, Netscape de facto is the most widely deployed software platform for building and running Java-based applications. Netscape has released its Java- and JavaScript-enabled Netscape Navigator 3.0 client software across the most widely used operating environments: Microsoft Windows 95, Microsoft Windows 3.1, Macintosh, and UNIX. Netscape servers started shipping with server-side Java in 1996, enabling easier and quicker distribution of network-centric applications.

As a foundation for Java applications, Netscape has introduced Internet Foundation Classes, which offer developers prebuilt objects that will form the core of many Java applications. These IFCs are written entirely in Java, so they are cross-platform. The source code is available to developers at no charge. In essence, these IFCs provide the underlying machinery so that developers can focus on the value-added functionality of their application. For example, the

IFCs have drag-and-drop and windowing classes that a developer can use for his or her application; this eliminates a significant amount of programming and helps accelerate software development. These IFCs are vendor neutral; they can run on any Java Virtual Machine. Netscape also added Internet Inter-ORB Protocol (IIOP) support in its products in 1996. IIOP allows for objects distributed on a network to communicate and interact, and Netscape's implementation supports Java as well as platform-specific languages. IIOP significantly improves connectivity between Java applets, servers, and databases, enabling robust distributed applications. It also allows for server-to-server or client-to-client object communication, which enhances the capabilities of any client or server application.

All of this points to more use of Java for both Internet and intranet applications. Java is built into the client and server products with the largest market share. Java-powered intranet applications have been developed that use the unique advantages of Java. The fact that Java is cross platform makes it a useful tool for breaking down barriers between departments and geographic entities. Its graphic, dynamic, and smart client capabilities make it particularly applicable to the new wave of customer-focused as opposed to back-office-focused computing. Several Java-powered applications are included in Netscape's AppFoundry. They offer advantages to the user in their functionality and speed. They offer advantages to their developers in terms of the time they took to develop and the time they take to deploy to users.

APPFOUNDRY FOR CORPORATE INTRANETS

The on-line availability of beta versions of the Netscape Navigator early in the life of Netscape Corporation was a key factor in the browser's rapid market acceptance and development. As of January 1, 1997, there are an estimated 48 million users of Netscape Navigator. The give-away-the-beta strategy obviously worked. New rules have been written for software release in a world moving at Web speed. The involvement of customers helped improve the product and the improved product generated more customers. Armchair critics of this approach have been swayed as on-line availability of beta products is now standard practice. Users can take test drives before they purchase.

AppFoundry is released in a similar way. It offers intranet business solutions that users can download and try. The program was launched in September 1996. Its intent was to enable enterprise developers and IS managers to download, customize, and demonstrate business-focused intranet applications. Netscape sells technology and infrastructure. Demonstrating tangible business solutions drives the sales of technology infrastructure.

AppFoundry was initially envisioned as an avalanche of applications that would demonstrate Netscape ONE business solutions. Three main objectives were outlined:

1. Elevate Netscape's message in the realm of solution providing.

2. Illustrate Netscape's view of an intranet: practical, cross-functional, easy-to-deploy business applications.

3. Provide a high-value partner program.

"Appalanche" as a program name had its proponents—one could even envision recasting the early on-line Netscape mascot, Mozilla, as a rescuing St. Bernard dog. However, the Appalanche name did not resonate in market tests, and AppFoundry was coined.

The iron-smelting image on the home page of the program is appropriate: the AppFoundry is a place to transform raw Web technologies into practical business solutions. It is a place where our third-party developers, Netscape, and business partners and customers come together and meld their ideas and applications. There is heat and light and motion implied in the image of the foundry, and AppFoundry has that: free, customizable business applications that come with documented source code; development tools suited for building and modifying these applications; on-line discussion forums for applications and tools; technology resources; and deployment case studies.

AppFoundry, as of January 1, 1997, has 19 business-focused intranet applications. These applications talk the language of business: there are practical finance, human resources, information system, marketing, sales, distribution, and other applications. For example, there are applications for training registration, contact and project managing, a sales and marketing encyclopedia, and re-sume- tracking. These can be downloaded, customized, and applied to the specific needs of a business. Corporate "champions" can try an application, demonstrate its utility, and make a case for a full-fledged implementation.

All the applications in AppFoundry are built on Netscape ONE, and use Java as well as other technologies, including JavaScript on the client and server side, HTML, and LiveConnect. By providing reusable code that adheres to a common style, AppFoundry speeds up the development of intranets. You more easily achieve a com-mon look and feel despite having a number of different third-party vendors develop the application. Each application leverages the common infrastructure of the Web and a common AppFoundry style guide.

At AppFoundry, there are also links to tools used to build these applications. Hyperlinks take the user to a description of each tool as well as information on how to download a trial version with on-line documentation. There are six specific intranet application building tools on the AppFoundry site, and links to over 34 other tools available on the Netscape site.

Two intranet development tools of note are NetDynamics' Studio and Symantec's Visual Café. Both these tools are focused on rapid development of Java applications.

NetDynamics' Studio is designed for rapid database application development. Rapid development is achieved through using graph-ical wizards, palettes, and a friendly interface to automatically gen-erate applications. The generated application is all server-side Java code. The tool hides the complexity of building Web and database applications and reduces the cost and effort of deploying those ap-plications. The tool is designed for corporate MIS developers look-ing to build wide area network (WAN) Web/database applications.

Visual Café is designed for rapid development of Java compo-nents, and rapid gluing of components into applications. The tool uses visual development, drag-and-drop, hierarchical project views, and other techniques to simplify rapid development, even for non-Java developers. Netscape's IFCs ship as components within Visual Café, further increasing development speed. Hard-core developers enjoy the ability to modify Java code directly and seeing the results take shape in the visual environment.

Other AppFoundry tools include Borland IntraBuilder, Media Share Site@rchitect, NetObjects Fusion, NeXT WebObject Enterprise, and Powersoft Netimpact Studio. These tools simplify the creation and management of an intranet. By being included on App-Foundry, they save the MIS developer time in researching and trying out new tools.

Also on AppFoundry there is a comprehensive guide for IS professionals that includes a directory of content developers, consultants, Java and JavaScript programmers, system integrators, and Web site designers, and a library of easily searchable technical information, frequently asked questions, and white papers.

There should be sound with the AppFoundry image; there are dozens of on-line forums where IS professionals and corporate developers can ask questions, discuss, collaborate, and share information with each other and AppFoundry experts. On-line demonstrations and case studies allow end users to test drive some of the applications right on their desktop, without downloading and setting up a server test.

The recently added virtual intranet allows users to view how the various applications and network services can be pulled together and deployed within a company. Users can navigate to any department and use relevant applications and networking services. Web publishing, collaboration, searching, and business applications are all available for use directly on-line. The company is fictitious, but the solutions are real.

APPFOUNDRY ADVANTAGES

Netscape's AppFoundry is an enabling tool for corporate developers, visionaries, and communicators to rapidly deploy intranet solutions that solve real business problems and maximize return on investment. There are a number of key benefits.

Fire for effect. With AppFoundry, corporate developers and communicators can quickly demonstrate network-centric business intranet applications that have useful functionality, are written quickly and inexpensively, and can run on their intranets right away or with minor modifications. This proof of concept can go a long way toward demonstrating the practical use of AppFoundry applications, and the quickness of development. An HR professional, looking to cut costs and increase employee satisfaction, for example, can initiate a project for 401K asset allocation, benefits enrollment, training registration, and job posting or applicant processing. He or she can do this working with the MIS department. An expensive, proprietary, outsourced programming project is avoided.

©1996 Netscape Communications Corporation. Used with permission. All Rights Reserved. This image may not be reprinted or copied without the express written permission of Netscape.

Figure 7-5. Netscape's AppFoundry is a collection of applications, advice, and trial versions of intranet tools. Innovative corporate developers can try applications, prove their validity to senior management, and start intranetting.

Style Guide. At the outset of the effort, Netscape provided the third-party developers with an application style guide. The various applications in AppFoundry adhere to basic style guidelines, which simplifies the task of modifying and deploying applications. Installation and configuration is similar across applications. Database-creation scripts are invoked using the same mechanisms, and follow similar naming schemes. Of particular note is the on-line help facility. Based on the NetHelp SDK, the on-line help provides HTML help that looks the same on any platform, while providing robust functionality with powerful customization features. Getting context-sensitive help is as easy as point-and-click, and developers only need one or two hours to populate the help template with content. Applications obtained from different third-party vendors have a similar look and feel. An integrated, powerful intranet that works together is possible.

Reusable Building Blocks. Since the source code for each application is provided, corporate developers can modify it however they want, and even use pieces of an application as building blocks for other applications. A generic graphing applet could be used for custom applications. Likewise the on-line help template can be used. This is an advantage to the developers of a company's style guide; reprogramming an on-line help application is unnecessary. New content is required, of course, but the development time to create a unique help functionality is significantly cut back.

Leading-Edge Tools. Development tools are provided in App-Foundry for a trial period from leading vendors such as Borland, MediaShare, NetObjects, NeXt, Powersoft and NetDynamics. Trial versions of these tools are available on-line. The development tools allow corporate developers to build their own intranet application if they wish to access existing databases, or to modify the App-Foundry applications.

A Support Network. The AppFoundry On-line Community includes forums for IS professionals and corporate developers. This is a place where developers can ask questions, find answers, and interact with their peers in other companies facing the same intranet challenges.

All the applications in AppFoundry leverage the open development technology of the Internet and the WWW, which has implications for crossing company boundaries. For example, the job-posting application works with managers, human resources, and all employees inside a company, and works with job applicants outside the company. Resumes can be submitted, and then tracked, routed and databased internally. A single application runs both inside and outside the firewall, with the same interfaces, similar functionality, and appropriate levels of access and visibility. Having one application is faster and less expensive to maintain than having two applications.

Using AppFoundry, corporate developers easily and quickly can prove concepts to senior management. They can demonstrate what cross-platform, cross-database, scaleable technology means for their company. The speed of development and speed of deployment are large factors in the cost justification of corporate intranet. Why create a 401K application from scratch when some of the work has already been done for a cross-platform application, particularly when this is customizable? The same rhetorical question holds for other corporate intranet applications.

Users tend to agree: 30,000 AppFoundry downloads took place in the last four months of 1996.

SORTING OUT THE REBELLION

Organization charts are ubiquitous in companies, and usually out-of-date and hard to maintain, particularly for companies moving at Web speed. Putting complex organization charts on an intranet sounds like a great idea, if they are accurate, accessible, linked to databases, linked to e-mail addresses, and dynamic. The real value is in making the structure and contacts obvious; employees from anywhere in a multinational, multidivisional firm, for example, can more easily find out who does what and then contact that person directly.

DTAI, a software development company located in San Diego, developed an interactive organization chart for AppFoundry. The application was developed totally in Java.

There were a number of reasons for choosing Java. The application itself required drill-down navigation, to go deeper and deeper into an organization chart. It required a high degree of interactivity. Graphics were essential; the application was not envisioned as a list of names. For simplicity of use it required drag-and-drop capabilities. And to do the job right, it needed database connectiveness. The application was not envisioned as static: people would join the company, the structure would change and would be updated by any number of privileged editors. Java had the characteristics to meet those needs—the graphic, interactive, network-centric, and security needs. Java also offered significant development advantages in terms of time and programmer productivity.

The interactive organization chart displays a pictorial overview of an entire organization. It has hierarchical organizational diagrams and who's who listings. From anywhere in the chart you can navigate to different sections and levels. Employees can see detailed information on each department by clicking on a department manager. They can find information on employees with names, job titles, e-mail addresses, and personal URLs. Links can be created to e-mail systems and reference databases. Click on an employee's box and leave an e-mail message. New positions or employees can be graphically added to the organization chart. Modification privileges can be limited to selected users within the organization. For data entry, there are pop-up dialog boxes that offer error messages, warnings, information, questions and custom dialogue. Graphical objects (badge identification photos, for example) can be added and linked to the application. The key to the success of the application is that any employee can view and navigate the information without requiring special downloads or applications.

This dynamic organization chart application is a great example of the rapid development and rapid deployment possible with Java, as well as its graphic and interactive capabilities. DTAI developed the AppFoundry version of the Interactive Org Chart in eight weeks. Several hundred organizations test-drove this application during the following eight weeks. A commercial version of the Interactive Org Chart was launched in January 1997. A newsgroup on the App-Foundry site provides a support community for this application.

IN JAVA TIME

As we move to a service-based economy, efficient tracking of service becomes a key requirement. The primary way of tracking service is measuring time spent on various tasks. Keeping track of time spent on projects by individuals and teams and by categories of work applied to the project can be challenging. Geographically dispersed teams increase the challenge.

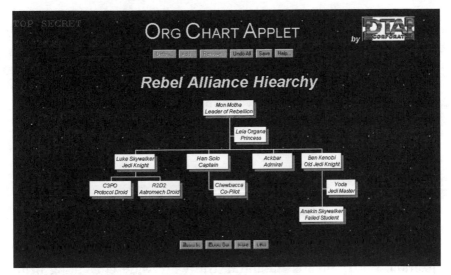

©1997 DTAI, Inc. Used with permission.

Figure 7-6. Sorting out the rebellion. The interactive organization chart created by DTAI for AppFoundry lets you create organizational charts that can be viewed by any employee throughout the alliance.

An AppFoundry time-tracking application called Tock, developed by Internet Media Services, Inc., of Palo Alto, California, enables employees or contractors on any platform, from any location, to quickly and efficiently record the time they spend on projects for billing purposes, payroll purposes, or project management purposes. The application is easily customizable and has an intuitive and easy-to-use interface.

Tock is a hybrid application: part Java, part JavaScript, part Live-Connect, part HTML. The application uses cookies to remember a user log-on and password information, so users only have to log on once. Cookies are a general mechanism which server-side connections can use to both store and retrieve information on the client side of the connection. Report data can be configured for export into spreadsheets and back-end databases, and various access levels can be created for accounting, team leaders, and team managers. A Java-generated graph provides a quick visual analysis of where the time has gone. Various reports can be customized and created.

Tock is a good example of how Java can be seamlessly integrated with other technologies to meet a business need. For example, when the user enters hours into an HTML form, JavaScript notifies the Java hours display applet of the new hours. The hours graphical display is then immediately adjusted as the information is entered.

A full-featured commercial version of Tock was introduced by Internet Media Services in 1996.

SPENDING HABITS

There are a number of routine and obvious intranet applications. The power of intranets, however, can be applied to fairly complex business needs. Take the need to identify, analyze, and diagnose opportunities to improve purchasing across a large, distributed organization. Booz, Allen & Hamilton, the worldwide consulting firm, created a purchasing analysis tool that is a part of AppFoundry. The tool provides access to key data on a firm's suppliers, purchasing categories, and spending levels. It helps propagate best practices and consistent purchasing rules across a distributed organization, and can help companies achieve continuous improvement in their purchasing process.

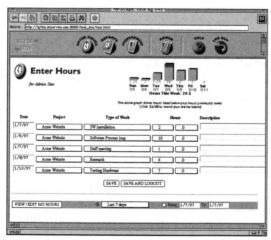

©1997, Internet Media Services, Inc. Used with permission.

Figure 7-7. The AppFoundry application Tock provides a graphic, intuitive, and easy-to-use tool for tracking time spent by teams and individuals on various projects.

The application uses Java and JavaScript on both client and server. Java applets and JavaScript perform graphical operations and dynamic Web-page creation. Java is used to drill-down into a purchasing database and pivot, filter, and select various parts of that database.

Booz, Allen & Hamilton's application demonstrates the graphical power of Java, as well as its utility as a means of connecting, accessing, and manipulating data from relational databases.

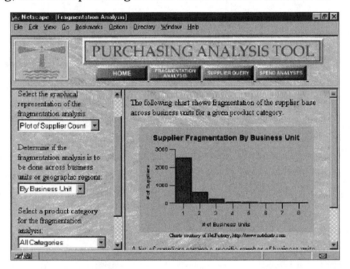

©Copyright 1997 Booz, Allen & Hamilton. Used with permission.

Figure 7-8. Part of the strategics sourcing process involves analyzing current purchasing patterns. The purchasing analysis tool created by Booz, Allen & Hamilton provides access to key data on a firm's suppliers, purchasing categories, and spending levels.

JAVA INTRANET APPLICATIONS

These three AppFoundry applications demonstrate the utility of Java and JavaScript for intranet applications. The applications meet real business needs. Several thousand copies have been downloaded for evaluation. Rich Kadal, the senior programmer at DTAI largely responsible for the interactive dynamic organization chart, commented: "Java is now the programming language of choice. We estimate that we are five to ten times more productive with Java than with C++ because of Java's strong compile-time and run-time error checking, exception handling and reporting, garbage collection to relieve the burden of pointer maintenance, simplicity of the language, and prudent selection of language features."

AppFoundry business applications use other technologies as well. Client-side JavaScript is used in 14 of these applications, several of which use JavaScript to communicate with Java applets. Server-side JavaScript is used in 18 of these applications, and HTML is the unifying application medium in almost all of the AppFoundry applications.

SOME LIMITATIONS

Java programs currently run slightly slower than platform-specific compiled code like that in C or C++. The speed issue is fast disappearing. Advances in just-in-time compilers and healthy vendor competition will keep these improvements coming. The end result will enable Java to move from the typical client-side scrolling stock-ticker type of application to full-scale, complex applications.

A lack of robust tools also has impeded development of Java applications. That situation is rapidly changing as well. Second-generation tools, such as those featured in AppFoundry, are well on their way. There are tools to make life easier for the sophisticated Java programmer, as well as drag-and-drop tools for the nonprogramming users. The availability of tools will make Java applications easier to create. Symantec's Visual Café has won several awards as a Java development tool. The network applications tool segment is seeing heated competition, more than any other tool segment. This virtually assures that the best development tools will be available to intranet and Java developers.

The Java environment has also lacked maturity, which has had an impact on the development of applications. Some implementations of the Java Virtual Machine are more robust than others. Some AWT components do not act identically on all platforms. Netscape fully supports the JavaSoft 100% Java initiative, which will protect the integrity of this rapidly evolving network language. Advances in Internet Foundation Classes, which offer developers pre-built objects that can form the core of many applications, is also helping with consistency.

The addition of server-side Java, shipping with Netscape servers, is an indication of language maturity. This enables developers to distribute applications over networks and better leverage the network for programming. Java network services can be created and tied into back-end databases.

There have been difficulties with Java applet, server, and database connectivity, as well as creation of complex distributed applications. Standardization is helping this particular issue. Netscape has added Internet Inter-ORB Protocol (IIOP) support to its products. Internet Inter-ORB Protocol is part of Common Object Request Broker Architecture (CORBA), an open standard for distributed object communication. This simplifies life for programmers, and simplifies the linkage between browsers and back-end legacy systems.

Despite some limitations, Java has been used to create viable intranet applications that are working today in thousands of corporations, applications that themselves use components of browsers and servers built with Java. Improvements in the language will accelerate Java's use in intranet. The rapid pace of Java tool evolution will also accelerate use, as will the experience and education of programmers.

RAPID DEVELOPMENT, RAPID DEPLOYMENT

A number of developers have reported significant productivity gains in programming in Java rather than with C or C++. There are some built-in advantages to Java in terms of programming. There is automatic garbage collection of disconnected and inoperable code, which may be the biggest time advantage. This means that a programmer does not waste time chasing down memory leaks. Since Java is object and component based, it has a high degree of reusability; you can take the graphing function from the Tock application, for example, and use that in another intranet application. Reusability increases productivity. A component can be taken and used without even looking at the source code, and it can be integrated in a seamless way.

Iterative prototyping is easier with a language such as Java. Continuous improvement is also simplified. Try it, fix it, and make it available on the server. All users are now running the latest version.

With Java, developers do not have to worry about porting to different platforms, another time-saver. On-line resources, such as Netscape's AppFoundry and the Gamelan directory of Java applications, also accelerate development. A developer can find applications similar to the one he or she is developing, or get ideas from applications that have similar functionalities.

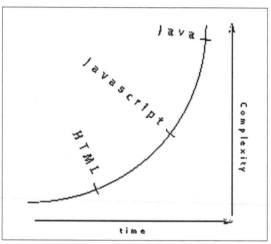

Figure 7-9. Developers can begin with simple HTML publishing, then easily start using JavaScript as they become more experienced, and lastly migrate from scripting to full-blown Java applications. The gradual learning curve allows more developers to easily learn the language by removing the barriers imposed by large technology discontinuities.

Deployment is rapid. Build an application with Java and Web technologies, and it can be instantly available across a multinational, multidivisional corporation on different computer platforms. The network administrator does not have to run around to every PC and workstation to make sure everyone got the latest update. Applications can be managed centrally, and if something changes, it can be done once and the updated programs are quickly available throughout the network. Take the time-tracker application; your best programmer thinks you ought to track development time by language as well as by project. You add a field of pull-down language choices on your Tock application, put it up on the server, and your distributed team of programmers from inside and outside the company see the new variable and can start filling it in.

Consider modeling the time it would take to develop and deploy a proprietary version of the 19 applications in AppFoundry. Chances are it would take much longer, and several times the investment, and by the time you get there, the business need would have changed.

Intranets benefit from the flexibility of having separate, modular applications. They can reference and link to each other. Even within a given application, a service-based approach allows for distribution of key objects across a network. For example, a central LDAP directory can provide human resource and finance applications with user authentication and privilege information. However, the application modules can be modified or updated separately.

THE WHOLE INTERNET CLIPBOARD

For an intranet developer, Java offers a key advantage. The language lives on the network; it's communicated on the network. Pieces of it can be easily reused for other applications. Metcalf's law of the utility of networks increasing exponentially with the number of users holds for the utility of the network language, it would seem. The whole Internet becomes a clipboard. Objects within a program have a high degree of reuse. For intranet developers, this means it will become easier to find applications to meet specific business needs, to use the pieces that make sense for their business, and to feed the network with their new creation.

Future additions to AppFoundry and future Netscape products will increase the use of Java in corporate intranet. Java technology underlies the new Netscape Communicator, an open e-mail, groupware, and browser suite introduced in 1996. Java also plays a key role in Netscape's new workspace component Constellation. Constellation will let users customize the information and applications they care about in a simple, unified, network-centric environment. It makes the intranet and Internet an integral part of their native environment. Constellation is built with HTML, JavaScript, and Java. It will enable users to receive netcast messages and updated Web site information automatically to their computer, and have roaming access to this information from any machine in any location. The embedded Castanet tuner will enable updating of software applications over an intranet, reducing network administration time and simplifying version control. Constellation will further integrate the Internet and intranets. New AppFoundry applications will flow into this new tool—literally, with the netcasting capability.

Java will power an increasing number of these applications, as well as the servers, the browsers, and the channels. The language has ubiquity: it crosses platforms, can be used with any operating system, and has the Internet as its clipboard. Java's ability to cross mainframe, workstation, PC, and device hardware platforms makes it a natural candidate for corporate intranets. It has proven utility for the intranet, exemplified in the AppFoundry applications. And Java offers economy: development time is faster and deployment is faster.

Bottom line: it will be easier and more cost-effective to work with people inside and outside the enterprise. Java will help break down the walls.

END NOTES

1   *The Intranet: Slashing the Cost of Business,* by Ian Campbell, Collaborative and Intranet Computing, International Data Corporation, Five Speen Street, Framingham, Massachusetts, 01701. The report is available on-line, with registration, at cgi.netscape.com/comprod/announce/roi.html

CHAPTER 8

NJC/LANL: IMPROVING PATIENT CARE WITH JAVA

James L. Cook, Mimi N. Hackley, National Jewish Medical and Research Center

Richard L. Phillips, James E. George, David W. Forslund, Los Alamos National Laboratory

The National Jewish Medical and Research Center, located in Denver, Colorado, has focused on diagnosing and caring for patients with tuberculosis and other respiratory diseases since 1899. Los Alamos National Laboratory, in Los Alamos, New Mexico, is a U.S. government research laboratory that does basic and applied research. Physicians and computer scientists from the two institutions developed a telemedicine application called TeleMed to more easily create, archive, and retrieve patient medical records. A Java version of TeleMed was later developed with significant advantages in access, distribution costs, and development time. There were some performance limitations in the beta versions of Java used during development, and a lack of third-party off-the-shelf media tools, but the advantages of Java outweighed the difficulties. This Java-based medical application has major implications for better treatment of chronically ill patients; patient records can be pulled up at remote sites with a standard PC rather than a proprietary and expensive workstation; patient records can include voice and image annotations; patient records are stored and retrieved more quickly and intuitively. The application also offers tremendous potential for connecting medical consultants with physicians in remote areas.

TeleMed is an integrated, virtual patient record system with significant implications for health-care services and costs. TeleMed provides physicians with a user-friendly graphical interface, the Graphical Patient Record, that allows a comprehensive overview of the entire clinical history and related ancillary data of a patient with TB or other mycobacterial infections on a single computer screen. Two of the objectives of TeleMed are to decrease physician time spent acquiring and synthesizing clinical data before initiating patient care and decision making and to facilitate physician sharing of primary patient data during remote, clinical consultations. TeleMed is being converted to a Java version to allow wider access and reduced costs for physicians using the system to share patient data between distant sites. Java offers graphic, interactive, and development time advantages that have boosted TeleMed's potential for use with other chronic illnesses and its potential to support physicians involved in a variety of areas of healthcare, and physicians servicing widely dispersed populations in remote areas.

TELEMED'S ORIGIN

TeleMed originated with a patient need: limited access of patients to subspecialists at National Jewish Medical and Research Center. The project also was initiated to address the volume and increasingly complex nature of medical information.

Tuberculosis, an infection caused by a member of the bacterial family called *mycobacteriaceae,* is a contagious infection which, in the modern era, is usually limited to the lungs. Non-TB mycobacteria (NTM) can cause similar infections that may be equally devastating for the infected person but are not contagious.

Since 1899, National Jewish has been committed to the diagnosis and management of patients with TB and NTM infections. In the early years of the existence of National Jewish, all of the efforts of its physicians and other personnel were focused on the care of large numbers of TB patients who came to the center from across the country. More recently, National Jewish has continued to be a national referral center for patients with TB or NTM infections that have failed to respond to conventional therapy, but has also increasingly become a source of remote consultative support for physicians caring for such patients at other centers across the country.

Many forces have changed the ability of patients with mycobacterial infections to come to the National Jewish for their medical care. Among these forces is the increasing limitation on the ability of patients to obtain health-care outside of their local, insured systems due to restrictions on patient referral imposed by the current managed-care model. Other factors that can limit patient referral to National Jewish include problems with transportation of people with contagious TB, patients' resistance to receive care for TB or NTM infections away from their home towns, and restrictions on the movement of certain patient groups, such as those in correctional facilities. Therefore, National Jewish faces the challenge of continuing to offer its physicians' expertise nationally to patients and physicians seeking advice at a time when increasing numbers of patients are either unable or unwilling to travel to Denver for medical care. This question, faced by many referral centers, has obvious financial implications for clinical operations of this center and for others who support wide areas of patient referral.

In addition to the problem of increasingly limited access of patients and their physicians to consultants at National Jewish, there is a growing problem of time and information management for all physicians who care for patients with chronic illnesses. An example of an average physician follow-up visit with a National Jewish patient with chronic mycobacterial infection serves to illustrate this point. Patients with refractory TB or NTM infections who come to National Jewish for diagnosis and initiation of treatment usually stay at the center for two to three weeks and then return for follow-up evaluation at three- to six-month intervals during treatment periods that often last for two or more years. There is a large quantity and variety of data collected during the initial visit and in the intervals between return visits.

When a physician from the infectious diseases division walks up to the door of the clinic to see one of these patients who has returned for reevaluation, that physician is confronted with a complex set of clinical data. There is usually a thick paper chart that contains previous clinical history in the form of typed and handwritten sheets, both bound and loose previous and recent computer printouts from the bacteriology and pharmacokinetics laboratories, and a radiology film jacket that may contain from 10 to 50 separate films (rarely in chronological order).

There are two sets of expectations that color the environment in which the physician must assess and use these clinical data. There are the patients who properly expect the physician to know "everything" about their clinical problems and related data. There is also the specter of the clinical administrator who expects that the physician will work more efficiently each year to maintain the flow of clinical revenues for the institution. With the growing complexity of medical information, poor clinical data management is increasingly unacceptable.

The conventional approach taken by the physician at the clinic door is to take the chart to another room to leaf through the previous textual information and then to try to integrate into this story the relevant clinical laboratory data (often by rewriting key data in chronological order) and radiology information (almost always by reorganizing films and putting them up on a light box for review). The time lag between picking up the chart at the clinic door and the first step into the room to see the patient may be 15 or 20 minutes, depending upon the complexity, availability, and organization of the data that must be reviewed and whether the physician must leave the clinic to review films in the radiology suite. Obviously, if these clinical data are difficult to manage efficiently at the point of patient contact in the clinic, it is certain that the problems will be compounded when trying to use these data for remote interactions between a referring and consulting physician trying to discuss a patient problem by telephone. These data management and time utilization problems have driven the collaborative telemedicine project, TeleMed, between National Jewish physicians and Los Alamos computer scientists.

COMPLEMENTARY ASSETS OF THE NATIONAL JEWISH PHYSICIANS AND SCIENTISTS AT THE LOS ALAMOS ADVANCED COMPUTING LABORATORY

A series of discussions between the director of radiology at National Jewish and a visiting computer scientist from the Advanced Computing Laboratory at Los Alamos led to the stepwise process that evolved into the TeleMed project.

The first discussions centered around improved ways to manage and analyze data from computerized axial tomograms (commonly called CAT scans) of the lung. After this work began, it became apparent that it would be valuable to integrate radiology data analysis into the context of a clinical problem, rather than working on lung-imaging studies in isolation. Since lung CAT scan images are key components in the diagnosis and follow-up evaluation of patients with chronic mycobacterial infections, it was logical to extend this collaboration to the Infectious Diseases Division at National Jewish.

The Infectious Diseases group at National Jewish already had a basic graphical structure into which to expand this radiology work. TB and NTM infections have well-defined parameters useful for diagnosis and follow-up of infected patients during courses of therapy. These include the clinical history common to all patients, bacteriology data, radiology data, and the results of assays of serum-drug-level monitoring, as well as the relationships between antibiotic treatment and clinical outcome. Over the years, physicians in the Infectious Diseases Division had developed a graphical template used to combine key aspects of the patient history with a longitudinal record of drug treatment. This template was called the "drug-o-gram."

During early meetings with Los Alamos computer scientists, it became apparent that the drug-o-gram could be expanded to provide a rapid view of key components of the patient record in a single, integrated graphical record that was named the Graphical Patient Record. It was also apparent that the expertise and previous experience of the Los Alamos Advanced Computing Laboratory in building distributed, high-performance, scalable applications would be invaluable in the development of TeleMed. From that point, Los Alamos drove the object design of the software based on clinical case material provided by National Jewish and also worked to develop a computer infrastructure for TeleMed that would support extensibility and the addition of numerous additional services as they were conceived during the course of the project. The Los Alamos experience with the Internet resulted in a project design that was Internet-oriented with built-in security to protect data integrity and patient confidentiality.

This combination of clinical and computer expertise in the collaboration between National Jewish and Los Alamos created a natural working relationship for the iterative process required to develop a user-friendly physician tool.

DEVELOPMENT OF A SOFTWARE INFRASTRUCTURE DRIVEN BY MEDICAL NEED

One unique aspect of the TeleMed project is that it was developed from the ground up, around the needs of physicians using *their* concepts about the most effective way to view and manage patient data, rather than trying to force their ideas into a preexisting database structure. The primary objective was to develop a physician tool that would address the problems faced when confronted with that stack of poorly organized clinical data at the clinic door and, at the same time, would provide a means by which to improve the effectiveness of remote consultations. There were numerous advantages envisioned for such a tool: less time spent collecting and reviewing clinical information, more time spent with the patient, increased cost efficiency of physician visits (decreased overall time for a clinical encounter), increased quality and speed of data sharing between referring and consulting physicians at remote sites, and new business opportunities through remote delivery of consultations via the Internet.

This new approach to clinical data management became the technological embodiment in the clinical setting of the old saying that a picture is worth a thousand words. The "picture" in this analogy is the Graphical Patient Record. The GPR can provide the physician in the clinic (or two physicians at remote sites) with an instantaneous, graphical overview of the entire course of the patient's illness. At the same time, icons in the GPR timeline can provide any detail that is needed to provide a more comprehensive view of the picture. The physician is then ready to get on with the business of clinical decision making, patient education, and implementation of a treatment plan. This point of contact with patients is where physicians would like to spend their time, not in the bowels of the hospital's medical records, radiology, and laboratory departments or information systems.

We have come to think of this attribute of TeleMed that reduces front-end delays in data collection and analysis as its ability to "get the physician to the point of decision." It is likely that, once fully implemented at the center, others will think of TeleMed differently. Our patients will think of it as the catalyst that gets us into their clinic rooms more quickly so that we spend more time addressing their concerns and planning the next steps in their treatment. Our administrators will think of it as the mechanism that allows us to see more patients per unit time, while maintaining a high-quality workplace. The overall importance of this type of conceptual advance in the management of clinical data is that it is easy to imagine that it will improve many aspects of patient care, both within the clinic and across the distances between two physicians seeking to solve clinical problems through consultation.

DESCRIPTION OF THE TELEMED SYSTEM

INTEGRATION OF DIVERSE CLINICAL DATA USING THE GRAPHICAL PATIENT RECORD

A first step in clinical data management is development of a baseline summary of the history of the patient's illness. This provides the background and infrastructure upon which to hang the ancillary data and from which to evolve the course of the patient's illness and response to therapy. This is a problem that faces all physicians treating patients with chronic illness, whether they are primary care physicians or consultants, and whether they are in clinic or communicating across a distance. Once the initial patient history is acquired, it should be possible to retrieve it easily and review it quickly during both the initial synthesis of the clinical problem and subsequent patient encounters or consultations. After their creation, conventional paper versions of patient histories are buried in charts in medical records departments or, worse yet, in storage facilities. Any time-use analysis would show significant delays in responses to clinical queries linked to retrieval and review of such paper records.

Another problem faced when caring for patients with mycobacterial infections (and other chronic illnesses) is that most of the ancillary data (e.g., radiology films and clinical laboratory data) that must be related to the clinical history during decision making are stored in various (and usually different) forms in multiple databases or files. Reports of these ancillary data are located in different sections of the paper record; therefore, it is not possible to see these data in the same plane with information on the clinical history. It is also common for the primary data, especially radiology films, to be stored at locations (offices, clinics, hospitals) that are separate from the paper record. In fact, radiology films must be stored in a central facility, usually the hospital's radiology department. Therefore, only summaries of the radiologist's interpretations are available in the paper record. If physicians want to view the actual films, rather than just read reported interpretations, they must either request that the radiology folder be transported to the clinic area or go to the radiology suite to view the films. Furthermore, hard-copy radiology films that reach a certain age are either moved to a storage facility or destroyed. In cases where the physician wants to review the course of a chronic lung abnormality over time, the only data available may be the paper report.

Reports of laboratory studies, such as the bacteriology and serum-drug-level information used to follow patients with chronic mycobacterial diseases, should also be in the paper record. These paper reports are printouts of computer database information and, as such, may be incomplete due to delays in transfer or may be lost in transit.

These problems with clinical data management are presented here from the perspective of a single clinical unit at one location. However, when we consider remote consultation, all of these problems are compounded many fold when physicians try to share and manage data collected and stored at different clinical locations. Integration of all of these types of data in the Graphical Patient Record makes it possible to visualize the patient history and ancillary data on a single computer screen (Figure 8-1).

The core information located in the initial patient history can be viewed at two levels of detail. The essence of the history of the illness can be entered into the window represented by the patient history icon (the hand icon in the upper center of the GPR). With a click, the physician can recall and review this information (Figure

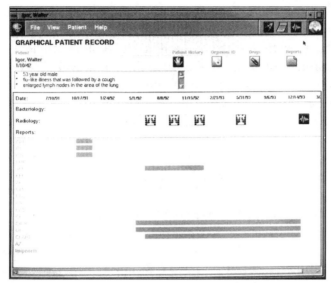

Figure 8-1. A graphical patient record (GPR) summarizes all pertinent patient information.

8-2). There is no longer a need to try to find the paper page(s) containing this information.

All patient histories have certain key elements that set that patient apart from others. Physicians use these memory pegs to distinguish one patient from another and to get oriented as they prepare to review the interval changes in the patient's clinical course. The summary box toward the top of the GPR containing bulleted information allows the physician to select and display those key elements of the history at the same time that the treatment history and ancillary data are viewed.

Antibiotic treatment regimens are represented using horizontal histograms next to the abbreviations of the antibiotics used (left-hand column of the GPR, Figure 8-1). Icons displayed in rows across the top of the GPR represent files containing data on bacteriology and radiology (X-ray) files and progress reports describing changes observed during the course of treatment. Any of those icons can be clicked to open a detailed data window superimposed upon the GPR. For example, if the physician wants to view a specific X-ray or CAT scan study, a click of the X-ray icon will open the study for viewing on the desktop (Figure 8-3). Physicians no longer need to re-

quest, unpack, reorganize, and mount radiology films in the clinic
or the radiology department. Again, physician time saved translates into more time with the patient and a more efficient (and less
costly) clinic visit. The same ease of access is available for detailed
bacteriology information and measurements of drug levels
achieved in the patient's blood.

When a physician reviews these data either before or during the
patient visit, he or she often desires to make a notation in the
record for reference when synthesizing the important events from
that encounter. Two methods are available in the GPR for physician
notes.

If the physician wishes, typed annotations can be entered using a
sticky note that can be dragged and dropped from in the upper-
right-hand corner of the menu bar of the GPR (Figure 8-1) to the desired location anywhere on the GPR. These typed annotations can
also be added to selected X-ray screens to store comments made on
observations during review of radiology data. If the physician does
not want to take time to type a note (and even those who know how
to type may not want to take the time to do so), there is an audio annotation option that can be used in the same way as a sticky note.

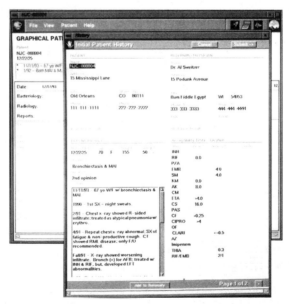

*Figure 8-2. Clicking on an icon in the patient's record will drill
down into a patient's history.*

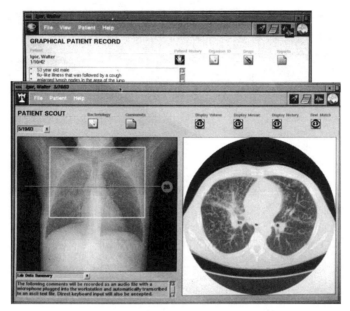

Figure 8-3. Simpler and faster X-ray studies are accessible on a desktop with TeleMed.

The physician simply drags and drops the audio icon from the upper-right-hand corner of the GPR menu bar (just to the right of the sticky note) to any location on the GPR or radiology window (Figure 8-4). Upon activation, this icon can be used to enter verbal notes, orders, or other instructions.

Textual or audio annotations can be used in a variety of ways, depending on the physician's style. These notes can be recovered by a secretary for formal entry into that day's progress note or for action on a physician order (for example, a test to be performed or drug to be ordered). An advantage of these annotation capabilities is that the physician can use the GPR to replace any manual note taking, order writing, or other written interactions normally done using the paper record. This allows the physician to spend more time on patient interactions and decision making and less time on chart management and paperwork. That work can be left to support personnel in the clinic or office, while the physician goes on to review new data and make decisions about the next patient to be seen in clinic.

Figure 8-4. Physicians can add audio annotations to enter verbal notes or orders.

In summary, a single screen in the GPR can be used by the physician to obtain the historical information and ancillary data needed to get to the decision and action stages of the patient encounter and to implement the plan of action without ever resorting to the paper record or other files that are currently used in patient care.

LONGITUDINAL ACCUMULATION AND MANAGEMENT OF DATA DURING A CHRONIC ILLNESS

By definition, chronic illnesses require longitudinal management of the same variety of clinical data discussed above. The added complexity is that the data must be integrated and analyzed as they change over the course of the illness.

The standard way to follow such data is to review serial paper records at each patient visit, incrementally adding interval data. Once again, the problem is that clinical data review, as usually done, cannot be accomplished using a single document, but requires the physician to develop a mental or written mechanism with which to combine a variety of textual, numerical, and radiological data. For patients with chronic illness who return to the clinic periodically but infrequently, the physician repeatedly assembles and reviews the same data to regain an understanding of the situation up to that point and then adds another textual entry into the paper record to describe interval changes and the new treatment plan. The advantage of the GPR for this longitudinal process of clinical data integration is that it provides a single, compressible time line on which all of the key data can be presented on a single screen.

The initial patient history and all interval textual notes on patient progress can be reviewed at any time. The physician can also choose combinations of textual notes and audio annotations to speed the process of preparing for the next patient encounter. For example, once the physician has identified key components of the patient history, interval reports, and ancillary data required for preparation for the next visit, the physician can voice record those notes he or she will want to review just before seeing the patient on the next visit. Imagine the increased efficiency, as a physician, of being able to verbally set the stage for yourself as you are about to approach a complicated clinical decision-making situation.

A powerful aspect of the TeleMed system for physicians reviewing data over time is its ability to display the history of any type of ancillary data upon command. For example, physicians often need to review a series of CAT scans of the lung when evaluating disease progression or response to therapy. Rather than having to request, sort, and mount all of the radiology films required for this analysis in today's clinic, the physician of tomorrow using TeleMed will be able to click "display history" in the X-ray window of the GPR and view a chronological series of matched CT scan images taken at different times over the course of the patient's repeated visits (Figure 8-5).

If the physician wishes to view entire sets of CAT scan images of the lung, that can be done by clicking "display mosaic" in the same window (Figure 8-6). In essence, the physician can use the TeleMed window to access any radiology study or compare any pair of studies stored on a patient without leaving the clinic room. The ease of manipulation of radiology images can also be useful for the physician educating the patient about the changes occurring as a result of therapy.

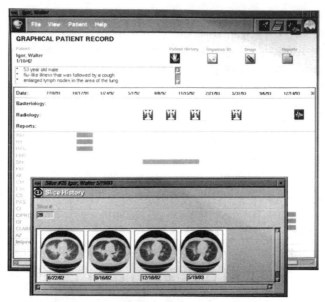

*Figure 8-5. Retrieval and comparison of CAT scans over time
for a patient with chronic illness is simplified with TeleMed.*

This same concept of historical data review can be applied to longitudinal integration of any type of ancillary data that the physician would like to view over time. For example, Figure 8-7 shows one format being developed in TeleMed to follow the bacteriology results of cultures of patient sputum specimens tested for TB bacteria over time after beginning antibiotic treatment. Identification of the types of cultures represented are not important for this discussion. What is important is that, once again, it is possible to use the picture-is-worth-a-thousand-words approach to greatly speed the ability of the physician to analyze complex data over time. For both semiquantitative assays (for instance, sputum smear results on the top row) or assays that yield only positive or negative data (for example, BACTEC culture results on the second row), the physician can quickly inspect the graphical display of the history of the bacteriology data to determine whether there is a trend toward improvement (in this case, decreased positivity of the bacteriology data) or relapse.

As with other types of laboratory data, conventional analysis of bacteriology data using the paper record can be quite time consuming and often requires manual note taking to summarize the flow of the data over time.

SHARING CLINICAL DATA USING A MASTER PATIENT INDEX

For the power of the GPR to be shared by multiple health-care providers at different sites, standards of patient identification must be developed that are both rapid and secure. Once such a convention is accepted by multiple users, it will be possible for those with proper access to identify and share databases that relate to the patient in question.

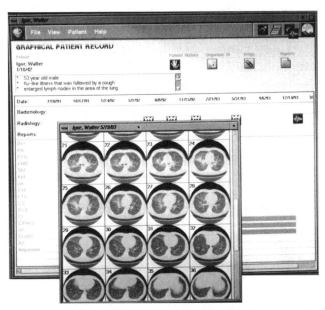

Figure 8-6. Entire sets of CAT scans can be viewed.

The distributed nature of the TeleMed system requires the registration of patient data from multiple databases. Although the existing database capability was built around Object Design's Object- store, the CORBA infrastructure was designed to handle multiple databases. However, to present an integrated record from multiple locations, one must be sure that the data from the different locations corresponds to the same patient. This is the role of the Master Patient Index. Until recently, medical records were the domain of a single institution and contained in a proprietary medical information system, so a patient index was only needed for that institution. As the TeleMed system becomes used among different institutions, there will have to be some agreement on how patients are identified and how medical record locations are specified.

An example of a Master Patient Index currently created for patient data at National Jewish is shown in Figure 8-8. This is the first view of TeleMed encountered by a physician seeking patient information. Either an alphabetical list of patient names (for example, Dennis, Bruce) or a list of hospital numbers (for example, NJC-48625) can be used for patient identification. Once the health-care provider has gained secure access to the system, a click on the patient identifier will bring the GPR and all of its associated data icons to the desktop. Any number of valid users can share the GPR simultaneously, thus allowing both data use by primary care providers and data sharing by referring and consulting physicians at different sites.

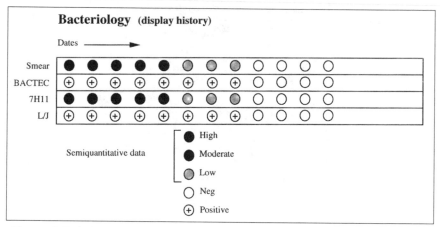

Figure 8-7. A fast visual look at complex lab data over time is available.

The approach to data accession and assembly using what is called distributed object technology allows data to be stored at a central location and then formatted on the fly as it is requested at various end-user sites. This is important when data are stored at different sites and must be assembled for viewing by different

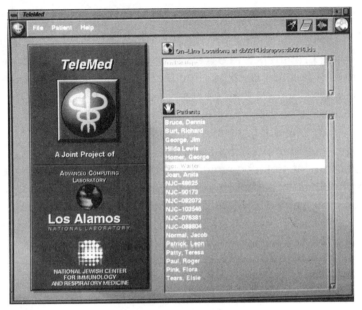

Figure 8-8. Simultaneous access of patient records is possible with TeleMed.

users. A contrast between the way electronic laboratory data are handled in many systems and the integrated approach possible with TeleMed is useful here. Through a secure password, physicians at National Jewish can access clinical laboratory data on their desktop computers from the laboratory's current information system. These data are preformatted to provide a computer screen view of the laboratory printout found in the paper chart. Access to these data is better than it would be if one had to request the paper chart to view it, but is not integrated with any other part of the patient record. Furthermore, these data must be printed or handwritten to be compiled with other parts of the paper record or viewed in the clinic. In contrast, when various types of ancillary data are managed as distributed objects as they are in TeleMed, the data are only formatted upon request by the user and then are integrated into the GPR to provide an assembly of information that is all seen as a single document. This approach also allows data stored in different formats at different locations to be configured similarly for common use during remote consultation.

VALUE OF CORBA AND A MERGED PATIENT RECORD

The increased mobility of patient populations and changes in health-care providers and payers has resulted in a patient's medical information being accumulated in a variety of locations—hospitals, HMOs, and doctor's offices—frequently with no links between them. Because of these multiple points of entry of patient information into the health-care system, both health-care provider and payer get a fragmented picture of the patient history. Due to the extended time of data accumulation, this problem is exaggerated when physicians deal with a patient with a chronic illness. This fragmented view can occur over a regional network of clinics as well as over the entire country. We call this requirement for multiple entry points into the health-care system "distributed health-care." This increasingly wide diffusion of the patient data require them to be accessible in an organized manner on a national scale, independently of the health-care provider or payer. There are a variety of standards bodies looking at various aspects of facilitating data interchange.

The impact on the health-care industry of making health-care information securely available over wide areas, while maintaining patient confidentiality, will be quite profound. Besides enabling better management of the individual patient, the integration of health-care information, for example, could enable "data mining" to be used in a routine manner. "Data mining" could be used to discover and analyze associations between disease entities and previously unknown risk factors (recorded in the patient history), to test hypotheses regarding putative risk factors, or to study disease distribution using demographic data. Applications of "data mining" could also include enabling a physician to do a comparative analysis of a particular patient's clinical presentation with that of other patients with similar or different diseases. Having wide-area access to health-care information would also allow for more intelligent video consultations. During these consultations, specialists in multiple locations could simultaneously see the video and annotate a patient's record. HMOs could do a better job of outcomes analysis, physicians would have access to better decision-support information, and patients could be better educated to manage their health. All of these applications require advanced pattern matching techniques beyond simple database searches.

Through a virtual patient record, distributed health-care data are made available through references (analogous to hypertext links on the World Wide Web) and are only brought together (or created) on demand by the end user. Since users generally access components of a record rather than the entire patient record, data movement is minimized. In the distributed system, reference counting capabilities and distributed transaction processing maintain the integrity of the data. Thus, full asynchronous access of the record enables multiple physicians, other health-care providers, and health-care payers to update the patient record.

Distributed object technology was chosen for the implementation of the TeleMed system to carefully define the roles of the client and the various servers in a formal way. Objects can be made to closely represent the medical domain in a natural way in which data and services are encapsulated. This provides better support of the software and the ability to add very complex capabilities to the system in a fairly simple way. Objects, for example, can represent a patient's medical history, audio annotations, or a lung CAT scan series.

Common Object Request Broker Architecture (CORBA) is the most mature and widely supported distributed object infrastructure (or middleware) and thus was chosen for the TeleMed development. This enabled use of commercial software for the integration of the objects and provided automatic support for a variety of heterogeneous hardware systems. In addition, it provides multiple language support so that the client does not have to be written in the same language as the servers. A variety of services are available for linking multiple locations in a straightforward manner. With the introduction of IIOP (Internet inter-ORB operability protocol), CORBA provides a vendor-independent way to link multiple databases with full transaction processing driven from the client-side. Using CORBA, it is possible to provide a merged medical record (or virtual patient record) in which patient information from various databases are presented to the physician in a unified way.

Although CORBA was selected for TeleMed development in 1993 because of its strengths, it lacked robust support within the World

Wide Web. The Web has grown in popularity and capability since then. Even today, however, the HTTP protocol provides poor support for database transactions as well as limited simultaneous connectivity. With CORBA, for example, we can activate multiple sites simultaneously with a single mouse click. With the advent of Java and the integration of IIOP with Web browsers, one can take advantage of the ubiquity of Web browsers while providing the power and scalability of CORBA.

The language independence of CORBA enabled us to migrate our client-side to Java as that language became popular without changing our basic design or reengineering the server side.

BENEFITS OF THE TELEMED SYSTEM FOR CHRONIC MYCOBACTERIAL DISEASES AND OTHER CHRONIC ILLNESSES

IMPROVED EFFICIENCY AND EFFECTIVENESS IN PATIENT CARE

TeleMed's success depends upon improving physician access to the data needed for patient care. At National Jewish, we have begun an in-house, clinical testing phase of this system. Three clinical situations will be tested. TeleMed will be used by physicians in the Infectious Diseases Division to (1) review data for new patients referred to the center for consultation and care, (2) prepare for follow-up visits with patients previously seen at the center, and (3) advise physicians at remote sites who are caring for patients previously seen at the center. After limited testing, it is already apparent that TeleMed improves physician preparation for visits to the clinic through improved access to integrated clinical data. A study contrasting the conventional (paper record) approach to patient care with that using TeleMed to replace reliance on the paper record will be used to define the advantages and limitations of this new method.

INCREASED ACCESS BY PRIMARY CARE PHYSICIANS TO SUBSPECIALTY CONSULTATIONS

After the in-house analysis in the clinic setting is complete and needed modifications are made to TeleMed, the system will be tested at selected remote sites to evaluate its ability to enhance the quality and effectiveness of remote consultations. To date, this has been done on only a mock basis. However, it is already apparent that, once the data are entered and can be seen and discussed in TeleMed by two physicians during telephone conversations, clearer questions can be asked and answers given when primary (especially radiology) data are used rather than interpretations of information relayed verbally. In addition to real-time discussions between referring and consulting physicians, it will also be possible for consultations to be sent, reviewed, and answered at the convenience of both physicians.

This type of data management is not in common use at medical centers or physicians' offices. Therefore, one problem to be solved during implementation of TeleMed at multiple sites will be adaptation of support personnel to a new form of data entry and transfer. In the short term, textual data entry will continue to require secretarial support. In the long term, it should be possible to replace much of this with voice-recognition technology.

It will also be necessary to maximize links with any existing databases at remote sites (for example, laboratory systems, radiology systems) to minimize redundant data entry. Automated radiology data entry into TeleMed is already possible using today's technology, and automated entry of clinical laboratory data is not far behind. Once these various forms of primary data can be managed by the average medical center as distributed objects, remote consultations between primary care physicians and consultants at National Jewish will be possible. It is inevitable that a learning curve will be required for those who use this technology. However, each successful application will make the next easier. One such project is already under way in which many of the basic infrastructure components of TeleMed will be tested by linking rural sites with remote medical centers.

GENERALIZATION OF THE BASIC CONCEPTS OF TELEMED TO OTHER CHRONIC ILLNESSES

One advantage of chronic mycobacterial disease as the initial paradigm for TeleMed development is that many of the same basic categories of data used to manage these patient problems will also apply to management of data from patients with other chronic illnesses. Among the key clinical parameters used for the diagnosis and follow-up evaluation of patients with TB and NTM infections are patient history, bacteriology data, therapeutic drug monitoring, and radiology data. Patients with other chronic infectious diseases can be followed with many of the same parameters used to follow our patients with mycobacterial diseases. For example, in patients infected with the human immunodeficiency virus, HIV, that causes AIDS, it is necessary to follow patient history, microbiological data (both for HIV and for other infectious agents that cause disease in these immunocompromised patients), drug treatment protocols, and radiology studies. There are also clinical parameters that are unique to the management of AIDS patients. But these clinical data are still amenable to the same logic that has been used to manage the other forms of clinical information—quantitation of the parameter, conversion wherever possible to a graphical display, and integration of data across the time of patient follow-up.

This comparison can also be extended to noninfectious chronic illnesses. For example, patients with various forms of cancer are evaluated and monitored using changes in the same basic parameters including clinical history, laboratory data, drug-treatment records, and radiology studies as well as using disease-specific parameters. The same general extrapolation could be made to other common chronic illnesses. The essential point is that, once basic clinical parameters are considered as distributed objects, it will be possible to use the fundamental infrastructure of TeleMed to create applications for a variety of diseases.

IMPORTANCE OF JAVA AND CORBA FOR IMPLEMENTATION OF THE TELEMED SYSTEM

INCREASED ACCESS TO HEALTH-CARE PROVIDERS USING DIFFERENT PLATFORMS

With the inclusion of Java support (and thus CORBA support) in the most popular Web browsers and the introduction of powerful but low-cost 32-bit computer systems, TeleMed has the capability of being deployed in a very low-cost environment. The necessary equipment to run a TeleMed client is accessible from large discount electronics stores and the software is downloaded on demand to the client using the Java virtual machine (JVM) in the browser.

DECREASED COST OF DISTRIBUTION RESULTING IN AN INCREASED SPECTRUM OF END USERS

The browser enables a fully distributed computing environment to be created on the client machine without the troublesome issues of distributing the software through some external channel on a cyclic basis as the software is improved. At this point TeleMed can be deployed even in a rural setting using POTS (plain ordinary telephone system) as the local delivery vehicle. Thus a powerful architecture combined with a low-cost ubiquitous delivery vehicle makes TeleMed accessible to even a rural health clinic. This, in fact, is underway through an NTIA grant recently awarded to Northern New Mexico Community College in Española, New Mexico, in which the Java TeleMed software will be a key component to the delivery and use of a virtual patient record.

INCREASED RATE OF ITERATIVE IMPROVEMENTS IN APPLICATION OF TELEMED FOR MYCOBACTERIAL DISEASES AND OTHER CHRONIC ILLNESSES

It has become clear during the development of the TeleMed system that multiple rounds of development, clinical testing, and modification will be needed to optimize the system for daily use in the clinic. Using conventional software development strategies, it would be necessary to upgrade the software at each user site after every modification. This approach tends to encourage the accumulation of suggestions on the client user (in this case the physician) side and the implementation of software changes at relatively infrequent intervals. A more desirable approach involves rapid feedback and modification between clinical test sites and the sites where program modification are occurring. This is one of the theoretical advantages of a Java TeleMed application. As improved features are ready for deployment, only the server side of TeleMed will need to be changed, and then all client users will automatically be upgraded at their next use. Furthermore, everyone will be running the same version at all times during development and clinical testing.

Another advantage of a Java solution is that the layout of the Java graphical user interface can adapt to its environment more flexibly because of the underlying support available on the users' computing platform, giving users a display tuned for their computing environment. Additionally, the user interface can be incrementally developed to provide different views for different patients or physicians. For example, one can envision specialized GPR forms for different chronic illnesses (e.g., mycobacterial disease, AIDS, and cancer) all driven from the same serving database.

DISADVANTAGES OF JAVA IMPLEMENTATION

Our original client environment (based on Gain Momentum) enabled very rapid prototyping and automatic support for a variety of multimedia types, including sound, imaging, and even video. Ultimately, Java will provide this kind of capability in third-party software. Today, however, such environments are not available. In addition, there are a number of bugs in the implementations that make Java-based software development slow, and the current versions of the Java virtual machine need improvement in performance for them to be competitive with other client software systems. Maturing Java also requires modifications of the support software, such as browsers, as well as the distributed object software.

Despite these limitations, the advantages of the Java approach outweigh the difficulties, in our opinion. Java is new and the pace of development for corrections, enhancements, and additional features is unmatched in the computer industry. Java has developed and matured in its first year as much as C++ did in ten years. In fact, the pace of change has been a challenge for developing our leading-edge TeleMed system with the distributed Java software environment.

BETTER HEALTH-CARE

Use of the Java version of the TeleMed system has several advantages for both the primary care physician and physicians at remote sites sharing decision making for patients with mycobacterial infections and other chronic illnesses. Before the physician sees or discusses the patient, all relevant clinical information can be assembled on the physician's desktop computer in an integrated Graphical Patient Record. The graphical interface provides physicians with a rapid overview of the entire history of the patient's illness and of relationships between therapeutic interventions, diagnostic studies, and follow-up progress reports. This interface provides data views that mimic patterns of data organization that have long been in use by physicians but does so in a single plane of the computer screen. Physicians will no longer need to acquire, review, and synthesize clinical information from paper records, laboratory databases, and radiology folders. All of this work can be done by support personnel and automated data accrual methods before the physician ever reviews the record. The ability of physicians to use TeleMed to preview well-organized patient data will decrease preparation time required before seeing patients and will focus the physician efforts on direct patient interactions and decision making, rather than data recovery and organization.

This reallocation of physician time should increase physician efficiency without compromising the quality of physician-patient interactions. In fact, ready access to the entire spectrum of patient data in the clinic room should increase physician effectiveness in explanations of the clinical diagnosis and the status of the disease during discussions with patients. In addition to its utility for direct patient care, TeleMed also provides a method that can be contrasted with the paper record approach to health-care delivery for cost-benefit analyses of the use of electronic patient records.

Work remains to be done on automation of data entry, definition of the needs for data compression technology, and ensurance and acceptance of security standards by the medical community. However, as these questions are answered, it will be possible to proceed quickly to clinical testing and maturation of the TeleMed system between multiple medical centers.

The power of TeleMed for the primary care situation is amplified when two physicians seek to share patient data between remote sites for consultation. Infectious diseases physicians at National Jewish respond to numerous telephone consultations each week. In almost every instance, a summary of the clinical data is shared by telephone, but relevant primary data (especially radiology information) is usually unavailable. When TeleMed can be used for these remote consultations, the quality of data upon which opinions and recommendations are based will be greatly improved.

In this era of managed health-care, the TeleMed approach to remote consultative support is likely to have other effects on patient care. Physicians working in a managed health-care organization will have access to remote consultations that may be limited currently. Perhaps more important is the fact that physicians working in managed-care organizations will not have to send their patients out of their system to obtain expert consultation. For example, a physician working at a managed-care facility or caring for a patient whose health-care is supported by a managed-care organization will be able to submit all relevant, primary clinical data to TeleMed and have these data reviewed by a remote consultant with the needed expertise. Consultation questions can be discussed and recommendations made based upon relevant information that can be viewed simultaneously by the referring and consulting physicians. The TeleMed system also makes it possible for such consultations to be submitted and reviewed at separate times if that is more convenient for the referring and consulting physician. This ability of TeleMed to support synchronous or asynchronous consultations within the same framework while maintaining full data integrity is unique in the field. Throughout the entire process, the patient does not need to be moved out of the primary care clinical setting.

There are analogous situations where it may be undesirable to move a patient but a consultation is needed. Patients may be too ill to travel or may be constrained from travel for financial or other reasons (for example, a patient who is an inmate in a correctional facility). In all such cases where there is a primary care physician on site to collect the data, oversee its entry into TeleMed, and implement the recommendations of the consultant, an Internet-mediated transfer of Java-based TeleMed data can be used to obtain needed guidance from an expert in the needed subspecialty area.

From the perspective of institutions like National Jewish, which has historically been a national referral center, this increased accessibility of referring physicians to center consultants can have financial, as well as academic, advantages. Not only can the center study the effectiveness of TeleMed delivery of consultative care in outcomes analyses, but the maturation of these TeleMed capabilities can be included in the long-term business strategy of the institution.

For TeleMed to have maximum value as a clinical tool, its basic concepts must be generalized to chronic illnesses that are more common than mycobacterial infections. There is inherent value of the TeleMed technology for on-site and remote management of patients with refractory mycobacterial infections. However, these infections are relatively uncommon on a national scale. Future TeleMed development must include identification of other chronic illnesses where TeleMed can improve primary and consultative management of clinical data.

This development of TeleMed comes at a time when there is an active national dialogue about the values and limitations of various types of telemedicine applications. The TeleMed project should become part of this national debate as medical, legal, ethical, and security issues are confronted and resolved.

CHAPTER 9

F. HOFFMANN-LA ROCHE: JAVA FOR THE PHARMACEUTICAL INTRANET

Enrico Bondi, Department CSE, F. Hoffmann-La Roche AG

Gabriela Keller, Ergon Informatik AG

F. Hoffmann-La Roche, with its headquarters in Basel, Switzerland, is one of the world's largest pharmaceutical and biotechnology research and manufacturing firms. With activities in over 100 countries, and all most 50,000 employees in some 150 affiliated companies, Roche has been innovative in its use of information technology to develop its business. Roche implemented an "intranet" before the term became popular. Using Java, Roche developed an application that cut the printing costs of their Safety Data Sheets and accelerated worldwide distribution of these voluminous, regulatory-required documents by three months. Worker access to these Safety Data Sheets was improved and safety information was made available more readily. The "front-end" Java application took four weeks to develop and has been deployed since the beginning of 1996. At the time of the development, there were limitations with Java availability for Windows 3.1, which have since been resolved. Response to the SDS application has been positive. While improving access and safety, Roche has cut administrative and print costs. Java solutions for a heterogeneous IT infrastructure proved effective. Roche is also utilizing Java to increase access to a creative process modeling application on its intranet.

It is important for workers in the chemical and pharmaceutical industries to have up-to-date information on the materials they are handling, with clear and accessible information on the storage, chemical properties, and first-aid measures associated with those materials. Various standards groups and regulatory agencies have defined the content of what are called Safety Data Sheets. Continuously publishing and distributing several thousand data sheets in a multinational, multidivisional organization is very challenging and time-consuming. Using Java and a robust Intranet, the department of Corporate Safety and Environmental protection (CSE) at F. Hoffmann-La Roche has implemented a significantly faster, less-expensive and more accessible means of continuously publishing Safety Data Sheets to several hundred locations in the Roche group.

Founded in Basel in 1896, F. Hoffmann-La Roche is the parent company of one of the oldest Swiss multinational groups, and is active in over 100 countries. The Roche Group employs about 50,000 persons, mainly in Europe and in the United States. The Roche Group is one of the world's leading research-based health-care groups active in the discovery, development, manufacture and marketing of pharmaceuticals and diagnostic systems. The Group is also one of the world's largest producers of vitamins and carotenoids and of fragrances and flavors. In 1996, as one of the leading international pharmaceutical corporations, Roche has celebrated its first 100 years.

The responsibility of Roche for safety and the environment are key issues laid down in the policy of the company. For appropriate support in this field, Roche has established the department of Corporate Safety and Environmental protection (CSE). This group ensures compliance with regulatory and government standards and is committed to going beyond those standards in its environmental and safety mission.

ABOUT ERGON INFORMATIK AG

Ergon Informatik AG, founded in 1984, is a software development company with 15 high-qualified engineers, working on a variety of demanding projects. Ergon was one of the first companies in Switzerland to focus on UNIX programming and is now one of the leading Java development companies. Ergon has been working on a data warehousing application for Roche since 1989 and has partnered with Roche in its development of innovative Java applications for its Intranet.

THE ROCHE INTRANET

Given the size and complexity of Roche's business, and the competitive pressures of the pharmaceutical industry, Roche views information technology as a strategic imperative. As one might expect, the Company has evolved a very heterogeneous and distributed information technology environment. The computing environment needs to be flexible and adaptable to different business sizes and demands depending on the department and country. At the same time, the Company needs to maximize the interoperability between departments, locations and platforms.

To help achieve that goal, the Company has taken a number of steps. The Roche Intranet was created in 1993. Most of the workplaces in the entire Roche group can be connected to the Roche Intranet, whether they are using PCs or Macs.

Standards have also been set. The strategic direction is: enterprise servers (for databases and infrastructure) run under UNIX, workgroup servers run under UNIX or Windows NT. Recommended clients are PCs with Windows NT. Workstations running under UNIX are only used for special purposes such as computational chemistry. Similarly, Macintosh computers are mainly used for special purposes such as desktop publishing and multimedia.

The strategic client/server connectivity will be done with TCP/IP. In terms of World Wide Web access, Netscape Navigator is currently widely used within Roche.

In terms of IT direction, prepackaged solutions are used whenever possible to save time and avoid proprietary, time-consuming customized programming. Similarly, mature technology with appropriate risk levels is typically used. As a standard practice, Roche is not dependent on a single vendor. In view of the already existing heterogeneous computing environment, there is interest in technology to more easily manage this with less direct intervention. There is a desire to migrate away from multiple-purpose servers to a three-tier client/server computing architecture that strikes a balance between one monolithic system and a heterogeneous nonintegrated environment. Roche wants to balance the flexibility of providing business solutions with the need to have efficient, cost-effective system management and support. Maximizing interoperability and availability of information across platforms is critical. Of increasing importance is the portability of applications.

In this environment Java technology is becoming more and more interesting. The Java compiler creates a platform-independent intermediate code that only has to be executed in real time by a hardware dependent interpreter. Java-written software can be offered on a Web server. Whoever has access to the Web server with a Java-capable browser can use it immediately; it is available to everyone across the organization. We also found that the Java learning curve is short with someone familiar with object- oriented programming. Application development is fast.

BUILDING A DATA WAREHOUSE

In 1989 a major IT project was initiated at CSE to warehouse all of the information needed for safety and environmental protection across the Roche organization. The volume and importance of this information made the warehousing an obvious decision. It would enable the CSE group to fulfill their responsibility for providing information to managers, engineers, and specialists. The data warehouse project was named SEISMO for Safety and Environmental Protection Information System for Management Orientation.

SEISMO was split into fourteen subprojects. In terms of data warehouse hardware, Sun servers and workstations were utilized. These allowed access to the already existing hardware (IBM and DEC). PCs were integrated in the local SEISMO net through PC-NFS and work partly with X-emulation. This means that there is a very heterogeneous environment, not only within the entire organization, but also within the project group itself. This heterogenicity puts a premium on software that works on different platforms and may be distributed in a easy way. Sybase was chosen as the database management system.

Table 9-1. The Safety Data Sheet project is part of a larger and long-term IT initiative by Roche's safety and environmental protection group to create a data warehouse of information. Given Roche's IT infrastructure and the success of the SDS project, Java will play a role in a number of other SEISMO projects.

Roche "SEISMO" Project Components	Description
Infrastructure project	Evaluation and construction of a network; optimized implementation of the client/server principle
Core database management, "Core Data"	Centralized management of core data (e.g., partner, products, location); mandatory for all future SEISMO databases
Office system	Compilation/exchange of compound documents
Document management system	Archiving of all relevant S+E documents
Basic product data for risk analysis	Management of S+E basic data for products; central function for SDS and risk analysis
Safety data sheets	Compilation, evaluation, assignments of SDS for risk analysis; views of basic data
Waste data management system	Management, control, monitoring, statistics of waste data
Management Information System (MIS)	Access to selected, condensed data; key figures, tables, diagrams, material flow sheets; WWW/intranet
Incident/accident management	Management of accidents and incidents information; interpretation

(continued)

Table 9-1. (continued)

Roche "SEISMO" Project Components	Description
Laboratory management system	Management of laboratory tests, analytical and sample data (e.g., safety lab)
Materials management	Management of equipment; location, maintenance, service
Investigation methods management	Compilation, management of testing methods
Partner capacities planning	Scheduling of audits, appointments, or presence time
Safety+Environmental Protection courses	Management of courses for risk analysis, fire fighting, etc.

One of the fourteen subprojects was the databasing of Safety Data Sheets (SDS). An SDS provides basic information on the hazards of a product to people and the environment. Based on physical, chemical, toxicological, and ecotoxicological data the most important hazards are described together with measures for a safe handling and storage. In addition, emergency measures in the case of spills, including fire-fighting or first-aid are given. The content is defined by the ISO (International Standards Organization)—standard 11014, the EC (European Council)—directives 91/155 and 93/112, as well as the ANSI (American National Standards Institute)—standard Z-400.1-1993. According to these regulations and standards, a SDS contains 16 chapters each with several attributes. A complete SDS has about 50 to 60 attributes from a set of 150 different types of attributes. There are three types of products: substances (pure chemical substances), mixtures (e.g., vitamin mixtures), and kits (diagnostic products containing substances and mixtures). The information given in these Safety Data Sheets is integrated into the standard operating procedures of the individual workplaces taking into consideration the local technical possibilities. In addition, the Safety Data Sheet provides background information on the product in question, as well as quick reference in case of emergencies.

Before the SEISMO project, all Safety Data Sheets were written with a PC word-processing program. This limited their utility across a network, and for other applications such as risk analysis. Distribution was difficult and time-consuming. Twice a year CSE sent the updates of SDS to approximately 450 locations. Those locations had to put the updates in different Safety Data Sheet folders and distribute them locally to different departments and people. Thus in the worst case the latest version of an SDS required up to six months to get to the end-user. Over and above the distribution issue, there were concerns about easy access and updating of SDS files. There was no way to ensure that new SDS were put in the right place at each workplace, or that files were actually updated.

The complete set of SDS issued by CSE consisted of about 1,200 Safety Data Sheets representing some 6,000 sheets of paper. This delivery vehicle was quite expensive, time consuming, and not at all ecological. There were significant costs associated with producing, translating, and printing.

STATE OF THE SDS PROJECT

The complexity and volume of the SDS program made a relational database approach obvious. The design of the database scheme and the application for the database access were completed in 1995. The data is entered and maintained with a generic database tool for relational databases, called TableTool, written by Ergon Informatik. This generic tool has been enhanced with project-specific business rules and functions for the composition of the Safety Data Sheets.

The different attributes of a product are stored in a database with almost 700 tables and views. The structure of this database follows the 16 chapters of an SDS and allows the parallel generation of Safety Data Sheets in several languages. Different content providers enter attributes on products into this database. SDS redactors then compose an SDS out of the entered attributes. After an electronic evaluation process the Safety Data Sheet is validated. The final SDS is built with a database publishing tool, called ReportTool, written by Ergon Informatik, and stored on disk in the Adobe™ Portable Document Format (PDF). The SDS are offered in this PDF format in the database application where they may be viewed on screen or printed on paper locally for further use. This PDF format can be displayed by a platform independent reader.

Updates of SDS have to be well documented and earlier version have to be archived. The database application helps the editors to build an update of an SDS while storing older versions. Attributes may be changed, added or removed. After another evaluation and approval process this update may be validated. This forces the creation of the new Safety Data Sheet with the database publishing tool.

PUT IT ON THE NETWORK

With the development and increased use of the Roche intranet, the idea came up to use the intranet to publish the Safety Data Sheets in the whole Roche group. In this way users would have immediate access to the latest SDS.

The goal was to develop an effective intranet application for the search and access to Safety Data Sheets. However something was needed that would run in the whole Roche group on different platforms with very little distribution effort and always the latest versions of the Data Sheets. Java offers the possibility of writing a Web-application with different windows that looks very similar to the database application. There is no distribution effort for those who have access with a Web browser to the Roche intranet.

JAVA CONNECTION

A working Java applet was constructed in four weeks, fast by any programming productivity standard. The applet was relatively easy to create, although there was a need to have it hook into the database and pull out the specified PDF file. No commercial middleware existed to do this at the time, so a middleware program had to be developed and implemented.

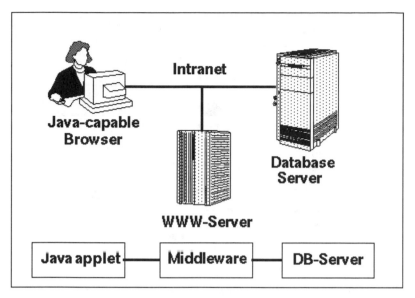

© 1997 F. Hoffmann-La Roche. Used with permission. All rights reserved.

Figure 9-1. The diagram shows the three-tier architecture of the application. The Java applet is connected via a socket or an HTTP/CGI gateway to a middleware server. The middleware server translates the requests of the Java applet into SQL commands which are executed on the DB server. The Safety Data Sheets are generated with a report writer, converted to PDF and then stored on the Web server for faster access.

There is a three-tier structure to the application: the Java front end; the middleware data access; and the database itself. The Java applet is connected through an HTTP/CGI gateway to the middleware server. This middleware is connected to the database server. The middleware translates the requests of the Java applet into SQL commands which are executed on the database server and sends the result back to the applet. At the moment, the Safety Data Sheet is set valid, the PDF file is created on the fly, and then stored on the file server.

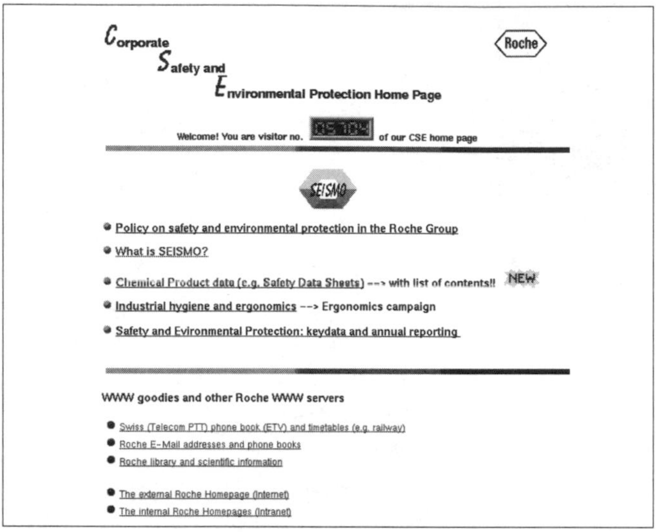

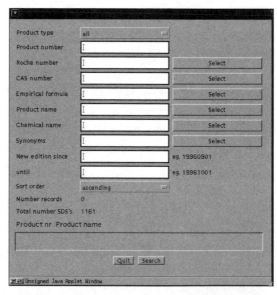

© 1997 F. Hoffmann-La Roche. Used with permission. All rights reserved.

*Figure 9-2. This is what the end user sees as the entry point to
the Seismo home page. To get to the Safety Data Sheet application,
he or she clicks on the SDS link.*

© 1997 F. Hoffmann-La Roche. Used with permission. All rights reserved.

*Figure 9-3. A search browser comes up enabling the user to search based
on the type of product, its product number, empirical formula, and product name. Searches can also be conducted by date and date range.*

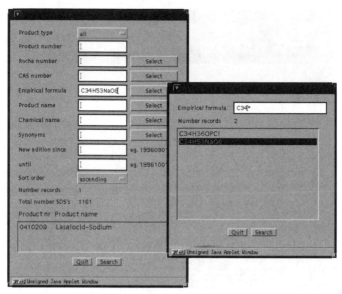

© 1997 F. Hoffmann-La Roche. Used with permission. All rights reserved.

Figure 9-4. For some search fields there exists a selection browser that comes up when one of the Select buttons is clicked. This is a browser that shows the values stored in the database. This helps the user to compose their query.

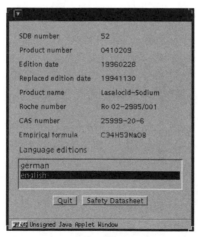

© 1997 F. Hoffmann-La Roche. Used with permission. All rights reserved.

Figure 9-5. With a mouse click on a row, a view on this data record is brought up, showing more details about the selected Safety Data Sheet and the available languages. The selection of one of the language versions activates the Safety Data Sheet button.

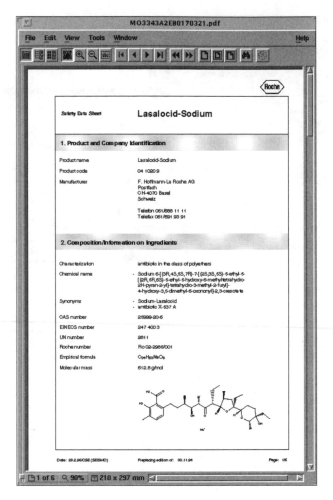

© 1997 F. Hoffmann-La Roche. Used with permission. All rights reserved.

Figure 9-6. The click on the Safety Data Sheet button brings up the Safety Data Sheet in the PDF format in the Adobe™ Acrobat™ Reader. The SDS may also be printed on the local printer.

USER RESPONSE

The on-line SDS has been accessed 2,500 times in six months from all over the Roche world. Based on e-mails and phone calls, the Roche community has responded well to the application and find it easy to use.

There are a number of obvious and not-so-obvious benefits to the end user. Paper updates no longer need to be dealt with, which saves time and costs. Immediate, direct access to the latest information is always available from all who have access to the Roche intranet with a Java-capable Web browser. Earlier CSE sent the complete set of SDS to 450 locations from where they were distributed to the end user. Now each end user has direct access to all available SDS. Electronic searches are faster and more convenient than searching through SDS folders and papers. Most users only require a small part of the entire SDS collection; now they can categorize and target their searches. There are plans to expand the number of languages in which the SDS documents are available.

In addition, repetitive costs for the sending of the paper updates has disappeared. This includes costs for paper, the organization of shipment, mailing costs, and the labor for updating the individual SDS folders. Last, but not least, it is an ecological gain. A lot of waste paper is avoided, about 100,000 pages every year.

USING JAVA

The development of this Safety Data Sheet applet including the middleware for the database access was written in four person weeks. This was with competent programmers who had little Java experience at the beginning of the project. They found the language easy to learn and easy to use. Java was a very cost-effective way to build a graphical, user-friendly interface to an existing database. It demonstrated new ways to publish and disseminate information within a large multinational, multidivisional company.

At the time the project was developed, a productive version of a Web browser supporting Java was not available for Windows 3.1PCs. A lot of the Roche PCs still run with these systems, and this lack of Java resources was an impediment. A second Web access with simple HTML pages had to be written. This was done with CGI scripts written in Perl. Database access was done with Sybperl. At the moment both search possibilities are still offered on the Seismo home page. Recent announcements of Windows 3.1 Java support will change that situation. After the realization of the Roche desk top standard (Windows NT) the possibility for usage of the Java solution will also increase.

The database connectivity demonstrated with the SDS program has implications on other parts of the Roche intranet and the SEISMO project. The speed of development of Java applications is apparent. The speed of deployment throughout the Roche intranet is also apparent. Users have responded well to the interactivity of Java. As more tools become available, and more functionality becomes available, we expect the use of the language to increase significantly. The initial results are promising. SEISMO has its arms around the Java mascot, Duke, and we expect they will be doing a lot more work together.

CHAPTER 10

NATIONAL SEMICONDUCTOR: ACCELERATING TIME TO MARKET FOR DESIGN ENGINEERS

Phil Gibson, Director, InterActive Marketing, National Semiconductor

Saif Kantrikar, Senior Programmer Analyst, National Semiconductor

National Semiconductor is a leading developer and marketer of semiconductor components. National Semiconductor and CADIS®, Inc., developed the first commercially viable Java business application: a parametric search engine that has made information on 23,000 products instantaneously accessible to National's customers. By having easy, immediate access to information, design engineers cut days and weeks off design cycle times, giving them a competitive advantage. National Semiconductor has significantly improved customer service while reducing print, CD duplication, and distribution costs. There were start-up development challenges as this was an early Java business application, but the Java-based search engine, deployed for over 14 months, has proven reliable and effective. Additional Java applications are projected for National's industry-leading Web site and for its intranet.

N ational Semiconductor develops and markets semiconductor components. These small, fingernail-sized, electronic devices make it possible to operate your computer, telephone, automobile, and most electronic equipment. The $2.4 billion company (fiscal year 1996 revenues) serves a large worldwide customer base of original equipment suppliers in communications, personal computer, consumer, and manufacturing markets.

The key decision maker in the purchasing process for National Semiconductor's products is the design engineer. He or she is a technically skilled professional who is responsible for the design and development of the next generation system for their companies. The essential information that these designers must have to complete their projects is contained in Data Sheets and Application Notes.

The Web offered National an explosive opportunity to deliver this information instantly to every engineer that wanted it. A million customers around the world could pull down exactly the information that they wanted and they could do it on demand at any time of the day or night. National's Internet strategy was to jump on this opportunity and to make 40,000 pages of data sheets and technical information on 23,000 parts available anywhere, anytime at a designer's whim. A second goal was to develop a search capability to enable the designer to quickly find the "needle in the haystack" that solved their technical requirement.

To achieve this goal, National partnered with Cadis in the summer of 1995 to develop the first commercially viable Java business application, the parametric search engine. The application was demonstrated at Sun headquarters in November 1995, at a major Java launch event. There was a lot of excitement about Java leading up to this launch; the language was seen as the first truly object-oriented, totally platform-independent language for the Web. But could it be used for business applications? Most of the demonstrations of its utility had centered around applets, scrolling tickers, and tumbling animations. These were useful and attractive, but had limited business appeal and interest. The CADIS parametric search engine, however, clearly demonstrated the power of Java: its graphic, interactive, and connective power. This application helped National meet a real customer need and has resulted in a faster diffusion of deeper information to a much broader audience.

NATIONAL'S WEB STRATEGY

National's InterActive Marketing group is responsible for National's external Web site and its Marketing Intranet. This group has one strategy: "Be Dynamic; Be First." Instant delivery of useful information to the designer whenever he or she wants it is the objective.

Twenty-four months ago, people were skeptical about the Internet for information access; today it is a given. National's monthly visitor traffic has grown to 40 to 50 percent penetration of the potential engineering user base. A key reason for that growth was National's parametric search engine.

Frequently, a customer has only a rough idea of the device that is needed for an end system. The necessary device may be broadly classified according to general functions, but specific characteristics may be needed for the end system. This includes voltage, speed, package size, price and temperature requirements. Imagine searching for information on a part with input characteristic voltage in the range of 10–50 volts and input current in the range of 10 mAmps to 50 mAmps. With 23,000 products to look through, locating a part with these characteristics is challenging.

The solution to finding a specific part with the desired characteristics among the products in National's portfolio was to create a parametric search engine using Java. This capability enables engineers searching National's Web site to type in component attributes and receive a selection of possible devices that meet the required specifications. This search functionality is only possible today using CADIS' Krakatoa® Web Catalog Publisher™ search engine.

BUSINESS UTILITY OF KRAKATOA

National is reducing the typical information delivery cycle by at least two weeks by providing fingertip access to the selection criteria that every designer needs. Before the Web, the design engineer had to wade through stacks of data sheets or volumes of data books to find specific parameter tables. If the designer did not have the necessary data sheet for a project, he or she had to order or cajole the information from the local distributor or rep and then wait two weeks or more for delivery by mail. This included bouncing through voice mail, missed commitments, and confused messages. Worst of all, if the wrong data sheet or material was delivered, the designer had to restart the entire process and suffer another two weeks of frustration.

Data sheets, by their printed nature, are created in bulk and it is expensive to store, ship, and archive them. Oftentimes, these printed documents are out of date with the latest revisions of semiconductor devices. If a designer gets a data sheet but not the errata document that goes with all of the recent changes to a part, their design is doomed to subsequent unexpected changes. Finally, price and availability, key inputs to every design decision, were never accurate in print. They are available on the Web today for any designer and are the result of any search through the Krakatoa™ tool.

JAVA RATIONALE

The nonplatform-specific nature of Java was the main reason it was chosen as a critical component of our search technology. Its rich interactive interface allows an enhanced user experience because of its intuitive nature and ease of use.

The front end for the parametric search engine during the start of the National project was very platform specific (either Windows 3.1 or Motif). National needed a Web front end that would work across multiple platforms and browsers, Design engineers are typically UNIX and/or Windows based with an occasional Macintosh thrown in. As a result, the major requirement for a Web front end to the parametric search tool was that it had to be totally cross-platform. National also needed a simple and easy-to-use interface that could download information from the Web site at the user's request. Java was the natural choice since it is the only true programming language supported on the Web (excluding the scripting languages of course).

There were several theoretical and practical advantages to choosing Java for the search application.

Cross Platform. The Java applet can run on any browser supporting the Java virtual machine on any platform. All that a client needs is a Java-enabled browser, which is now available on almost all platforms. The applet uses Netscape's Navigator and Microsoft's Internet Explorer on the PC, Macintosh, and Sun platforms. It has the same look and feel across these platforms. Unique coding and compilations for different platforms is no longer required as it was using traditional programming languages like C and C++.

Intuitive Interface. The applet is intuitive since it closely resembles an existing product, which has been tested successfully in different industries.

Client/Server Paradigm. The applet has been built as a true client/server application, with the Java front end acting as the client and the search server acting as a server. The joys of distributed computing are that the server just has to provide the necessary data and the client will handle all the processing involved.

Object-Oriented. Since Java is object-oriented and a close cousin to C++ (in most aspects), the algorithms created previously for the Windows/Motif version (which was written in C++) could be carried over with just the language changes, but not functional changes.

Easy Version Updates. Since Java is distributed via the Web and the applet downloads to the client's Web browser each time he or she accesses it, the Java version could easily be upgraded at the server side and the client would automatically download the latest version of the software.

Fewer Client Licenses. With the Web front end, we just needed one client license, a major benefit over having to purchase lots of licenses for our customers who are ever changing and on the move.

Quick Learning Curve. It is very easy for a software programmer familiar with object-oriented language like C++ to pick up Java. No extensive training is required.

Lower Cost of Software Distribution. By providing a central location for customers to get the software, the cost of distribution is greatly reduced.

There were several disadvantages to this cutting-edge technology in 1995. There were early performance issues due to the unstable nature of the Java environment, specifically the Java virtual machine code, in the browser. There was also a firewall problem with Java applets. They could not communicate using traditional network programming techniques like sockets through a company's firewall. At the time, all browsers did not support Java. There was also a long initial download time for the entire applet. The most significant barrier in 1995: no sophisticated development environment or tools were available and documentation on working with the language was nonexistent.

Those disadvantages have largely disappeared. The language

has matured. The processing speed at the client side has been significantly increased by the advent of just-in-time (JIT) compilers in the two major browsers. A solution was found to the firewall issue. There are major new development environments and tools for Java, hundreds of technical books, and more Java expertise.

There were alternative approaches to developing the search engine application. An HTML/CGI version was created to support non-Java browsers. It was not intuitive, but it served the purpose of being compatible with earlier and different browsers.

Having the two versions highlighted the performance advantages of Java. With the HTML version, each drill down requires the browser to first pass the relevant information to the Web server. The Web server then runs common gateway interface (CGI) scripts, which are written in C and C++ computer languages. These scripts call the parametric search server, and the server does a query on the database, passing the results of the query back to the CGI script. The CGI script packs this into an HTML page, which it then passes on to the Web server which in turn serves it to the engineer's Web client. All this page serving and connectivity take a toll on performance and execution is slow. The pages themselves take user-infuriating time to download for each query.

Java does away with a lot of these back and forth connectivity issues. With the Java version, the initial download time for an applet is significant but later search queries are much faster. The only time you need to connect with the National server is to do the actual query and download the results quickly. All the other processing, such as sorting data, for example, can be done on the client side.

SIMPLIFIED SEARCHING

The Krakatoa Web Catalog Publisher application is very intuitive, fast, and specific. It is geared towards the busy design engineer. A visual drill-down will give you an idea of the capability of this application.

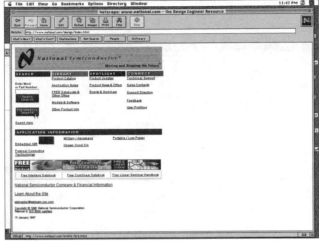

© 1997 National Semiconductor Inc. Used with permission. All rights reserved.

Figure 10-1. Many National customers bookmark this product information page, which has links to the Krakatoa parametric search engine. The National site was a finalist in the National Information Infrastructure Awards program in 1996.

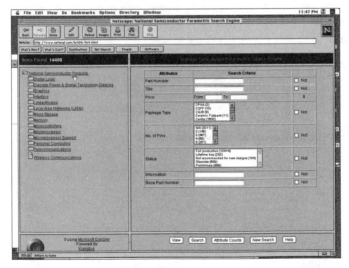

© 1997 National Semiconductor Inc. Used with permission. All rights reserved.

Figure 10-2. The Java-powered parametric search engine first comes up with a screen split into two halves: the left side denotes the position the user is at according to the parts classification; the right side denotes the attributes that apply to that specific part of the tree on the left. "Items found" qualification count denotes the number of parts found at each particular level.

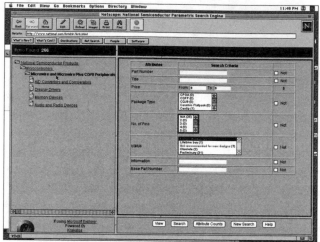

© 1997 National Semiconductor Inc. Used with permission. All rights reserved.

Figure 10-3. As you further drill down the tree to the specific category that you are looking for, the attributes reflect the specialized parameters applicable for that part. The item count also shows you how many parts are available at that level. You can set any search criteria for the parameters at any level and the counter shows the number of parts that match it accordingly. When the Krakatoa "Items found" results number is manageable for viewing, you simply click View to see the available parts in a spreadsheet format.

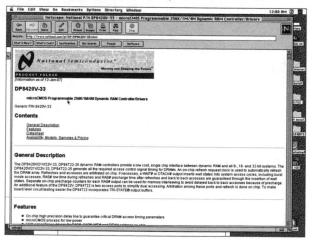

© 1997 National Semiconductor Inc. Used with permission. All rights reserved.

Figure 10-4. One of the parameters for the part is a URL link that takes you directly to a product folder containing all the information about the part, including availability, detailed models, samples, and pricing. A color data sheet can be printed by the engineer through an Adobe Acrobat PDF file.

WHAT MAKES IT SIMPLE, FAST, AND INTERACTIVE

Behind the application there are three interacting components: Java clients, a Java-powered proxy server, and a main server with a knowledge base (see below). These are basic components of the CADIS Krakatoa Web Catalog Publisher, with which we built our Parametric Search application.

The Java client is an application downloaded to a user's browser when the parametric search option is clicked at the National Semiconductor Web site. Once on the user's browser, the application presents an interface for conducting parametric searches, viewing search results, and accessing additional information about any single query result item. (There is also an HTML client which is a programmed set of HTML frames that are invoked and modified during interactions with the server, allowing the user to conduct parametric searches and link to associated URLs with non-Java enabled browsers.)

The Java Proxy Server is a security feature of the Java implementation that is a relay service between the main server and many clients. Connection information is maintained about each connected client; inactive clients are removed. Several patent pending mechanisms are used to provide security insulation for the main server. If an attack is detected by the proxy server, it breaks the errant connection while allowing other client connections to continue with normal operations.

The main server is an object-oriented knowledge modeling engine that serves Krakatoa knowledge bases. It supports very high speed query performance, dynamic class management, and drag-and-drop authoring, as well as links to data in other databases via URLs. Using the parameters supplied by the client software, the server can quickly reduce large amounts of data into manageable sets of data that meet the client criteria.

A Krakatoa knowledge base is a sophisticated index to data stored in any type of database in Web-readable format. The knowledge base is an object-oriented classification structure, or schema, that is populated with instances, usually with URL links to the original data page or image. Knowledge-base objects can have many attributes of the following four attribute types: numeric, enumerated, Boolean, or text.

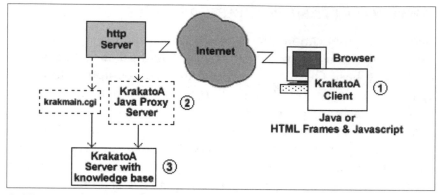

© 1997 National Semiconductor Inc. Used with permission. All rights reserved.

Figure 10-5. Basic operation of the Krakatoa Web Catalog Publisher with which NSC built its parametric search engine. (1) The URL is requested by a browser and the Java client application is downloaded to the browser. The Java client makes requests of the main server through the proxy server (2) and/or CGI. The main server (3) returns data to the client.

Access to a Krakatoa knowledge base can be accomplished with both Java-enabled and HTML-enabled browsers.

Internet connections are established between the Java client and the main Krakatoa Server through the Java proxy. This connection is established using a TCP/IP socket, or an HTTP simulated socket if firewalls are present in the connection path.

CLIENT AND SERVER FIREWALLS

The Krakatoa Web Catalog Publisher has been designed to inter-operate with Internet firewalls, at both the server and the client locations. When no firewalls are present, the Java client interacts directly with the Java Proxy Server. If firewalls are present, HTTP simulated sockets are used to transport the data between the client and the proxy server. The simulated sockets use existing Web protocols as a transport for the client/server data. The proxy server implements several patent-pending mechanisms to guard against outside attacks. When an attack is detected, the server closes the connection to the attacking client and continues operations with the remaining clients.

When client connections are made to the proxy server, the simulated socket mechanism does not accept any external address information. As a result, external sources are prevented from providing inappropriate address information that would result in an operation being attempted with an unintended host. This security feature requires that the Java proxy server and the HTTP server run on the same host. However, the main Krakatoa server may run on a different host.

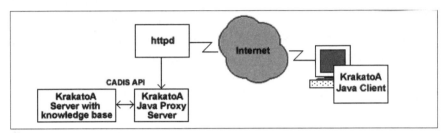

© 1997 National Semiconductor Inc. Used with permission. All rights reserved.

Figure 10-6. Java-powered client operation: no firewalls. Here's the sequence of events: URL is requested by browser. Java application is delivered to browser. Java client makes successive requests of Java proxy server. Java proxy server relays requests to main server via API. Java proxy server replies to Java client with requested data.

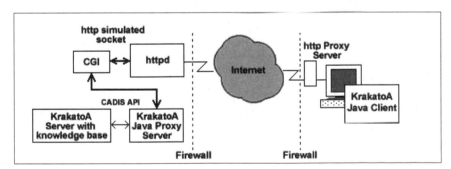

© 1997 National Semiconductor Inc. Used with permission. All rights reserved.

Figure 10-7. Most of National Semiconductor's customers work behind firewalls, and the parametric search application had to work across firewalls. Here's the sequence of events with Java-client and server firewalls. URL is requested by browser through local HTTP proxy server. Java application is delivered to browser. Java client makes requests of Java proxy server via HTTP-simulated socket. Java proxy server relays request to main server via API. Java proxy server replies to Java client with requested data via HTTP-simulated socket.

OPTIMIZATION AND PERFORMANCE

The Krakatoa server has been designed for optimum performance in a number of ways. Navigation and attribute selections negotiated between clients and the server are accomplished using a single client/server exchange (RPC call). The Krakatoa server is highly tuned for managing sessions among a large number of clients. The main server uses an object-oriented model that is iteratively discovered by client queries, dramatically improving performance and flexibility. Knowledge bases represent data in compact structure, minimizing memory requirements. The Java proxy server provides multithreading of read-only knowledge bases.

All of these features benefit the speed and reliability of the search engine. An important technical point for business: The application is scalable from a stand-alone PC to a large enterprise-wide server. In addition, the attention to firewalls and security addresses a major business concern.

WHAT CUSTOMERS THINK

From customers' perspective, it is very easy to use and find parts using Krakatoa. They do not really care about the search engine at all: they are interested in getting the information they need as quickly and painlessly as possible. With the Krakatoa parametric search engine, all the customer has to have is a general idea of what kind of a part is desired. Then he or she goes down the tree to the specific level relating to the part characteristics, such as high speed analog devices, enters the search criteria for the parameters required, and, instantly, he or she gets all the parts that match the criteria. The customer can then either refine the search to very specific parts or take a look at the parts in a spreadsheet format and get all the information needed. No more searching through tons of paper data, scanning characteristics for the parts desired, and no more learning about the supplier's part-numbering scheme. What used to take a customer seven to eight weeks to discover takes two or three minutes with the parametric search engine from CADIS.

Every customer service business must constantly evaluate and improve on the quality of the service it delivers. The goal of the Web

team at National was to make our Web site the number one preferred Web site for design engineers by June of 1996. This goal was
set in July of 1995 when our Web site was just getting off the ground.

We had to know how we stood to start with so we conducted sur-
veys, focus groups, and many, many one-on-one interviews to
benchmark our customer's needs and our competitor's status. We
continue this outward focus today because we are determined to
maintain the position we have achieved. We learned much from
those initial studies. Our site has evolved to meet our customer's
demands and today it is intuitive and easy to use. We can give all of
the credit for that result to the early efforts at end user research.
Designers were straightforward about new features to add but what
was equally important was what they told us to delete. Our site today uses minimal graphics with intuitive links and we strive to make
the designer's visit to the site as productive and brief as possible.
The objective is not to increase the "hits" to our site that so many
companies boast about. The objective is to get the designer to the
specific information that they seek as effortlessly as possible and to
allow them to get back to work so that they can complete their designs.

We offer everything for the designer in one place: specifications,
models, price, availability, literature, automatic updates, easy feedback, and even free samples. Currently, the National Web site is visited by 500,000 to 600,000 unique visitors each month. The
parametric search, using Krakatoa, is the second most visited page
on National's site. That popularity signifies the importance of the
information, as well as the usability of the search tool. Over 7,000
data sheets a day are now delivered to customers and prospective
customers on-line, and over 1,000 e-mails a day are received from
our site users every business day. Register design engineers are
growing at a rate of 20 percent per month.

These are some quotes from our customers about our
Web site:

From a senior engineer, NovAtel Communications:

"This site is the best that I have seen for ease of searching
and completeness of information. Technical data on

parts is provided in a good format. E-mail option on PDF files is a great idea. On-line sample ordering is excellent. I had parts in my hand in Calgary in two days. That's faster than my local reps can get them to me. Please keep up the good work."

From a senior design engineer at Network Equipment Technologies:

"Congratulations! You have set up a very useful Web site. I found that using the library section of your WWW site provided all the initial information I need, in a clear and helpful manner. The use of PDF files for your data sheets and app notes combined with the availability of IBIS models and on-line pricing made my job and the process of component selection much easier. Keep up the good work."

From an applications engineer at Teradyne:

"Yours is the best organized Web site of all the semiconductor company sites I have seen so far. Having the part number search utility at the home page saves me from having to search through several layers of information to find the information I need. It's a real time saver. Good job!"

From an engineer at Packet Engines Incorporated:

"Excellent work. Saves lots of trees and time. I recently took both routes: your 800 data book route and this route—guess which I will use in the future?"

From a senior design engineer at Lasergraphics, Inc:

"Just a quick note to say how impressed I am with your site. The National Web Site is, without question, the most usable, least time wasteful semiconductor manufacturer presence I have seen. Great job! I will be back often."

And this quote from a design engineer sums it all up:

"This Web site has been designed by a design engineer for a design engineer."

RESULTS AND LESSONS LEARNED

The success of the Krakatoa parametric search engine is evident in the daily number of accesses, downloads, and e-mails. Customers have responded favorably in quantitative market studies and qualitative market focus groups and interviews.

A hidden value: With the amount of information on-line, the print distribution of the data books has been drastically reduced. Currently, National is offering its data books to be ordered on-line, but this may change since the information that the customer requires can be readily downloaded from the Web.

We also realized savings in programmer development time. With the Java language closely resembling C++ in its object-oriented approach, the learning curve for C++ developers is greatly reduced. The developers at CADIS were able to prototype the Java version of the parametric front end to the search engine in a record three weeks and found themselves more productive with Java than with C++.

A key development time factor was our partnership with CADIS on this project. The need for a parametric search engine was imperative and CADIS had early Java experience. They focused on building the engine; we focused on building the architecture specific to NSC in building the content and in making the engine work on our Web site.

This last point is important. To make the application work well on our Web site, all the information, search tools, and other databases had to be glued together. We obtained all the product data sheets from our product data base in PDF format. These are stored in a defined directory structure, which is then populated into the National's parametric search knowledge base along with information obtained from NSC's transactional database systems, like pricing, packaging information, etc. These transactional databases are updated on a weekly basis to have the most up-to-date information

available to our customers. Product folders for each part are created from existing systems in HTML pages with many scripts. All
these are tied intricately with the full text and parametric search engine giving users the usual comfortable feel to which they are accustomed on National's site.

Eventually, we expect a continuous rather than batch process
connection to our transactional databases. This will enable direct
ordering of components.

JAVA AT NATIONAL SEMICONDUCTOR

Java is a very viable tool for business applications. The parametric
search engine is complex, handles tens of thousands of documents,
and works on potentially millions of desktops, regardless of
whether they are PCs, UNIX workstations, or Macintoshes. Speed,
reliability, and happy users are the result of the first 18 months of
operation.

We see a great potential for Java at National Semiconductor. It
will continue to improve customer access to information and help
drive our growth and directions. Real-time technical support will be
enhanced in the future with Java, as customers will be able to talk
"engineer to engineer" while sharing simulation models, timing diagrams, and whiteboards. Customers will be able to test their designs by downloading a Java applet to execute local simulations or
potentially upload their information for execution on a much higher
performance platform. The applet could continue to monitor the
site and notify them of the task completion so they could download
the result. Beyond simulation and technical interactions, training is
an obvious migration for this technology. Any user, anywhere, any
time certainly has the right ring to it. On-line commerce will soon
become common in business-to-business applications, and Java
will definitely play a role in the front end and back end of that application as well.

Java has already helped National Semiconductor lead the new information era of the Web. It has helped us cut costs and build the
foundation for a highly productive, easy-to-use site. The most obvious benefit today is the advantage that Java gives us in helping
designers quickly find and select the most appropriate National

device. This accelerates their designs and our revenues as well. This is for today; key is to keep our creative thoughts open about the potentials for the future. A basic search engine is easy; Java's promise is that it will allow truly dynamic and interactive applications to come. Stay tuned to www.national.com and see what develops.

CHAPTER 11
@HOME:
CABLE JAVA

Mark Neumann, Director, Content Engineering, @Home

@Home is making high bandwidth connectivity to the Internet a reality for homes, schools, and businesses in areas of the United States. The high bandwidth access is provided through the cable TV infrastructure. @Home has optimized that infrastructure for the Internet with an innovative network architecture, physical improvements, and network-centric software tools like Java. @Home is using Java as a tool for its front-end Web site, and for distributing content over Castanet channels. Java is also a means of updating software versions over the Internet. Java is one of many tools @Home uses to optimize its high bandwidth connectivity: JavaScript, C++, PERL, and UNIX are all used. Java offers some key advantages: its cross-platform feature is very useful in the heterogeneous consumer market; development time is short with Java, and it is easy to make iterative improvements. Large and affordable increases in bandwidth have major implications for how businesses leverage the Internet for customers and employees.

The growth of the Internet is particularly amazing considering the slow download speeds using a 28.8 modem, the standard for most people. Some pundits call this the World Wide Wait.

233

But Hybrid Fiber Coax (HFC) cable technology is now available for providing local area network (LAN) access speeds into homes and businesses over existing cable television plants around much of the U.S., and offers opportunities for some areas of Europe and Asia as well. Split the cable coming into your home or business, run it up to your PC, add a cable modem, and you get a hundred times the bandwidth of your bandwidth-challenged colleagues. You watch MTV video clips while others weep about brownouts and bottlenecks. It is not quite that simple, but that is the idea; use the existing cable television infrastructure to provide high-speed Internet access and services to homes and businesses.

@Home focuses on making that a reality. The idea was born when John Doerr and Will Hearst of the Kleiner Perkins, Caufeld, Byers venture firm contacted Milo Medin, the man who led the NASA Internet effort, championed the TCP/IP protocol, and is a legend in network circles for his ability to help steer the Internet through various logjams and crises, and create its future. John Doerr also enlisted the backing of Bruce Ravenal of TCI, the largest cable operator in the US.

Today, @Home is owned by TCI, ComCast, Cox (the number one, four, and five cable TV companies in the United States), and Kleiner-Perkins. The cable companies bring their assets and infrastructure expertise, @Home provides the Internet expertise. And @Home has announced partnerships with other cable companies.

@Home is organized around three business units: The core @Home service provides Internet access to consumers; @Work is an Internet service provider (ISP) for business; and @Media is the content unit that works with partners to develop content that makes optimal use of high-speed, always-on Internet connections.

CABLE MODEMS: INTERNET FOR THE REST OF US

Cable modems are black boxes that sit between the coaxial and fiber cable of the cable network and the end user's PC. The end user's PC has an Ethernet card connecting to a standard Ethernet cable and then to the cable modem. The modem converts the signal from the computer to analog for transmission across the coaxial and fiber cable to the head-end facility where it is converted into digital, and vice versa for interactivity. The boxes themselves are more complex than standard phone modems and are usually leased to the end user as part of the Internet service; they cost in the $700 range, with costs expected to come down below $300 by the end of 1997.

HIGH-SPEED: 100 TIMES FASTER THAN 28.8 MODEM SPEEDS

Depending on the type of cable modem, computers connected to the same head end share 27Mbps for downstream content and 768kbps for upstream content. The bandwidth available to the end-user computer is further restricted to the 10Mbps total for Ethernet and by the network interface card, bus speed, and processor speed of the computer. This means that an effective 1.5-2.5Mbps for a typical PC[1] is now the bottleneck, but this is almost 100 times faster than 28.8 modem speeds.

Of course, the 27Mbps is shared, much like a LAN. Typically, the cable may pass by 500 to 2,000 homes. Tests by the cable modem labs have shown no degradation in service for 200 simultaneous users doing typical Web-browsing activities. An important benefit of cable technology is that further channels of the cable plant can be assigned as traffic demands, effectively dividing the user base across the additional channels. You access the Internet on channel 88 and your next-door neighbor uses channel 89, so you are not contending for the same bandwidth. This allows for maintaining good performance as the popularity of Internet access increases.

Table 11-1. Speed is a key advantage of cable modems.[1] For the dynamic Web with 3-D graphics, video clips, and interactive product catalogs, speed is a necessity.

Speed (bits) File Size (Bytes)	28.8 kbps modem	ISDN (128 kbps peak)	T-1 (1.44 Mbps peak)	cable (2.5Mbps effective)
56KB, 10-page text document	15.5 seconds	3.5 seconds	<1 second	<1 second
350KB, 1-page 600 dpi graphic file	> 1.5 minutes	21 seconds	<2 seconds	<1.5 secs.

(continued)

Table 11-1. (continued)

Speed (bits) File Size (Bytes)	28.8 kbps modem	ISDN (128 kbps peak)	T-1 (1.44 Mbps peak)	cable (2.5Mbps effective)
2.2 MB Quicktime Video	> 10 minutes	> 2 minutes	12 seconds	7 seconds
10.0 MB OS software download	> 45 minutes	>10 minutes	56 seconds	32 seconds

ALWAYS ON: NO CALL SETUP TIME

Similar to your cable TV box, a cable modem is always on. Users are always connected and do not have to wait for a call to be set up. It is a LAN type of connection. This will change the way people use the Internet and personal computers in general because information and services are more readily at hand. The Internet becomes as accessible as a CD-ROM or an application on your hard drive. Other computers on your virtual LAN can be icons on your computer screen; click and connect to your daughter's home page at college; click and connect to your supplier in Seattle.

Cable Modem Quiz

Can I watch The X-Files *on my television and log on to the X-Files Internet site simultaneously?*

Absolutely. There is plenty of capacity in the cable running to your home. The cable is spliced: one path to the television, one to the computer. No crossover, unless there is some paranormal creature on the program that evening.

What if the whole neighborhood watches The X-Files *on television and logs onto the X-Files Internet site at the same time?*

This depends on the size of the neighborhood. Two hundred to 300 users can be supported without any degradation in performance. With a larger group of users, additional bandwidth would be converted from more traditional cable TV service.

A key point: the underlying coaxial cable and fiber optic cable network has more capacity than the first-generation cable modems can handle. Second-generation cable modems will offer even higher capacity than the 10 to 27Mbps capacity of today's modems.

Can I upload as fast as I can download?

Several different methods are available for communicating from the end-user computer back to the network. Some modems split the bandwidth evenly, providing 10Mbps upstream and downstream. Others recognize that most traffic will be downstream, so they provide 27Mbps downstream and 728Kbps upstream. Finally, where it is prohibitively expensive to upgrade the cable plant to two-way, a conventional modem (telco-return) can be used to provide 28.8Kbps upstream, plenty for http requests.

CAUTION: A FOUR-LANE HIGHWAY ONTO A DIRT ROAD

When Milo first met with Will Hearst and John Doerr to discuss their ideas for accessing the Internet over cable modems, he pointed out the pitfalls of adding millions of high-speed connections to an already overburdened and sometimes unreliable network. The speed of a network connection is only as fast as the slowest link. And with the economics of today's Internet, where service to the user is not tied to usage, the situation does not encourage the existing Internet providers to upgrade their plant to handle the load increased by someone else, like @Home.

But Milo had a solution.

A MANAGED NETWORK: NEVER SEND THE SAME BITS TWICE

Milo proposed to build a separate network, an @Home intranet, to service @Home users and to connect to the Internet. This Intranet has a backbone network connecting regional data centers, where commonly used services and data are duplicated, dividing up the workload and localizing network traffic. These regional data centers balance the load and localize the impact of outages. In addition to e-mail and Usenet newsgroups, the data centers serve Web content specifically intended for the high-bandwidth-capable @Home users, such as video and large graphics. Web pages are created and replicated automatically to each center using @Home-developed replication technology. At each center, pages are updated automatically and replicated databases provide search functions.

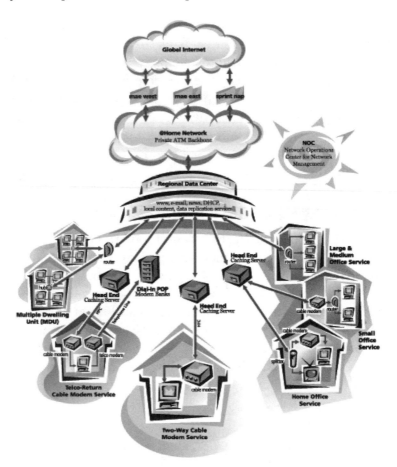

© 1997 @Home Corporation. Used with permission. All rights reserved.

Figure 11-1. The @Home network provides a separate backbone for Internet access. Replication takes place at regional data centers; this balances the network load and provides for redundancy. Caching takes place at cable head ends.

The regional data centers serve multiple cable company head ends, facilities where the Internet traffic transitions to the HFC plant used for two-way communications to the household. At the head-end facilities are computers that cache copies of popular data, further reducing traffic on the network and insuring reliable and consistent response times to users.

Why should everyone in Mountain View CA, for example, have to go to New York to pick up the electronic *New York Times?* The popular site is cached at a head-end facility using a proxy server, where any number of users can download and view.

This approach, keeping data close to the users and never shipping the same bits twice, avoids bottlenecks, husbands bandwidth, and makes the entire network more reliable and functional. The approach also requires some rethinking of popular techniques for publishing on the Web, which is where Java and JavaScript come in.

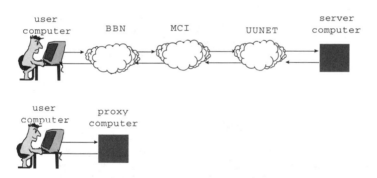

© 1997 @Home Corporation. Used with permission. All rights reserved.

Figure 11-2. @Home proxy servers at the head ends shorten the sequence of network clouds an Internet user has to navigate successfully through. The proxy servers bring the most popular data closest to the user.

CREATING DYNAMIC CONTENT WITH JAVA AND JAVASCRIPT

Today, most content on the World Wide Web is static, meaning that the Web pages are displayed the same way to every requester with no functional change. But many sites are striving to add value by dynamically generating the Web page based on information available to the site, either from a database or volunteered by the user. For example, @Home Web pages provide local weather to users in different geographic areas.

But if the Web page is created on the Web server for every request, then it cannot effectively be cached (although common elements of a page, e.g., an icon or graphic, can be cached). Sometimes the core data of the Web page depends upon user input, so the page cannot be static (like a search for a topic on the Yahoo! Web site). Sometimes the Web page is varied based upon information stored in client-side cookies (like a unique user ID, or user-selected preferences, or simple counters). Information stored on the client computer can be used to create a custom Web page, with specific advertising or other content. Today, this dynamic Web page functionality is provided primarily using server-side applications that apply programmer-defined rules to information provided by the client computer to create the Web page.

© 1997 @Home Corporation. Used with permission. All rights reserved.

Figure 11-3.@Home users have a home page packed with Java and JavaScript. This provides for a dynamic interface, without using cached or uncached network resources, helping optimize bandwidth.

The introduction of Netscape 3.0 and Internet Explorer 3.0 enabled programmers to develop Web pages that contain software which can be executed on the users' computers, reducing the load on servers and the network, improving response times, and providing fault tolerance. With 3.0, Netscape provided two important tools, a Java virtual machine, to execute embedded Java applets, and a scripting language called JavaScript, to execute scripting commands contained in the Web pages. By moving the application code into the Web page, the page again becomes static and can be cached.

© 1997 @Home Corporation. Used with permission. All rights reserved.

Figure 11-4. @Home's navigation bar is written in JavaScript.

Version 1.0 of the @Home Web pages includes a number of functions that all use Java and JavaScript to make the on-line experience more useful and dynamic, while at the same time husbanding and maximizing network resources. These functions include:

- Checking software versions for browser and for missing plug-ins. When users connect to the @Home default home page, they can be prompted to upgrade their software and taken to the download area. Or they can select a "bug me later" option. JavaScript is used for this function.

- Improving the user interface with more interactive controls. New users often are confused by the different methods for identifying a hyperlink. @Home has developed active buttons, which change color to show what options are available and/or selected. JavaScript is used for this function as well.

- Providing a Welcome for new users. First-time users are greeted by a video clip of the CEO of @Home, Tom Jermoluk, welcoming them to the service. The Welcome includes an introduction to the user profile feature, where they can enter their name in the service directory. Also presented is information for parents on how to protect their families from unsuitable material on the Internet. JavaScript is used for this function.

- Providing multimedia tours of the Web. Users can take tours of the Web where Web-jays (like MTV's veejays) appear in a pop-up window, while the main window displays different Web sites to narration. Eventually, users will be able to subscribe to their favorite personalities' view of the World Wide Web. JavaScript is used for this function.

- Branching to different content based upon user attributes: geographic location, user-selected options, time-of-day, etc. JavaScript is used for this function.

- Targeting advertising. Ads can be displayed based upon the content topic, PC type, user locale, and user-volunteered attributes. JavaScript is used for this function.

- Polling of servers for time-sensitive data. Headlines, stock quotes, sports scores, and other timely information can be pulled and refreshed on the current Web page. Java is used for this function.

- Providing different experiences for high-end and low-end machines. Now that the speed of the Internet connection is not the limiting factor, the capabilities of the consumers' computer are the limiting factor. @Home supports a broad base of users, from 386 computers to the latest Pentiums and Macintoshes. JavaScript is used to warn users about the possible limits of their computer when they are downloading videos. JavaScript is also used to display simpler interface elements to slower computers.

© 1997 @Home Corporation. Used with permission. All rights reserved.

Figure 11-5. @Home Network is customizable with local content, Java- and JavaScript-driven. The community promise of cable TV is carried over to cable Internet.

- Expiring content from the local disk cache. One problem with client disk caching is that old data may be displayed. The Netscape browser is configured to check the validity of a cached page once it is displayed after the browser is started. But since @Home is an always-on service, this is not frequent enough. The browser can be configured to compare the date of a cached page to that on the server every time the page is displayed, but this imposes an unacceptable burden on the network and slows response time. With JavaScript, our pages expire from the local disk cache after a set time, causing the browser to check the modification date of the page cached on the proxy server, which sends down a more recent page if it exists.

Java and JavaScript proved to be useful tools for creating interactive, dynamic content for the @Home user interface. The @Home Web entry to the Internet is now in use in tens of thousands of homes; the dynamic interface has proven useful in providing easy navigation and automating customer service activities.

There are other ways to add dynamic behavior and multimedia to Web pages: embedded plug-ins that enable a Web page to display video and animation, and play music. @Home installs a standard set of the most popular plug-ins, allowing @Home Web pages to contain video, music, and animations. These are installed by a data technician, who visits the home to install the cable modem and @Home software.

THE PROBLEM WITH PROPRIETARY PLUG-INS

Plug-ins have their limitations. They are updated frequently, and there are new plug-ins being developed and introduced. Users are prompted to download new plug-ins to view content at many Web sites. This can be tricky because some plug-ins may conflict with others. And there is no way for a user to be sure that a plug-in being downloaded does not contain a virus that could harm the user's computer. Also, since plug-ins are platform specific, cross-platform development is required.

Unlike plug-ins, Java and JavaScript provide a secure and cross-platform method for delivering applications over a network and can be used for both server and client applications. Plug-ins can only be used for client applications.

SERVER-SIDE JAVA AND JAVASCRIPT

@Home has been very successful using mostly client-side programming techniques to take advantage of our distributed managed network. But many data-intensive applications work best on a shared server. Servers are distributed, too!

@Home has four types of servers in its architecture:

- Publishing servers, where content originates from.

- Application servers, like personal Web page servers and user databases.

- Regional servers, which distribute content and provide common services, like e-mail, newsgroups, directories, search databases, user databases, and chat servers.

- Proxy servers, which cache Web pages and collect usage log information.

These servers consist of different models of Sun and SGI computers with varying capacities. Most of the software is commercial. Netscape provides the Web servers, proxy servers, newsgroup servers, chat servers, and e-mail servers. Oracle provides the relational database for storing a user database. Oracle's strong replication capabilities are used to keep the distributed data in sync. The public domain Harvest program is used for indexing content, though it may be replaced by a Netscape commercialized version of that program. And Tivoli supplies the software for software and file distribution.

@Home developed a number of user services, such as directories of people and content search using Netscape technology. Programs for accessing the user databases and for staging and distributing data were also directed by @Home.

An example of a publishing server application developed using JavaScript is the listings publishing system. Listings are @Home compilations of the Best of the Web, selected sites organized by major categories and subcategories (e.g., sports and football). @Home editors select these sites while browsing the Web. The @Home listings editor provides a Web page where the user can create new listings. Each listing consists of a screen shot, a headline, a description, and the category and subcategory assignments. The Web forms used are connected to an Oracle database using

JavaScript. When the listings are created, records are created in the database and a screenshot generated using the framegrabber on a Sun workstation. When the listings are published, the data is automatically exported in tab-delimited format and HTML generated using a PERL script.

LESSONS, LIMITATIONS, CONTEXT

JavaScript has proven to be a robust programming environment, even more reliable and faster than Java implemented to date. Many features that @Home originally developed using Java proved better when implemented in JavaScript. With JavaScript, the basic unit of code organization is the Web page, since JavaScript is contained in web pages and tightly integrated with HTML. On the other hand, this limits what can be done with client-side programming.

JavaScript objects and methods from the same Web site and frame set can be shared with other pages. On the other hand, a major advantage of Java over JavaScript is cross-browser support. Internet Explorer does not yet support all the JavaScript functions provided by Netscape. Recently, Netscape submitted JavaScript to a standards body, so hopefully this situation will improve. Meanwhile, Java is more standardized (although this, too, could change).

Netscape 3.0 provides a feature called Live Connect, which allows for integration of JavaScript functions, Java applets, and plug-ins. @Home uses this feature to control the presentation of audio and video on Web pages.

JavaScript has another limitation. Few debugging tools exist, forcing use of basic techniques to understand the execution of the code.

Java and JavaScript are not the only tools used by @Home to support its Internet service.:

- C++ is used for application development where performance is a concern. (At the time of this writing, the available Java virtual machines were not as fast as conventional compiled code for some applications.)

- PERL is used for many off-line programs.

- Shell scripts are used to glue many of the programs together.

- LiveWire, with JavaScript, is used to access Oracle databases and for some tools.

- Java is being used for several novel client-server applications, such as user voting or polling with real-time feedback, where IRC (Internet Relax Chat) servers provide data distribution.

In addition, standard UNIX off-the-shelf editors, version control systems, compilers, debuggers, etc., are used. @Home uses fairly standard industry practices with no standard development methodology or life cycle. The basic dictum is "use what you know" and "use what works."

DATABASE GLUE, AVOIDING THE PROPRIETARY TOOL TRAP

While developing the @Home network, we discovered that many commercial Web-serving systems, especially those used to dynamically create content from a central database, do not work well with a distributed network like @Home's. Most of these tools for page creation/serving, ad insertion, log processing, personalization, HTML message boards, and other functions were designed for centralized operation supporting a nonhomogenous browser software population on the Internet.

With the @Home network, a homogenous client-software base is provided, allowing a more integrated client-server approach with implications for both content and software delivery. And with Java and JavaScript, a common programming language can be used on both client and server.

Overall, however, Java and JavaScript have proven to be robust and useful. Given the rapid development needs of Web programming, both have proven easy to use and to debug. And the network itself provides for rapid turnaround and prototyping by making it easy to revise the software. ("Ship early, ship often" is the new software marketing mantra.)

JAVA: TAKING @HOME BEYOND THE BROWSER

While Java applets are supported inside the browser, much the way plug-ins are supported, the creation of stand-alone, network-enabled applications will allow optimal use of the high-speed LAN-like environment of the @Home network.

So far, @Home has used Java where the problem being solved requires more functionality than available from HTML. Scrolling headline carousels, user polling applications, and easy-to-use chat clients have been implemented as Java applets. As applets, these programs are constrained by the security model as implemented by Netscape. But the polling and chat applets take advantage of communication techniques not involving HTML and HTTP. (Note: these two examples use the IRC protocol.)

But Java *applications,* not applets, can access local storage and provide a more fertile ground for Web-site development. This is essential to doing true client-server development. Java applications do not execute inside a browser, but instead execute inside a Java virtual machine loaded on the client computer.

Java promises to be a major building block of @Home 2.0. With Java we can develop outside the constraints of the browser and HTML. At this time, @Home has prototyped headline carousel, floating navigation bar palettes, and vertical news tickers using Java and the Castanet technology from Marimba. These applications will co-exist with HTML browsers while providing more flexible and powerful network-aware applications. And the Castanet architecture of transmitter (content staging), repeater (regional servers), and proxy servers closely mirrors the @Home network architecture.

THE @HOME NETWORK FUTURE: DISTRIBUTED OBJECT MANAGEMENT

Looking out over the next 12 to 18 months, we see several technical and practical events that will accelerate the utility and user base for cable modem networks.

The Application is the Content. Today with the advent of client-side programming, the distinction between content such as graphics and text, and presentation programs, like the browser, video plug-ins, animation applets, etc., blurs. As @Home grows to millions of users, how will we keep all of the users' computers configured with the latest appropriate software?

All Users Automatically on the Latest Version. With Java applications, the content and programming can be more closely integrated, negating the need for a browser (although a consistent user interface, like that of a browser, will still be important). And several vendors, most notably Marimba, are addressing how to perform distributed object management. With Marimba's Castanet, users can subscribe to an application, receiving updates to presentation, information, and function at regular intervals.

The End of Version 2.0, Constant Updates. With tools like Castanet, the concept of "versions" will disappear. Applications will be composed of objects that will be updated as required. @Home has prototyped different functions currently performed by the browser or by applets in the browser using Java and Castanet.

© 1997 @Home Corporation. Used with permission. All rights reserved.

Figure 11-6. @Home has ported its News Carousel applet to a Castanet channel. This channel displays the headlines off the top news sites. Clicking on the headline launches the browser to the story on the site.

The Set-top Box Appliance Replaces the PC. Another factor driving @Home is the introduction of alternative devices besides the general purpose personal computer. These devices have often had no non-volatile local storage, hence much of the functionality is downloaded at run time. Eventually, there may be sufficient storage to cache the most frequently used data and applications. Of available solutions, only Java seems to provide the distributed applications support needed to support millions of PCs and appliance-type devices.

Finally, the Object Revolution Pans Out. During the early days of object-oriented programming, much was made of object reuse in different applications. Perhaps it took the phenomenon of the Internet to see the real value of sharing objects (or components) across different applications in real time with distribution of the objects over the network.

IMPLICATIONS FOR BUSINESS

There are a number of implications of fast, always-on Internet access provided by @Home and the cable network, as well as implications for @Home's use of Java and JavaScript.

- Seventy to 100 times the bandwidth means more content, and more dynamic multimedia content, is possible to deliver to customers. Customers will be looking for this. Some business applications, for example, in publishing and health care, simply require the transfer of very large files; the bandwidth of a cable network makes this fast and painless.

- Constant access to the Internet has implications on how often customers use the Internet and what they use it for. A cable connection is always live and is as accessible as a CD-ROM or a hard-drive application. Internet usage will increase.

- More bandwidth delivered directly to the home empowers telecommuters in ways that were previously impractical. The Internet becomes a large LAN for employees.

- Competing technologies will keep the cost of Internet access down. Cable modems and the cable network are the speed to beat, and have raised the bar on Internet speed and bandwidth. This is good for consumers—and for business.

- @Home is an early evaluator of Java-based Marimba technology. The use of channels instead of browsers offers another means of rapidly ramping up bandwidth.

- @Home is establishing a new infrastructure for high-speed, continuous Internet access. Architecture and hardware play a role; content and software play a role. Java has proven to be a reliable means of creating content and building bandwidth on both the server side and client side of the @Home system.

END NOTES

1   As reported by October 1996 *Cable Datacom News.*

CHAPTER 12

VIRTUAL VINEYARDS AND SUN MICROSYSTEMS: THE NAPA VALLEY WINE AUCTION LIVE, ON-LINE

Carl Meske, Internet Architect, Sun Microsystems, Inc.

Rob Reesor, Senior Software Developer, Virtual Vineyards

Virtual Vineyards, based in Palo Alto, California, is one of the most cited business success stories on the Internet. The company has innovated in electronic commerce, selling wines and gourmet foods on-line. You can buy rare wines from small vineyards in California and balsamic vinegar from farms in central Italy. The buying experience is designed to be informative, easy, and fun. Sun Microsystems has innovated in network computing and is the multibillion-dollar company that developed Java. Both companies teamed up to support a major charity event, the 16th Annual Napa Valley Wine Auction. They implemented the first real-time, Java-based on-line auction, intended to provide the look and feel of the live event, and enable on-line bidders to compete with live bidders. There were challenges: this had not been done before and the robust, multimedia Java experience was limited to high-bandwidth customers. A less robust alternative, however, was created for lower-bandwidth participants, and the event was a technical success that demonstrated Java's utility and potential for interactive, multimedia event marketing.

Virtual Vineyards, based in Palo Alto, California, is the leading retailer of food and wine on the Internet. Under the direction of proprietor Peter Granoff, it has become known for outstanding selection, excellent service, and a pleasurable shopping experience. Every day thousands of shoppers visit Virtual Vineyards' Web site to browse, to learn, and to buy.

Virtual Vineyards was founded in 1994 by Granoff, a well-known wine expert, and Robert Olson, a Silicon Valley engineering veteran. On January 25, 1995 the Virtual Vineyards Web site opened for business. It quickly became known as the leading wine and gourmet food retailer on the Internet and one of the few Internet business success stories.

In part because of its early entry into the Web retail business, Virtual Vineyards' staff of software engineers has designed and developed the entire database and program infrastructure that underlies the site. This layer of infrastructure implements Web page creation, transaction processing, shipping and payment algorithms, customer account creation, purchase history, shipment tracking, and the many other necessary operational aspects of running a successful retail Web site. This experience has given the Virtual Vineyards engineering staff a broad background in the technical issues of Web retailing.

With world headquarters in Mountain View, California, Sun Microsystems, Inc., is the global leader in enterprise network computing. The company was founded in 1982 on the premise that "The network is the computer." This simple, yet revolutionary concept helped change the face of the computer industry and has propelled the company into and now has a thriving $7 billion business. While promoting open (nonproprietary) interfaces, Sun has developed many of the core networking technologies that today are the heart of the Internet and corporate intranets.

THE NAPA VALLEY WINE AUCTION

The Napa Valley Wine Auction is an annual charitable event sponsored by the Napa Valley Vintner's Association. The original Napa Valley Wine Auction was designed to benefit St. Helena Hospital and Health Center and Queen of the Valley Hospital. Since 1981 the auction has expanded its list of beneficiaries to include many other health-care organizations and charities. The auction has donated well over $5 million to health-care since its inception.

By any standard, the Napa Valley Wine Auction is a regal social event and the 1996 auction was no exception. Held at Meadowood Resort, a very popular wine country spot, the event was attended by approximately 1,200 eager bidders and party-goers vying for 201 auction lots. Typical auction events include barrel tastings, food and wine tastings, vintner and grower hospitality events, the Vintner's Ball, and the Twilight Finale. Food is prepared by acclaimed chefs and wine is auctioned by auctioneers from Christie's. The lots themselves included wine, exotic wine tours and cruises, and wine and food combinations. One auction lot included a trip to Paris and a reenactment of the famous 1976 Paris tasting by Chateau Montelena and Stag's Leap Wine Cellars.

Since the event necessarily is kept relatively small, attendance is by invitation only. In order to broaden the scope of the auction and raise more money for Napa Valley health-care, the Vintner's Association decided in 1995 to offer a Web-based component for those who wished to bid but could not physically attend.

In 1995, Virtual Vineyards worked alone with the Vintner's Association to offer a Web-based silent auction covering some of the auction lots. In 1996, the decision was made to expand the Web presence and include real-time bidding, audio, video, and to offer the capability for Web users to view the auction without actually committing to bid.

One of the Napa Valley Wine Auction participants over the past years is Bob Bressler, the chief scientist for networking at Sun Microsystems. After attending a few Napa Valley Wine Auctions, Bressler had a number of interesting ideas for how Java technology and Sun's Netra servers could be used to create a live bidding atmosphere on the Web.

The combination of the Napa Valley Wine Auction, Sun Microsystems, and Virtual Vineyards made for an irresistible opportunity to apply Java server and applet technology to an interesting problem and enable people who could not attend the auction the ability to participate in and experience the excitement of a live auction.

BUSINESS GOALS

The three entities involved all had, as might be expected, similar but different business goals and objectives in creating a Web-based component of the auction.

The Vintner's Association hoped that by extending an auction invitation to Web surfers, they could raise more money for area health-care. At the same time, the Vintner's Association had an understandably fine line to walk. People physically attending the auction pay a great deal of money for the privilege. Part of the reason that so much money is raised each year is that the auction takes on a very exciting and special aire. The Vintner's Association had to balance the possible additional income gained from Web bidders against the possibility of losing the rarefied feel by making the auction feel less exclusive.

Sun Microsystems saw an opportunity to showcase the Netra Internet server and the Java product. The Netra Internet server was deployed both as a Web server to deliver the auction to the Internet, including the Web and MBONE (Internet multicast backbone), and as an intranet server at the site to manage the auction state, including the bidding, video, and audio broadcasts. Java applets were deployed to receive the video and audio feeds, and bidding applets were used to submit real-time bids and to receive those bids during the fast-paced auction. Both Netra and Java were put through their paces, and were shown to be ready for real-time, on-line business transactions and applications.

For Virtual Vineyards, there were three main business goals: marketing, public relations, and engineering education. Virtual Vineyards essentially markets to two groups. One is potential retail customers who visit its Web site and purchase wine and food. The other group is the producers of the products that are featured on the Web site, many of which are based in the Napa Valley. The Napa Valley Wine Auction gave Virtual Vineyards the unique opportunity to be in front of both of these groups simultaneously and allowed Virtual Vineyards to gain customers in both of the groups.

The Napa Valley Wine Auction is a very good cause whose participants include the who's who of the local wine and food industry. Virtual Vineyards, as a major Web retailer of wine and food, was happy to take advantage of the public relations and image-building aspects of the auction while donating time and effort to the cause.

Finally, the auction and interaction with the Java experts at Sun provided a great opportunity for Virtual Vineyards to come up to speed with Java and the surrounding technology using a real business situation.

TECHNICAL GOALS

The main technical goal of the project was to create a bidder registration and payment system, a bidding server, live video and audio, and client applets that would all work together to give the Web bidder the sights, sounds, and excitement of attending the auction.

Virtual Vineyards has a great deal of expertise in customer-account creation and credit-card transaction processing, so that Virtual Vineyards was responsible for creating the registration and credit-authorizing applications.

Sun took on the large task of creating the Web server, bidding server, the live video and audio servers and applets, and the client-based bidding applets.

AUCTION SYSTEM OVERVIEW

The first task taken on by the team was creating the Web site for the event. This site is still operating and can be found on the Web at www.nvwa.org.

The site was designed to be easy to navigate, visually attractive, and content-rich. It provided a great deal of background information on the event itself; its rationale, its history, its sponsors—and the charities it supports. Helpful background information on the wine lots up for auction was provided, with links to the winery information and playful interviews with the winemakers and proprietors of those wineries. Wine labels and photos were part of the content. There were profiles and interviews of the auctioneers, as well as links to the best wine sites and wine jumping off points on the Internet.

Logistics information for physical and virtual attendees was also included. Schedules, parking, and transportation information was available for the physical attendees. The virtual attendees could find background on the technical requirements along with an explanation of the bidding process.

© 1996 Napa Valley Wine Auction. Used with permission. All rights reserved.

Figure 12-1. The Web site for the 1996 Napa Valley Wine Auction, with the theme "A Symphony for the Senses." The site extended the reach of a major charitable event, which contributed over $2.3 million to health-care organizations in the Napa Valley.

All this information was viewable as standard HTML Web pages, and there was pre-event, actual event, and post-event content on the site.

For the on-line auction itself, the system was designed to provide sites and sounds of the event. Tasting the product is an enjoyable part of the auction. But even the most powerful servers and widest bandwidth available could not offer that. There were two modes of transmitting the sights and sounds: high bandwidth and low bandwidth. The high-bandwidth mode was appropriate for cable modem networks, ISDN lines, and university or corporate T-1 and T-3 lines. It relied on the multicast backbone, or MBONE, of the Internet—a special part of the Internet infrastructure accessible to most corporate and university networks. To access the MBONE, users required UNIX audio and video tools or a PC with MBONE tools.

The low-bandwidth mode was constructed for 14.4 or 28.8Kpbs modems, or for attendees without MBONE access or viewing tools. For these attendees, RealAudio was used for the audio component. For the visual component, a series of JPEG images was created on the fly from the MBONE video feed; users could get a visual sense of the event similar to a slide show without using up a lot of bandwidth. A Java applet was programmed to help create the visual effect. RealAudio is a browser plug-in; JPEG images are viewable using most browsers. The JPEG visuals were effective during the event and were archived as still images after the event.

At modem speeds less than 14.4Kbps the video and slide show visual effects were too large and time-consuming, but the rest of the site was available for browsing, listening, and filling in forms.

The network and hardware infrastructure needed to stage the event had to be powerful, fast, secure. Bidders were leaving their credit card numbers and billing information. There were live audio and video feeds and a need to synchronize bidding. Sun Workstations, Cisco routers, PCs, and various servers were used at the auction site itself and at the Sun campus. The Meadowland Resort was connected to the Sun campus with a T-1 phone line.

From a business perspective the network topology was complex; from a technical perspective it was well-integrated, robust, and functional.

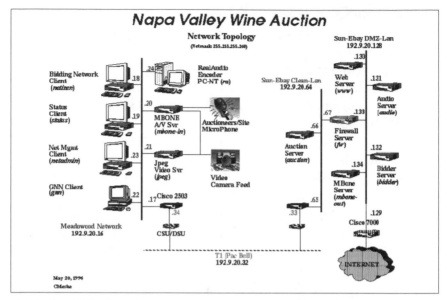

© 1996 Napa Valley Wine Auction. Used with permission. All rights reserved.

Figure 12-2. The network topology of a live, multimedia, transaction-intensive event looks complex. All of this was behind the scenes. The user had speed, reliability, a rich multimedia experience, and secure and simple transactions.

"GOING TO THE WOMAN WITH THE RED POWERBOOK"

For the bidding process, on-line attendees bid right along with the physical attendees in the tent at the Meadowood Country Club. A person in the audience with a Sun Workstation, referred to as the "proxy bidder", represented the on-line bidders.

The on-line bidders had two tools to bid with. The first was an HTML form accessed through their Web browser where they could place a bid before the live auction actually occurred. With this tool, on-line bidders went to the lot they were interested in and submitted a maximum bid. When the lot came up for auction, the computer system flagged the proxy bidder.

The second tool was interactive and live, and allowed on-line bidders to raise their maximum bids in real time. It also kept them posted on the current bid for the item and notified them if they were the current high bid or if they won the bidding process. This tool was implemented in Java.

Attendees were able to listen in and view the auction even if they were not registered bidders.

SIGNING UP FOR CHARITY

On the day of the live auction, bidders needed to be able to come into the www.nvwa.org site with a bidding paddle number, and be able to bid. At the same time, our application needed to be able to relate a paddle number to a real person and be assured that the person had the money to cover their bid. So before being able to bid, we required the prospective bidders to come to the site and register. Registration, in this case, meant the bidder provided his or her name, credit information, desired bidding limit, billing address, and shipping address. The bidder could either provide a credit card number through a secure link or provide all the other information and then phone in the credit card number.

On the final page of the registration, we provided the bidder with the Napa Valley Wine Auction terms and conditions and asked the bidder to print and sign the page and mail or fax it to us. Upon receipt of the signed terms and conditions, we activated the bidder's database record so the account was enabled and live bidding could take place.

At the time of registration, we only checked to see that the credit card number was valid. However, the evening before the auction, we authorized and placed a hold on the credit card for the desired bidding limit. We provided a phone number so the bidder could call at any time to release the hold. After the auction, we immediately released the hold on any money not spent.

HTML-BASED REGISTRATION

We assumed that some bidders who wished to register would not be using Java-compatible browsers. Therefore, the registration process had to be created so it would support non-Java-enabled as well as Java-enabled browsers.

The first registration page welcomed the bidder, pointed out the Napa Valley Wine Auction terms and conditions, provided an e-mail address and toll-free number in the event of problems, and explained the secure connection option and asked if the bidder wished to use it. The second page asked the bidder to choose a user name and password. There were two reasons for this. First, bidders might wish to return to the site and update their registration information. Hopefully, they would want to increase their desired bidding limit! Second, on the day of the auction, the bidder must have some way to signing in to the bidding applets.

The next step in creating a bidding account was for the prospective bidder to provide credit information. The desired bidding limit is the amount that will be authorized against the bidder's credit card just before the auction. This page is error checked to determine if the bidder has entered the required data and if the credit card number and expiration date make sense for the selected credit card type.

On the next registration page, the bidder was asked to enter his or her billing information. Error checking is done to make sure all entries make sense. This is followed by a registration page for shipping information.

The next registration page reiterated to the bidder the information just entered, explained that a hold would be placed on the credit card on the evening before the auction, and reminded the bidder that a registration fee would be charged to their account— for charity. When the bidder pressed the Continue button at the bottom of this page, the on-line portion of registration was finished.

The final page of the registration process was the terms and conditions page. This page thanked the bidder for registering and asked them to print, read, and sign the terms and conditions page and mail or fax it to the registrar. When the signed form was received, the bidder's registration was activated.

REGISTERING WITH SERVER-SIDE JAVA

At first glance it is reasonable to expect that the registration forms could be created using HTML alone. However, under the surface of the forms a great deal of processing must take place, including all manner of input error checking, session tracking from page to page, credit card verification and authorization, creation of databases, and the generation of paddle numbers.

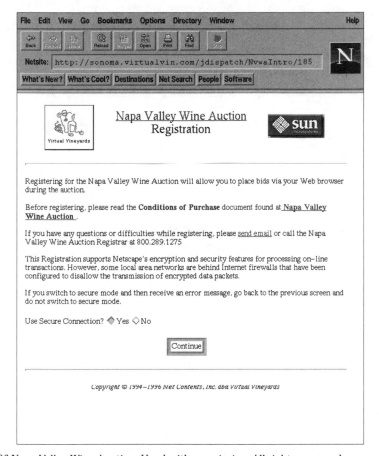

© 1996 Napa Valley Wine Auction. Used with permission. All rights reserved.

Figure 12-3. A sequence of bidder registration forms sets up a secure account for participating in the on-line live auction.

The Web server used to host the registration application is of the CGI type. We at Virtual Vineyards pondered whether we should write our CGI scripts in PERL, which is very common, or in some other familiar language, like C++. At the same time, we were very interested in getting our feet wet with Java and to get a feel for what it may offer in terms of the ongoing work on the Virtual Vineyards Web site. After a little self-convincing, we chose Java as our CGI language. We wanted to create some truly reusable class libraries that could be used not only to generate the pages of the Napa Valley

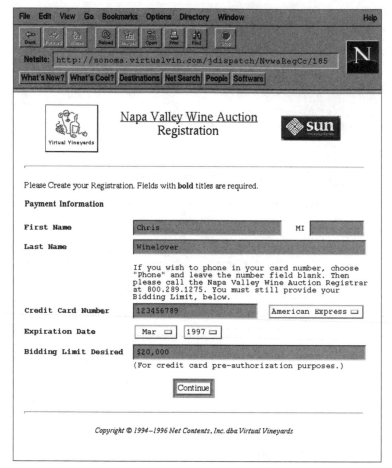

© 1996 Napa Valley Wine Auction. Used with permission. All rights reserved.

Figure 12-4. On-line credit-card payment accounts for more than 80 percent of Virtual Vineyards income. Security procedures used by Vitural Vineyards were applied to the Napa Valley Wine Auction.

Wine Auction registration form, but would be useful, in general, as we moved forward using Java in the Virtual Vineyards site.

One of the first tasks undertaken was to create a set of classes each of which implemented a useful HTML construct. For example, we created a text input class whose various class variables specified such things as its length, whether or not there is a title, title placement, modifying tags, and so forth, as well as a display method. Similar classes were created for all HTML constructs needed for the Napa Valley Wine Auction registration forms.

We also created utility classes for tasks like reading and parsing the values of an HTML form, various kinds of file I/O, money and phone number formatting, validating credit card numbers and dates, and calculating shipping rates.

On top of these utility classes, we created a class for each page we wanted to generate. For the most part, these classes contained hash tables for holding form values, vectors for holding errors, and so forth. Methods implemented the generation and display of the page, reading the page, error checking, and moving on to generating the next page. A harder task that we did not undertake, but may someday, would be to create a generic page creation class that understands current state as opposed to creating multiple-page generation classes.

TIME AND REUSABILITY ADVANTAGES

Though clearly not the best project metric, the registration code and all the utilities, including the HTML generation classes, came to 12,000 lines of Java code. This is code that includes fairly heavy use of program documentation and liberal use of white space.

Though quite familiar with object-oriented programming, this was our first server side Java application. As such, we learned the language and the environment as we went. Still, the registration work took just about four weeks to implement, test, and release. We found this to be quite acceptable, particularly since it was a new language to us, and we are happy with the foundation classes we now have for use at Virtual Vineyards.

The end user did not require a Java-enabled browser for registration; the Java work was done on the server side.

JAVA MULTIMEDIA

One of the promises of Java is its delivery of rich multimedia content. Java's built-in multithreading feature means that graphical applications and GUI functions are high performance. Live video and full audio of the nation's largest charity wine function, along with an interactive bidding process, were powered by Java.

Once the audio and video signals were captured, Java programs on the staging servers delivered the data to the applets on the Internet. The audio signal had to be relayed to a server outside the firewall. The video signal was sent directly from the video server at the event. The video applet allowed the browser to see what was going on at the auction. The streaming audio applet allowed the participant to listen to the audio segment of the event, which at times was quite hectic and lively.

© 1996 Napa Valley Wine Auction. Used with permission. All rights reserved.

Figure 12-5. Live video and its low-bandwidth JPEG facsimile provided a window to the actual event for thousands of virtual attendees.

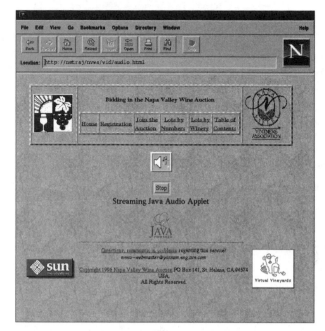

© 1996 Napa Valley Wine Auction. Used with permission. All rights reserved.

Figure 12-6. Users could select sound only from a streaming Java audio applet, created by Sun Microsystems. A RealAudio plug-in was an option for low-bandwidth attendees.

JAVA BIDDING WARS

After perusing the Napa Valley Wine Auction site, the bidder followed a link to the registration pages. Here the bidder provided, via a secure connection, a user name and password, credit information, desired bidding limit, billing address, and shipping address.

After registering, the bidder could log in to the auction and bid either on silent auction lots or during the live auction.

Bidders logged onto bidder.nvwa.org with a unique ID and password, and accessed a Web page that presented the bidder with a number of options by which he or she could participate in the auction.

They included:

- Preliminary bidding via an HTML page (available only before the live event; disabled during the event; Java-powered on the server-side).

268   JAVA FOR BUSINESS

- Active bidding via a Java applet.

- Active viewing via a Java applet.

- Active viewing via the MBONE.

- Active viewing via a client-pull of JPEG snapshots (Java-powered image sizing).

- Active listening via a Java applet.

- Active listening via RealAudio.

The bidder had the opportunity to select any or all of these options, depending on connectivity to the Internet.

If the bidder could sustain a greater throughput, the ideal configuration was a page with the video, audio, and bidding applets, all simultaneously delivering data from the event and transmitting bids from the bidder.

© 1996 Napa Valley Wine Auction. Used with permission. All rights reserved.

Figure 12-7. Sights, sounds, bidding from the remote sites expanded the audience for the charity wine auction. The video, audio, and bidding applets were developed by Sun Microsystems.

There were a number of other Java applets that enabled this production. During the bidding, a status applet, running on the status server, maintained the synchronization of all the active bidders on the Internet. This Java applet was used to maintain the current lot being bid upon and the current bid accepted for the lot. It also received the bids from the Internet and presented the current high bid to the bidding applet that was managed by a participant at the actual auction.

Once the network bids were received by the status applet, the bidding applet was instantaneously updated with the highest network bid. If the bid was higher than the current bid on the floor, the person acting on behalf of the network bid would raise their paddle to acquire the bid. If the network bid was accepted by the auctioneer, the bidding applet would be updated to inform the status and Internet bidder applet that the network had the bid. This transaction was immediate and had to be synchronized with the fast pace of the auction. If the bid was to a person on the floor, the Java applet told the user that the "Floor has the Bid." The Internet-Bidder could still bid. But once the bid was sealed, or given to the highest bidder, the bidding applet for the lot just sold was disabled—the Java applet could not submit anymore bids. Game over!

The current status of the auction was maintained via the status applet. At the beginning of a given lot, a preliminary bid program looked at the list of preliminary bids and submitted a bid, on behalf of an Internet-bidder, to the status applet. This allowed the Internet-bidder to submit the highest bid for a given lot before the actual bidding event. If the Internet-bidder wished to bid over this high bid, he or she could supersede the bid by submitting a higher bid during the event.

AUCTION OUTCOME AND OUTLOOK

The 16th Annual Napa Valley Wine Auction raised over $2.3 million for local health-care, about $500,000 more than was raised at the prior year's auction. It was the largest and most successful charity wine auction held in 1996 in the United States. Thousands viewed the event on-line and there were successful on-line bids for auction lots.

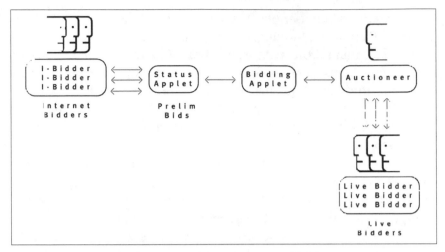

© 1996 Napa Valley Wine Auction. Used with permission. All rights reserved.

Figure 12-8. Flow of the bidding process. Internet on-line I-bidders had the same spontaneity and risk as live bidders in terms of raising their bids and responding to events on the auction floor.

One of the major bidders at Napa Valley Wine Auction over the years was not able to attend the auction in 1996 because of health reasons. The Web-based auction that we created allowed this bidder, and many others, to take part in the auction and to make successful bids. This alone allowed us to view the outcome of the project as successful. The Vintner's Association realized more income for charity, more people enjoyed taking part in and viewing the auction, and the Web presence had a positive public relations impact.

We all learned a great deal about Java. The ability to write multiple applications, including the video, audio, and bidding applets, and to run these on multiple platforms, gave a new meaning to the "Write Once, Run Anywhere" paradigm that Java has created. The event demonstrated the multimedia and interactive power of this networking language. Java has played a role in other major live multimedia events that Sun has supported on the Internet, including election night coverage in November 1996. For businesses and marketers, these events demonstrate the event-marketing potential of Java. We expect new tools and services to develop to make staging these events simpler and more common.

The registration portion of the Napa Valley Wine Auction system allowed us to get a feel for Java, not just as an applet language, but as a server-side, general-purpose programming language. In general, we liked what we saw. We found the language easy to learn and quite robust; the object model is clean and relatively simple; and the language seems to scale well as the project grows in size and complexity. Our project was implemented without the benefit of the newer just-in-time compilers and we still found performance, with few exceptions, to be adequate.

Virtual Vineyards plans to continue to use Java as our site continues to evolve. We have been experimenting with Java applets that implement tasting charts, shopping lists, and chat rooms. We are happy with what we've seen so far. We expect commerce and communication Java applications to be implemented, particularly as new development tools, Internet Foundation Classes and just-in-time compilers evolve.

Sun, of course, is committed to Java. It is the most exciting technology of our time, endorsed by major hardware and software vendors all over the world, and hailed as the future of network computing. From the hand-held PDAs to network thin clients and enterprise servers, from platform-independent software to service and support, Java computing is revolutionizing the computer industry.

And doing its bit for charity.

Authors' note: We want to recognize the scientists, engineers, and programmers who worked with us and gave their time and creativity to creating a successful event. Bob Bressler, chief scientist for networking, Sun Microsystems, Inc.; Boris Putanec, contractor to Sun Microsystems, Inc.; Owen Densmore, engineer, Sun Microsystems, Inc.; Befar Razavi, engineer, Sun Microsystems, Inc.; Michael Speers, engineer, Sun Microsystems, Inc.; Jeff Spirer, Virtual Vineyards; Ruth Colombo, Virtual Vineyards.

CHAPTER 13

HOME ACCOUNT NETWORK: BANKING ON JAVA

Charles A. Atkins, President, Proprietary Financial Products

David J. Brewer, Chief Technology Officer, HOME Account Network, Inc.

HOME Account® Network is a firm based in Charleston, South Carolina, focused on building on-line banking, investment, and financial planning tools. They are responding to industry need and customer demand. Banks and other financial institutions are changing the way they market products to and support their customers. More transactions are automated, more financial products and services are "disintermediated," more consumers want the speed and ease of use of networked customer service, more customers are market-savvy and on-line. HOME Account Network started using Java in the summer of 1995 and has developed a number of Java-based applets, applications, and servers . It has also provided the genesis, the architectural foundation, and half of the development team for the early development of the Java Electronic Commerce Framework (JECF) and the Java Wallet, a breakthrough application for on-line payment and commerce. The developers at HOME Account Network were early adopters and had problems with the alpha and beta versions of Java. Initial development time was limited by the lack of reusable Java components. Java is, however, the preferred language of the company and it offers database connectivity and cross-platform benefits for consumer financial applications. Security is a plus for Java. The latest versions of

Java and the deployment of the Java Wallet in millions of browsers and operating systems will further Java's utility for electronic commerce.

Bankers are staring straight into a challenging future, radically different from the present, for both their own institutions and the industry as a whole. Their present focus is on each other's competitive initiatives, paying far less attention to the more potentially costly threats posed by nonbank financial institutions. Over the past few years, bankers have learned that to increase profitability they must migrate from being public utilities to capture an increasing share of their customers' wallets and hold relationships for a longer duration. While emerging megabanks may create pressure in the near-term, some survey results suggest that bankers persistently underestimate the importance of the longer term contest with nimbler, more powerful nontraditional players that have been steadily gaining customer share of wallet.

All bankers and their competitors agree that to survive throughout the remainder of the decade and into the next millennium, they must move quickly to capture more customer value through developing and maintaining deep customer relationships. Industry experts estimate that between 3,000 and 7,000 financial institutions will offer advanced home banking services over the Internet by the year 2000. Associated studies have also asserted that the Internet will become the dominant electronic retail delivery channel in the not-so-distant future.

WHAT'S A HOME ACCOUNT?

HOME Account Network, Inc., was co-founded in February 1996 by a group led by Tucker Morse, chairman, who was the original general counsel and one of the early leaders of Federal Express. HOME Account Network is a pure investment in Javatized electronic commerce. Its foundation represented the fusion of the capabilities of its two predecessor companies and the knowledge and experience of its CEO, Andrew Barrett. Barrett, former managing director of Salomon Brothers, provided HOME Account Network with 20 years of experience in managing sophisticated analytical systems for billions of dollars of on-line investment and trading. Two predecessor companies, SolTech Systems Corporation and Proprietary Financial Products, Inc. (PFP), provided, respectively, a hotbed of Java programming talent and a decade of development of software and intellectual property for home banking.

HOME Account Network, Inc., offers financial institutions the two critical components for success in this increasingly competitive environment: a comprehensive relationship-management product that *The Economist* has referred to as "The Future of Home Banking," and cutting-edge multitier architecture with Java servers and thin client software to deliver on the company's product vision and transform financial institutions from commodity product providers into channel-based relationship managers.

The HOME Account pulls together all of an individual's financial activities—banking, brokerage, mutual funds, borrowing, and insurance—into a unified wealth account with tightly integrated financial analysis and planning tools. It provides automated accounting through networked connections to financial institutions' legacy transaction-processing systems; sophisticated financial analysis and planning tools with easy-to-use Java user interfaces; preauthorized and automatically adjusted credit facilities; and customized product offerings to a market of one through the use of customer information file profiling techniques.

HOME Account Network has built a suite of user-friendly network tools for financial planning through a person's cycle of savings, investment, and borrowing. This suite of tools initiates a financial planning, analysis, and management process and integrates all of a consumer's financial services into a single packaged product. This offers advantages to the consumer and to the institution providing the intelligent push-pull on-line service.

Key advantage to consumers: they can substantially increase their net worth with better financial management, increased savings, reduced borrowing costs, and more efficient tax and estate planning. There is also a major convenience advantage. From the consumer's perspective, what counts is the cumulative result of his or her savings, investment, and borrowing decisions. The HOME Account suite of financial tools makes the relationships between a customer's savings, investment, borrowing, and consumption decisions explicit. The patented product[1] systematically allows consumers to boost their savings for educational expenses and retirement as they provide for their current personal financial needs.

There are also benefits for financial institutions: improved operating efficiencies, better customer retention and penetration, increased duration of relationships and profitability, and better realization of opportunities for cross-selling financial products. These on-line tools also reduce the likelihood of delinquencies and defaults and therefore improve risk-management positions.

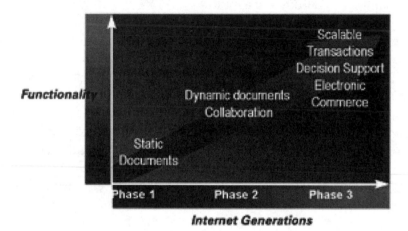

Figure 13-1. HOME Account Network's products and services are targeted at delivering value-added applications that are leading the deployment of phase three of the Internet evolution. According to Hambrecht and Quist and others, it is in phase three that highly robust transaction-oriented sites will become major players in the electronic commerce marketplace, and those that succeed in phase three will be dominate the evolution of the market.

There are significant benefits to both consumers and financial institutions in building on-line relationships. The efficiencies are obvious in comparing the costs of a branch office, phone center, and network-centric relationship. According to Booz•Allen & Hamilton, net on net, customers cost banks $1.07 each time they darken the doorstep of a branch and only $0.01 when they conduct transactions over the Net. Simple math. Although dramatic, looking only at the cost advantage of network-centric banking and financial management is misleading. There is much more value built into each on-line transaction in terms of customer profiling, segmentation, and measurement that can be used to better target and develop financial products and further improve customer service.

Table 13-1. There are cost advantages to building an effective on-line relationship with consumers. Improving customer satisfaction while simultaneously reducing costs is achievable with effective on-line tools.

Transaction Costs Compared

CHANNEL	COST
Branch, Full Service	$1.07
Telephone (Average)	0.54
ATM, Full Service	0.27
PC Banking (3rd Party Software)	0.015
Internet (World Wide Web)	0.010

SOURCE: 1996 Study by Booz, Allen & Hamilton

The network-centric relationship, however, is contingent on how it is executed. Savings will be ephemeral with a difficult-to-navigate, slow, and nonintuitive consumer interface. Connectivity and bandwidth are fundamental.

We believe that customer connectivity and bandwidth is growing faster than could have been anticipated only a few months ago as illustrated by the growth of Internet and on-line service subscribers. Forrester Research[2] estimates that 28 percent of households in the United States have personal computers today and 6 percent have access to the Internet. By the year 2000, they estimate that 42 percent of U.S. households will have PCs and 22 percent will be accessing the Internet. HAN believes that with major technology providers focusing on alternative delivery channels, increased access will occur sooner than later. The advent of cable modems that provide the bandwidth of traditional T1s at an affordable price ($20 versus $1,500 per month) in conjunction with continued development of low-cost Internet appliances with easy-to-use and entertaining user interfaces will accelerate acceptance in the market.

Given connectivity and bandwidth, the importance of financial analysis and planning tools becomes paramount. These tools have to be highly interactive, fast, secure, fun, easy to deploy, easy to develop, easy to maintain. They have to connect to back-end data-bases and run on any number of types of home computers and modem speeds. Unless an analytically robust agent technology like HOME Account Network's is used, in a couple of years we may look back and say, "Remember how easy it used to be before push technology and we had only 6,000 mutual funds to choose from?"

WHY JAVA?

Java offers compelling advantages in the financial industry. So profound was the impact of the Java epiphany for the founders of the HOME Account Network that we shifted away from HTML, Perl, and CGI programming for the Web in June 1995 and since then, we have exclusively focused on producing innovative Java programs for banks, brokers, mutual fund companies, insurers, and corporations with defined contribution plans. Java was an obvious choice. In a sense the Java decision was easier for HOME Account Network and its predecessor companies than for most firms: the HOME Account System is a highly interactive networked application that could not be done sensibly with HTML. Financial management is simply not a page-based activity, and HOME Account Network needed to move and move the financial industry to the post-HTML world. Simultaneously, we also had to solve the security, speed, and ubiquity/uniformity issues.

Management knew at the outset that we would be beset by the Beta-cubed problems (beta language, beta browsers, beta virtual machine), but we took the challenge and the risk so that our clients wouldn't have to. After 18 months of development of more than 180 Java Financial Classes, and an extensive suite of Java components, applets, applications, and servers, our suite of Java-based financial relationship tools will be rolling into financial institutions and processors in the second quarter of 1997.

The Java language is a platform-independent object-oriented programming language. Platform independence means that the Java programs you develop can be run on any platform (i.e., Windows

95, Macintosh, Solaris (UNIX OSs), OS/2 Warp, DOS) as long as the client (the computer viewing the Java applet) has a Java compatible browser. This gives the Internet, based on platform independence, a true language to develop applications.

In only a year and a half Java has gone from relative obscurity to the most talked about development on the Internet. Java fills the void left by simple HTML and inefficient CGI scripting. Although small applets, like animation and scrolling text, have been the focus of Java development, Java's ability to create platform-independent network-centric applications is becoming the driving force behind the Java language.

Most other languages today are compiled into the machine language for a specific platform, a particular operating system running on a particular processor. The operating system runs the compiled code directly, or natively. This is done for efficiency and speed, with the trade-off being portability between platforms. For example, if you create a program with the Microsoft C++ compiler running on a Windows NT platform, that same program will not execute on a UNIX operating system. Java compilers, however, eliminate this problem by compiling Java code to run on a virtual machine. Instead of being compiled to the machine language for a particular platform, Java code is compiled into byte code, which is effectively the machine language for the Java virtual machine.

All a computer needs to run Java is a Java run-time system, which is an implementation of the Java virtual machine for that computer's platform. The Java Virtual Machine (JavaVM) executes the byte code in a similar way that an operating system executes machine code. Compiled Java code can be thought of as being partially compiled and the JavaVM as handling all the specifics of a particular platform. A Java programmer need only concentrate on the development of an application and not on all of the operating systems and hardware configurations that the code will be run on. However, testing of the application on the different Java run-time systems is crucial to delivering reliable code.

A JAVATIZED FINANCIAL INSTITUTION

The HOME Account System comprises components in a multitiered financial framework that can be used individually or in combination with one another, depending on the medium for delivery. Tier one of the system is the client side of the intranet, Internet, or extranet; tier two is the server-side applications servers; and tier three is the domain of legacy applications. The three-tier architecture of the HOME Account System utilizes Java most heavily on the front end while providing Java-based on-line transaction processing and transaction monitoring and queuing connections to legacy applications via optional interfaces to CORBA[3] object request brokers (ORB).

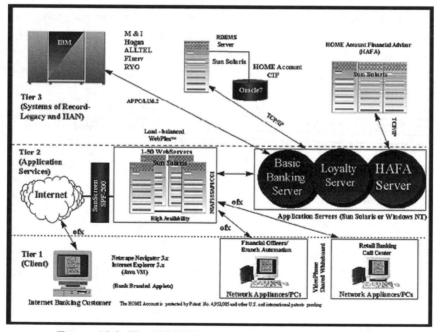

Figure 13-2. The HOME Account Network has a three-tier architecture: tier one is the client side of the intranet, Internet, or extranet; tier two is the server side for applications servers; and tier three is the domain of legacy applications.

All of the primary components in the HOME Account Network are Java-based applications, applets, or servers.

Table 13-2.

Tier 1. Components for the Internet, extranet, and intranet	Tier 2. Components for server-side applications
Java Teller Machine or JTM™	HOME Account® Financial Adviser Server (FAS).
The Balancer™	Basic Banking Server (BBS)
The Advisor™	Bill Payment Server (BPS)
Platform automation components	Brokerage and Mutual Fund server (BMFS)
Customer Call Service Center	WebPlex™: Web site balancing environment

WHAT THE CUSTOMER SEES

With the HOME Account Network, the customer has a Java Teller Machine or JTM™ on-line, which works just like an ATM—although, admittedly, cash does not spew out of your disk drive. But down-loading digital cash to a smart card is a feature we plan to introduce in the third quarter of 1997. Funds can be transferred, however, with the current version of HOME Account Network, and withdrawn and deposited electronically. There is access to personalized financial analysis and ways to interact with the financial institution for loan applications. Bills can be presented and payments authorized on-line as well.

BEHIND THE SCENES

For the customer, speed, simplicity, and security are important, not the technology. There is a lot going on behind these financial applets. The servers and legacy systems all interact to make it an intuitive and easy customer interaction.

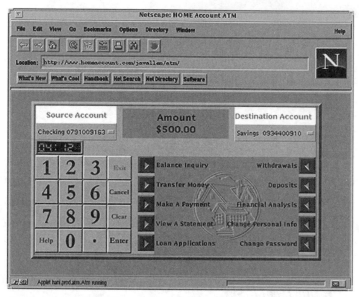

Figure 13-3. The JTM applet offers a very familiar interface to the consumer.

Date	Transaction Type	Payee	Memo	Category	Deposit	C-R	Debit
13-FEB-1997	MMAA	Cash	for some food	Auto			$896.85
20-MAR-1997	ATMC_BANK	Cash	for some gas	Misc Debit	$60.00		
14-FEB-1997	ATMC_BANK	Cash	for some food	Groceries			$66,667.00
17-DEC-1996	102	Cash	for some food	Utilities			$666.00
01-NOV-1998	ATMC_PURCHASES	Cash	for some food	Groceries			$96.69
23-FEB-1997	MMAA	Cash	for some food	Auto		C	$40.50
01-DEC-1998	ATMC_ATM_Native	Cash	for some food	Auto	$40.75		
02-DEC-1997	SCC_CHECK	Publix	groceries	Groceries	$777.77		
06-FEB-1997	Auto Payement				$33,333.30		
06-FEB-1997	Bank Charge				$3,333.03		
07-MAR-1997	ATMC_BANK			Auto	$333.00		
20-FEB-1997	ATMC_BANK			Auto	$333.00		
07-FEB-1997	Bank Charge				$333.00		
07-FEB-1997	WESAV_ATM			Auto	$3,333.03		

Figure 13-4. On-line banking has the same look and feel as paper banking, only faster, more convenient, and more cost effective. This applet we call The Balancer.

For example, the Basic Banking Server exchanges customer-account-related data between existing core processing applications and Java front-end applications or other application servers. It retrieves checking, savings, credit, debit or smart card account transactions for listing in the Java applet called The Balancer. It retrieves account balances for input to the Advisor applet. It can pay for a mutual fund purchase by debiting a customer's DDA or savings account through a transaction triggered by the Brokerage and Mutual Fund Server. It also provides data for the Java-based ATM or JTM to get account balances, transfer funds, pay bills, print an account statement, and perform other quick transaction tasks using the familiar ATM interface.

The Bill Payment Server routes electronic payment requests from banks or other financial institutions to Java front-end applications or applets that allow customers to initiate direct payment of the invoice. For example, a financial institution receives a payment request presented by a telephone company for last month's phone service. The payment request is translated into a customer request, when the customer elects to pay, and a check applet is created.

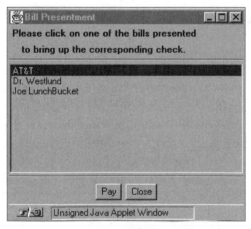

Figure 13-5. This HOME Account Applet displays due bills, and lets the customer decide on payment.

MUTUAL FUNDS ON-LINE

This server exchanges mutual fund account-related transactions and data between existing back-end mutual fund servicing applications and a Java PC-based mutual fund management product or other application servers. With this server a customer can submit a buy order for additional fund shares and debit savings or DDA account, initiate increase of monthly transfer from checking to mutual fund portfolio, and get account balances for input to the Home Account Financial Advisor (HAFA) Server.

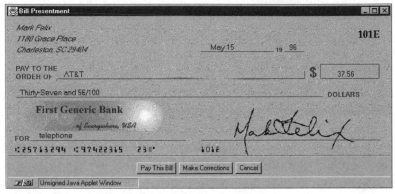

Figure 13-6. Payment in a familiar format: bill payment check image implemented as a Java applet.

INTEGRATED FINANCIAL ADVICE

The HOME Account Financial Advisor is an analysis and planning tool designed to help individuals save, invest, and borrow to meet their financial goals. These goals may be as simple as retirement, child's college tuition, or a new home, or as complex as achieving all three of these goals simultaneously and buying a new boat. The Advisor™ can be used for more immediate decisions, such as which mortgage to take when refinancing a home or how much to save this month to buy a new car next year, all the while balancing a customer's long-term goals and objectives.

The Advisor features the ability to optimize each savings, investment, and borrowing decision over hundreds of possible different economic scenarios, a forty-year planning horizon with annual review points, calculation of taxes on an annual basis (including the differentiation between income and capital gains), and transaction costs associated with buying or selling investments. The Advisor provides suggestions for customers, like where to invest, how much to save, and when and how to borrow. These action plans can easily be linked to existing product lines of financial services companies, resulting in immediate purchase of products or setup of regular sweeps from one account to another.

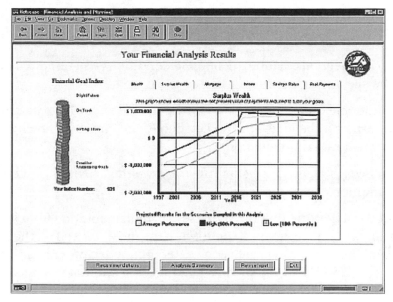

Figure 13-7. A very interactive and data-packed financial analysis tool is part of the HOME Account Network.

The front end of the Advisor is all Java. The compute-intensive legacy engine is composed of approximately 12,000 lines of C++ code. The Advisor has numerous applications, from personal financial management on the World Wide Web to total integrative risk management for banks and insurance companies using intranet Web technology. The Advisor's primary modules are the asset and liability allocation and optimization module, its scenario generation module, and population analysis.

The systems for conducting financial analysis and planning are based on well-established principles from financial economics. For example, risks are evaluated according to the likelihood of meeting specified goals over time. The core model incorporates these principles through a multistage process with decision rules. This methodology has been well-tested for large corporate pension plans and insurance companies by Towers Perrin, Frank Russell, ORTEC, and others.[4, 5] The HOME Account Network has extended the methodology to incorporate issues that face individual investors.

The Advisor system is designed in an easily extensible fashion so that:

1. any projections of future economic conditions can be added to the scenario generation;

2. additional asset categories can be included as long as the returns can be linked to the key economic variables (such as interest rates and inflation);

3. any well-specified decision rule for investing, savings, or consumption can be modeled.

Accordingly, the first three phases of implementation for a financial institution are aimed at identifying the most desired method for an individual and financial services company to interact with the Advisor. There is a wide spectrum of possible approaches by which individuals can input their financial information, see the results of the analysis with respect to their goals, and modify the input parameters to attain the best compromise and recommendation. Since The Advisor is a generic financial analysis and planning tool and not tied to a single product or economic forecast, the selection of the interactive elements and features is critical to the overall success of an implementation.

Population analysis utilizes the learning process called target analysis and a generalized form of sensitivity analysis to yield improved approaches for optimization, particularly where problems from a particular domain must be solved repeatedly. The resulting framework introduces an adaptive design for mapping problems to groups, as a basis for identifying processes that permit problems within a given group to be solved more quickly and effectively. Applied to a practical financial analysis application, HAN's approach succeeds in generating regions and representations that give an order of magnitude improvement in the time required to solve new problems.

HAN's framework incorporates user-selected trade-offs, and offers particular application opportunities in areas like financial planning, marketing strategy design, and product development. The new design is based on combining and extending principles from artificial intelligence and mathematical optimization. Population analysis may also be applied as a database mining tool to determine which new or existing products are uniquely well-suited to satisfy a customer's requirements.

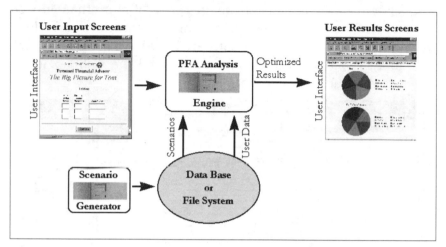

Figure 13-8. Flow diagram of the Home Account Financial Advisor.

MAKING IT SIMPLER FOR FINANCIAL INSTITUTIONS

WebPlex™ is a complete job management facility, developed by HOME Account Network, for managing networks of UNIX-based WWW servers. Within this UNIX complex, one or more servers can provide seamless, scalable, and reliable service to all users of a high volume Web site. WebPlex provides status and control of work scheduling, balances the network load, and routes Web clients to the most efficient server. A Java-based Admintool displays the system load for each server, and configures server processes to monitor the WWW servers and move them automatically through different states (on-line, off-line, maintenance, and standby). The WWW servers can easily be taken off-line for maintenance purposes, including hardware additions and software modifications, without disrupting the financial services being offered by a financial institution.

The WebPlex is the key to ending the World Wide Wait on intranets and the Internet. This is critical to internal and external customers of financial institutions. No one will stand in a virtual line on the Web any more than they will at a branch or an ATM machine.

Customers will take their business elsewhere. The same goes for internal customers. Customers for the WebPlex are the system administrators of corporate financial intranets and Web sites. They frequently have to administer the operation of more than 40 Web sites around the globe. They cannot do it with hardware-based load balancers; they have to use a software-based system that is scalable to up to 50 multiprocessor servers—and the WebPlex is the only one that can do it.

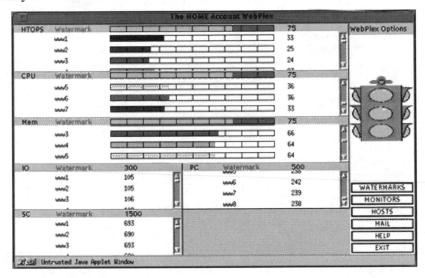

Figure 13-9. A Java-driven management tool simplifies management of the HOME Account Network for banks and other financial institutions.

A JAVA HEAD START

Java is what distinguishes the HOME Account System from basic banking as currently implemented in HTML by the few institutions that currently have working banking sites on the Web. Java enables us to do things that simply cannot be done in static HTML pages. For example, the HOME Account transaction register (also known as The Balancer) allows a customer to scroll through all checking, savings, or credit card transactions; sort on the fly by date, type of transaction, payee, dollar amount, etc.; dynamically reconcile records with the financial institution's legacy transaction processing system; graph balances, types of payments, and more.

In effect, the Balancer provides a simple interface that offers most of the functionality of the leading personal financial management software—but it does it with a simple thin client architecture that runs anywhere Java runs—from desktops to laptops to Nokia phones. The difference between HTML versions of home banking and the HOME Account Network's Java version is like the difference between the monthly paper statement in your mailbox and your favorite PC-based personal financial management software—same data, but in one case it's static and in the other it's very dynamic, and a lot more useful.

The initial implementation of the Balancer was big and slow. Indeed, it had to run as an application rather than an applet for download time reasons. The 1.1 version of The Balancer is an applet, and has been slimmed down by 75 percent—quite a diet. Development time on the two versions were 30 mythical man months for version 1.0 and 10 for version 1.1.

AGAIN, "WHY JAVA?"

1. Developer productivity through reuse, architecture, and modeling.

2. Almost "write once, run anywhere," including running on any type of ubiquitous computing device.

3. Dynamic executable content versus static pages.

The key here is that once the security and speed problems are solved (progress is being made), and an organization writes a few applications in Java, there is no going back. The efficiencies associated with using the Java platform overwhelm the rationale for using any other language.

THE KILLER APP FOR ELECTRONIC COMMERCE

The Java Wallet[6] is an open platform for payment methods and financial services that will be an integral part of the Java Development Kit (JDK) distributed to all Java licensees (IBM, Microsoft, Novell, Oracle, Netscape, etc.). JavaSoft's Java Wallet will provide a ubiquitous, extensible, scalable, and secure software platform for the deployment of home banking, shopping, and related financial experiences over the Internet.

The architecture is founded upon a framework, responsibilities, and services.

The merchant applet layer uses Java applets to enhance the shopping experience. Applets are an appropriate way to implement short-term customer relationships such as the shopping experience. Examples of consumer applets are shopping cart applets and content charging applets. Merchant applet layer code does not require a long-term customer-to-merchant relationship. Examples of bank applets include loan questionnaire applets and CD investment-selling-tools applets.

The cassette layer implements long-term customer relationships such as credit cards, home banking, and brokerages. Cassettes are a new feature that JECF adds to Java. Similar to applets, cassettes are downloaded from servers to client computers. Unlike applets, which disappear when users quit the browser, cassettes are retained on the customer's system. Cassettes store information in a database provided by the JECF. Cassettes may safely store valuable information, like public key certificates and transaction records, since the entire database is encrypted and they can retain long-term customer-to-institution relationships. Examples of sample cassettes include SET certificates and protocols, home banking, brokerage accounts, financial analysis, and planning software. Cassettes contain code, digital certificates, GIF images, and other resources. Financial institutions can use cassettes to deliver customer service features. Smart-card application developers can put smart-card reader-device drivers and application interfaces in cassettes.

The Java commerce package layer implements the infrastructure needed by the merchant and the cassette layers. Features at this layer include a user interface, an application model, a database, and access to strong cryptography.

The Java environment layer is the underlying browser or operating system.

THE SERVICES IN THE JECF

Applets and cassettes use several layers of service in the Java commerce package.

The GUI services layer provides a graphical metaphor of a wallet. The wallet depicts credit cards, ATM cards, membership cards, and other commonly found documents. The Wallet interface plays a central function in user interaction. GIF images implement the simplest card. Alternatively, a cassette may use all of Java's user interface components, such as JavaBeans, to create more elaborate animations and graphical user interfaces.

The application services layer implements common application metaphors. Initially, the Java commerce package supports metaphors most appropriate to purchasing. But future metaphors will include other financial services as well.

The foundation service layer includes the database classes, access to strong cryptography, smart card device access and various common utility classes such as Money. The Java commerce database provides a subset of the functionality of a relational database. The database is reliable and uses very little memory or disk resources. Although designed for computers with local or remote disks, the database is pluggable to meet the needs of diskless network computers. Third-party database vendors will create scalable commercial databases to provide software safe deposit boxes.

The Java Wallet is ubiquitous in the sense that it will be on more than 100 million computers in less than 12 months. Netscape, AOL, AT&T, IBM, Novell, Oracle, and Microsoft have all licensed Java from Sun Microsystems, and they will each implement all aspects of the language or functional equivalents.

SECURITY—A MINUS OR A BIG PLUS?

Providing security for banks and other financial institutions is the premier issue for conducting banking on the Internet. The more an organization has to lose, the less tolerance to risk it has. A bank's desire to provide superior customer service and ease of access to customer's data, by the customer, must be tempered with the most cost-effective security measures available. The security issue cannot be avoided, because the skyrocketing use of the Internet and World Wide Web is well-documented. It is extremely cost effective for the banks to reduce brick and mortar (branches) and turn to an electronic channel that someone else is paying for, but those cost advantages are for naught if the delivery mechanism isn't secure.

We shudder to think that the channel known as the branch (costly) is free to the bank's customer and some banks actually attempt to charge for Internet banking, which has a much lower cost per transaction. This paradigm shift is rapidly occurring and the security on the public channel known as the Internet must evolve quickly to keep pace.

The benefits associated with the enterprise deployment of the Java platform has been widely extolled in this chapter. However, the running of executable content over the World Wide Web, such as Java and ActiveX, has been hotly debated and has been addressed somewhat uniquely in their respective ways by Sun Microsystems and Microsoft. JavaSoft security experts have publicly stated that the fundamental goal for Java has been to provide maximum protection for untrusted code, and maximum configurability for trusted code—and to do it in an open manner, working with colleagues throughout the worldwide Internet security community.

JavaSoft's model for untrusted code enables the safe execution of applets downloaded from the Internet. In a browser environment, applets run in a sandbox, which prevents applets from gaining full access to the user's file systems, network connections, and other resources.

The applet Security Manager runs the sandbox, acting like the playground cop. The borders of the sandbox are strict: applets can't read or write to the local disk; they can't establish network connections except to the server they came from; they can't load libraries; they can't read sensitive system properties; etc. A description of the applet security policy is at java.sun.com/sfaq.

The sandbox and applet security manager build on the basic safety features of the Java language and Java virtual machine— strict typing, garbage collection, lack of pointer arithmetic, "private" and "protected" and "final" access modifiers, immutable strings, bounds-checked arrays, the lack of a preprocessor. All of these features are valuable for any developer trying to build more robust and safe applications.

These features make up the basic Java security model for handling untrusted code.

As more and more people use Java in intranets and other controlled networks, JavaSoft has started working on broadening the model to handle trusted code.

Banks must consider their security policy from two perspectives. One perspective is that of a bank customer who is accessing the bank's Web site to retrieve banking applets to run, and the other is that of bank employees who themselves access the Web and retrieve executable content to run internally. In both cases, the bank's internal systems cannot and must not be compromised. In the former case, the bank's Web site is trusted (via a digital certificate) by the customer, but what is unknown by the bank is what other sites the customer has visited and the question of whether any hostile applets have already been downloaded and are running in the same virtual machine (desktop) as the bank's applet(s). Fortunately, the developers of Java have considered this in their security model. With respect to untrusted code, the sandbox model described above protects the end-user's machine and networked computing resources from damage or theft by a malicious applet.

However, there are other issues that remain unaddressed by the sandbox model. Authentication is needed, to guarantee that an applet indeed came from the bank it claims to come from. Digitally signed and authenticated applets can be promoted to the status of trusted applets, and then allowed to run with fewer security restrictions. Encryption, such as that used with the secure sockets layer (SSL) can ensure the privacy of data passed between an applet client and an applications server on the Internet. Digitally signed applets are effectively shrink-wrapped in that the digital signature confirms that the producer of the code is a trusted entity and that the applet has not been tampered with in its transit over the Internet. In the JDK 1.1, JavaSoft has included Java Security APIs that include the ability to produce a signed applet; this signed file is known as a Java Archive, or JAR.

Thus far, we have addressed untrusted code and trusted code. A further extension to Java security is the gateway security model, which is being introduced in JavaSoft's Java Electronic Commerce Framework (JECF) initiative. The JECF will be the foundation for electronic wallets, point-of-sale terminals, electronic merchant servers, and other financial software. A product under development in that initiative is the Java Wallet referred to previously. The gateway security model extends the trusted code model and allows interapplication, cooperation, and auditability.

The gateway security model provides the means to implement contractual trust relationships. A good example of this would be a HOME Account Financial Advisor service cassette (Java Wallet component) that requires data from an investment account and money market account to produce a financial plan for a customer of the bank or financial institution. If the HOME Account Financial Advisor service cassette was provided by the bank to access the Advisor compute engine, and the money market fund and the investment account were at a brokerage house, both technical and contractual relationships between the customer, the bank, and the brokerage house must exist.

In this regard, there are three roles that exist: the broker, the financial adviser, and a money market fund reporter. Traditionally, the software that implements each role would only have access to data used by that individual role. Before Java, it was not possible to have reliable and secure separation between applications in the same address space, that is, running in the same machine, because applications in the same address space cooperate by sharing data and objects. Java and the JECF provide the appropriate technology for providing tight integration and yet maintain application data integrity. It is the extensibility of Java and the JECF features that allows a safe sharing of some data and the safeguarding of other data.

Nothing more can underscore the importance of these security features of Java than a recent hack into Intuit's Quicken program. A German group of hackers known as the Chaos Computer Club created an ActiveX control that was able to snatch money from one bank account and deposit it into another without having to enter the personal identification number. Chaos demonstrated the ActiveX control on German national television in late January 1997.

The incident underscores something that most computer security experts have known for some time: ActiveX is not as secure as Java. While Java applets are prevented from performing certain tasks, such as erasing files from a user's hard disk, ActiveX controls—small Internet programs that work mainly through the Internet Explorer browser—are able to do virtually anything on a user's computer that a programmer wants to, including installing a destructive virus.

BACK FROM THE BANKING FRONT LINE: LESSONS LEARNED AND PROBLEMS SOLVED

HOME Account Network, Inc., and its predecessor companies began serious Java development work with the alpha release of Java in June 1995. The principle rationale for our initial adoption of the language was not the rapidity of development under an alpha language bereft of tools, but the reality that we could not develop a truly interactive financial application in HTML. Accordingly, we suffered through the slings and arrows associated with development on a major application in a language that was not fully baked in order to get ahead of the curve. We sought solace in the fact that we knew we were on the right track, and that our early efforts would ultimately redound in saving our customers and clients, and in turn *their* customers and clients, the same agony.

For example, the Java interface for the HOME Account Financial Advisor took three highly talented young programmers (Jonathan Brown, Derald McMillan, and Doug Thomas) approximately three months of nonstop work using the alpha version of the language. The interface was demonstrated at Sun's booth at Networld-Interop in September 1995 with full animation and interactive graphing capability, and it was a spectacular success both in terms of its own capability and the properties of Java that were demonstrated to other developers. Unfortunately, with the deployment of the beta version of Java in November 1995, much of our prior work had to be redone—still with no development tools. Completion of the interactive graphing components of the HOME Account Financial Advisor with enhancements took only two thirds as much time—partly because of enhancements to the language and partly because of the increased skill and sophistication of our programmers.

As of February 1997, with the benefit of version 1.1 of the JDK, more than 180 HOME Account Java financial classes, a reusable treasure trove of Java components for financial services, and solid object-oriented modeling and code generation capabilities of Rational Rose—development time has been reduced by an order of magnitude.

The use of Java in the development of the HOME Account Balancer and WebPlex benefited from our early experience with the language. Both products were developed in 1996 with the attendant benefits associated with the enhancements in our development methodology and the stability of the Java language. Version 1.0 of the Balancer absorbed the full time and attention of a dozen programmers for 90 days and embodies the functionality of approximately 60 percent of complex PC-based personal financial managers—without the complexity. The Admintool for WebPlex was developed by two programmers in approximately 60 days.

In both cases we were able to take advantage of the efficiencies associated with an object-based language as opposed to one that is merely object-oriented (say, C++), and we were able to avoid the traps and pitfalls associated with the early versions of the language. What is more important, however, is that the innate design of Java enforces the object paradigm and generates the type of code reusability that will lead to ever increasing efficiency of HOME Account Network's development efforts. In short, we feel that our twenty-month lead on many other developers was well worth our investment.

Several large domestic financial institutions and three major processors of financial transactions are currently evaluating the HOME Account applications and have expressed an intention to license and implement our applications as soon as they are comfortable with the security, stability, and uniformity of the performance of Java under different browsers. Appropriately, the standards for performance in these three areas are higher for retail financial institutions than in almost any other industry. Java in retail banking means it will work in almost any environment.

Although these problems are being addressed in version 1.1 of the JDK and the Pure Java initiative, the initial releases of Java were not secure (beware untrusted applet), totally stable (not the curse of the AWT again!), and "not all Java virtual machines were created equal." The success of Java banking is premised upon reducing the cost of customer sales and service from the branch-based costs of $1.05 to the Web cost of $0.01. Banks and other financial institutions have absolutely no interest in having their customer call centers barraged with inquiries about errant results under different browsers.

Since the summer of 1995, our architecture and vision of the potential electronic commerce has been the foundation for initially Sun Lab's efforts and, since January 1996, JavaSoft's electronic commerce development. HOME Account Network has represented approximately 40 percent of the EC development team at JavaSoft since June 1996. In a sense, the Java Wallet is the most important distribution system HOME Account Network could ever hope for. As a part of the Java language, the Java wallet will be on every computer on the planet by 1998. It is a ubiquitous platform for the deployment of the HOME Account Network's technology. All of tier one software will be deployable as client service cassettes and our server technology will be redeployed as server cassettes.

Accordingly, the success of Java and HOME Account Network's implementation of Java-based home banking applications is dependent upon JavaSoft, Sun, and to some extent HOME Account Network solving the problems of security, stability, and uniformity.

Many early Java developers, such as HOME Account Network, continue to recite the inescapable rationale for using Java: platform independence; simplicity; reduced time to market; reduced cost over the complete development, deployment, and maintenance cycle, etc. One rationale not currently given is speed, and for good reason. Java is an interpreted language and it simply does not run as fast as C, FORTRAN, or other languages for compute-intensive operations—yet. The standing joke among the faithful is, "Wait until the JIT" (just in time compiler), but even with native compilers it is unlikely that Java will rival the speed associated with other compiled languages in the near term. Longer term, it is likely that Java will be used for complex and compute-intensive mathematical tasks as Java's designers have built in some of the best features of FORTRAN and other mathematically intensive languages.

BANKING ON JAVA

Several years ago, management of the HOME Account Network's predecessor companies envisioned where the financial industry was headed and what type of software platform was needed in order to bring about the promise of electronic commerce—a world in which the cost savings associated with electronic distribution and service are shared between consumers and financial institutions.

The arrival of Java in the summer of 1995 provided an answer to many of HOME Account Network's predecessor companies' prayers—finally there was the ability to offer dynamic executable content—real programs, not just hypertext—over the Web's overarching middleware.

The ubiquitous software platform for enabling electronic commerce detailed some 18 months ago has been rechristened as the Java Electronic Commerce Framework, now taking form in an environment in which banks and other financial institutions can participate. In this world, the financial institution's customers can benefit indirectly from reduced costs associated with the development, deployment, and maintenance of truly interactive, secure, and scalable Internet banking systems.

END NOTES

1   U.S. Patent 4,953,085, *System For The Operation Of A Financial Account,* date of patent: August 28, 1990.

2   Forrester Research, www.forrester.com.

3   *OMG, The Common Object Request Broker: Architecture and Specification, Version 2.0* Boston, Massachusetts: Object Management Group, 1995.

4   Dr. John M. Mulvey. *It Always Pays To Look Ahead, Balance Sheet,* vol. 4, no. 4, Winter 1995/96.

5   Dr. John M. Mulvey and Dr. Adam J. Berger. *The Home Account Advisor™, Asset and Liability Management for Individual Investors,* Financial Optimization, Cambridge University Press, 1997.

6   Sun Microsystems Computer Corporation and JavaSoft World Wide Web Servers, www.sun.com and www.javasoft.com.

CHAPTER 14

COREL: THINNING DOWN THE OFFICE SUITE

Chris Biber

Corel Corporation, based in Ottawa, Canada, is a leading developer and marketer of productivity applications, graphics, and multimedia software. Corel has created the first suite of office productivity applications totally written in Java, including word processing, spreadsheet, graphing, and other common applications. These network-centric, platform-independent applications can run on PCs and NCs (network computers). They offer new ways of working with documents and new ways of collaborating with colleagues. The applications are fully functional, and offer size, updating, version-control, and other advantages over traditional office productivity software. From prototype to Web preview, the development of Corel® Office for Java took four and a half months. Development tools and Java speed were barriers in early development, but these issues have been resolved. Thousands of pre-beta copies have been downloaded, and Corel has initiated a Corel Office for Java channel for customers, based on Marimba technology. This channel automatically upgrades versions of the software, simplifying distribution and accelerating development. Final product launch of Coral Office for Java is expected in May 1997. Beyond the office suite, Corel's innovative work has implications for the development, deployment, packaging and pricing of all kinds of software.

Since acquiring the WordPerfect group from Novell, Corel has reestablished WordPerfect as a serious contender in the $4 billion office productivity marketplace. Judging from this early success, the enthusiasm of users, and the positive feedback from third parties and OEMs, Corel's target of achieving a 20 percent share of this market seems achievable over the long run.

For Corel, Java is key to achieving and exceeding that target. The cross-platform capability of Java, along with its object orientation and built-in security make it ideal for deploying all types of applications, including a new generation of office software. The latter aspect is the focus of this case study: the development of Corel Office for Java, one of the most ambitious and far-reaching Java developments currently underway.

TODAY'S OFFICE SUITES

A comparison of today's office suites—Microsoft Office, Lotus SmartSuite, and Corel Office Professional—reveals a number of common traits.

All of Today's Suites are Platform Dependent. They were developed either for Windows 3.1, 95, NT, or Macintosh. While this allows them to take maximum advantage of the underlying operating system, platform dependency causes a range of problems in corporate environments where cross-platform environments are the norm rather than the exception. File transfer and document sharing between platforms becomes difficult, if the originating application is not available on all platforms deployed in the corporate network. A second aspect of platform dependency is the version dependency of documents created by these applications. A document created in WordPerfect 7 cannot easily be shared with WordPerfect 5.1. This holds true for all manufacturers.

Today's Office Suites are Amazingly Feature Rich. Competitive pressures have led to a feature war in this arena as well. As a result, office applications today offer almost every feature imaginable: for example, seven levels of footnotes, pivoting tables, a choice over the color underline of misspelled words. As you'll see below, not all these features are urgently requested by all users. Not surprisingly, these applications are hard-disk hungry. Their space requirement ranges from around 60MB (Lotus) to almost 200MB (Corel).

All of the Applications are Written with the Assumption of the Fat Client. A fat client is typically a powerful, often networked desktop machine with literally unlimited hard-disk and RAM capacity.

Does this mean that these traits are to continue into the foreseeable future? A closer examination of these commonalties reveals several problems with the underlying assumptions. While the rich feature set has become commonplace and an indispensable part of the marketing wars, most office users today use only a few of these features. Many users have never gone beyond the basic functions of their applications, have never heard of pivot tables, or never gotten lost in the nested footnotes. As in many other environments, the old 80/20 rule applies: 80 percent of users use 20 percent of the functionality (or less). This is even more true on desktops performing administrative tasks or single functions. It can thus be argued that not everyone needs the feature-rich application suite and the resulting fat client architecture.

The fat client architecture also requires a large MIS support effort. Figures by the Gartner Group and others indicate that support for a typical desktop PC costs from $10,000 to $12,000 per year, mainly due to the tasks involved in system maintenance, software and hardware administration and upgrades. The network computer architecture of a thin client addresses these issues: there are no movable parts and swapping desktops becomes a matter of replacing the physical units only. Java makes this possible: Software applications reside on the server and are downloaded to the client as needed, regardless of the client platform. This represents a whole new paradigm: applications are written for cross-platform execution, write once, run anywhere becomes the new way of software development.

Java's object-oriented nature allows the switch from fat clients to thin clients. Moreover, organizations are no longer required to upgrade their hardware to keep pace with increasing software demands. Java Virtual Machines as the enabling mechanisms are available for many different platforms, including Windows 3.1. In other words, rather than upgrading a Windows 3.1 desktop to run the latest generation of a Windows 95 client, Windows 3.1 can run Java applications and applets and thus be used productively in an intranet environment.

The server-centric model of Java and the network computer allows for central software maintenance and fluid upgrades of software. All software resides on the server and is downloaded to the client as required. This makes it easy to centrally upgrade to new software versions, install maintenance releases, or upgrade software with new features. In addition, technology like Marimba's Castanet allows for incremental updates of fat clients as well. Software can be installed locally and then be updated as new versions or features become available on the server. This results in drastically simplified software administration and consequently much lower cost of maintenance.

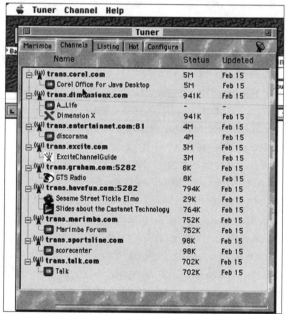

Figure 14-1. Screen shot of a Castanet tuner subscribed to the Corel Office for Java channel. New versions and features of the Corel Office for Java are updated transparently for the user. This is an efficient, cost-effective way to get the latest software updates automatically to Corel Office users. This greatly simplifies version control and updating for MIS departments, and accelerates distribution for Corel.

THE OFFICE OF THE FUTURE

In contrast to today's office applications, the suites of the future can be described by the following properties: they will be network-centric, with Internet/intranet functionality at their core. Functionality will in part reside on the server, allowing for smaller clients that receive features only when needed. The core features may originally be limited by the MIS administrator or the software developer, and additional features can be made available on the server as they are required. These features may be provided by either the original software developer or by any number of third-party developers of Java components. Deployment across different client platforms becomes straightforward because the software is the same across all Java Virtual Machine implementations on all platforms, including Windows 95, Windows NT, UNIX, MAC. Document sharing across platforms and software versions will become much easier, as required applets are simply downloaded from the central server for viewing and/or editing.

Under Java, these office suites can work in a number of ways.

SCENARIO 1: INTRANET & THIN CLIENTS

In this case, network computers are connected to a central application server. Only minimal software resides on the client—enough to boot and connect to a server. On start-up, the clients present the user with either a browser interface or a simple webtop environment with several tasks. After the user chooses the desired task, the appropriate Java classes are downloaded to the client and the applet executes locally. Documents and other work is saved on the content server for intranet-wide access. This also means that classes that are not required for a particular task are not downloaded to the client, saving valuable network bandwidth and memory space on the client machine.

SCENARIO 2: INTRANET & FAT CLIENTS

This scenario is similar to the one above. However, applications may reside locally and documents can be stored locally. As mentioned earlier, this model still allows the organization to benefit from central software administration through technology like the Marimba Castanet channel, and enables them to deploy and easily update a common set of applications across a wide variety of platforms.

SCENARIO 3: REMOTE ACCESS

In this scenario, a content server is accessed from a remote location with a Java-enabled browser. The browser downloads the required classes for viewing and—with the proper permission—downloads the classes for the users to edit the document. This is a scenario that is not possible with today's office suites, which require that the requesting client is on a particular platform and runs a particular application. With Java, a UNIX client may access a document that was created on a thin client and revised on a Macintosh. This is also true for documents created with different versions of the software. The client always downloads the required classes from the server, eliminating the versioning problem with today's software. In other words, the cross-platform capabilities of the suite extend beyond executing the applications on multiple platforms to allow for cross-platform sharing of documents as well.

SCENARIO 4: THE SUITE AS A BAG OF BEANS

Many of the components of Corel Office for Java are implemented in the form of JavaBeans. This makes it possible to use them in an entirely different context. A corporate developer is not able to produce custom applications such as forms and expense reports in Java by using these building blocks. Rather than developing applications from scratch, the JavaBeans architecture allows for the reuse of commonly used components such as text editing and spreadsheet engines. Corel Office for Java could thus aptly be called a Corel Bean Bag.

COREL OFFICE FOR JAVA

Corel Office for Java is the first suite of applications developed for the office of the future. Written entirely in Java, it provides a complete set of office tools for the Java computing platform. In its current beta form, it features fully functional word processing, spreadsheet, and charting components integrated into a rich GUI environment. A personal information manager with e-mail, address book and scheduling capabilities is also included. This version occupies less than 10MB of hard disk space and has been available for download since early April, at officeforjava.corel.com. The commercial version is slated to be available in late summer 1997 and will feature a presentation module with vector drawing components in addition to the components mentioned above.

Table 14-1 Corel Office for Java server and client architecture. The application leverages the network; the client side of the application is "thin."

Client architecture	Server architecture	
Document Object Storage	Spell Checker	Search/Replace
Persistent Class	Document Object Storage	Group Scheduling/-email server
App Components/Documents Word processing, spreadsheet, etc.	File IO and Filters	Groupware/workflow
	File Management System Printing and user logon	Database connectivity
Corel Application Framework		
Client OS and JVM	Java LDAP API	JDBC
	LDAP	SQL/Database
	Server OS Java Virtual Machine	

THE DOCUMENT-CENTRIC APPROACH

With Corel Office for Java, the application resides within the document rather than the document residing in the application. This means that users can seamlessly incorporate multiple components into their documents without ever leaving the main window. For example, a user can start creating a document using the word processor, embed a spreadsheet, chart the resulting data in a colorful bar graph, and the main interface always remains the same. Toolbars and menu items update as required.

In Microsoft Windows applications, the same effect is accomplished using ActiveX (OLE). This particular method for Object Linking and Embedding only works on Windows platforms (and is coming for Macintosh).

Corel implemented this document-centric approach using a container-component framework called Corel Application Framework. The Corel Application Framework allows containers to contain multiple components, which in turn can contain other components, and provides for the communication between components and containers, such as in-place editing of an embedded spreadsheet. This approach requires much less overhead than alternative approaches and is available across platforms, making it very useful for deployment in cross-platform environments.

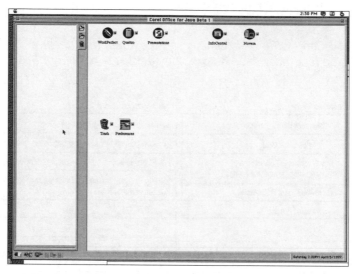

Figure 14-2. Corel Office for Java puts word processing, spreadsheet presentation, and other productivity tools right onto a desktop. This beta version was downloaded in less than 20 seconds, albeit with a cable modem. The beta version is less than 5 megabytes in size.

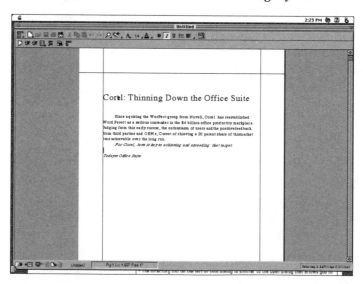

Figure 14-3. The network-centric word processing program works like any word processing program, with font, size, color options.

THE NETWORK-CENTRIC APPROACH

Unlike today's office suites, which are centered around a fat client, Corel Office for Java is network-centric. As a result of this network centric approach, maintenance of software is greatly simplified. To update an organization's productivity software simply requires an update of the software on the server. Software distribution and up-grading, version compatibility, and multiplatform environments are no longer an issue. This network-centric approach to computing also creates an ideal workgroup environment. Users can share any Corel Office for Java document across the network without giving a second thought to standards, file formats, or individual operating systems. Documents can be viewed with any Java-enabled browser. For example, one team member can edit a document's text and then return it to the network server so that another can change the chart formats while working from home. Meanwhile, server-based version control keeps track of the changes and controls user access.

MODULARITY

Corel Office for Java provides a suite of applications integrated into a rich user interface. However, only the components required by the end user are actually downloaded from the server. The components themselves are also modular: for example, spreadsheet functions are downloaded only when this functionality is required, leaving memory available on the client for local processing. The downloaded modules remain on the client either until the end of the session or until they are discarded from the client because they are no longer used and memory needs to be reallocated. The mechanism that accomplishes the latter is appropriately called garbage collection.

EXTENSIBILITY

Because Corel Office for Java is fully JavaBeans compliant, its functionality can be easily extended by adding Java applets for specific features or entire application components. To develop these extensions, programmers can either use pure AWT or take advantage of Corel's Developers' Tools.

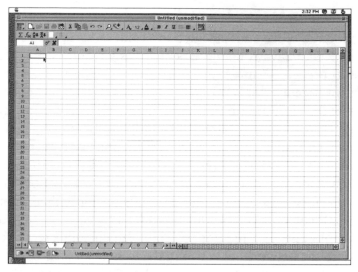

Figure 14-4. A fully functional spreadsheet with several hundred of the most used functions is pulled down by a client when needed. Obscure and underused features can be accessed on the network when needed instead of hogging local disk space.

Assume, for example, you need bubble charts for your once-a-year long-range plan. The charting application can be extended with bubble chart libraries.

MAXIMIZING CLIENTS AND SERVERS

As a network-centric productivity tool, Corel Office for Java incorporates both client and server components. All client components are integrated in a familiar graphical user interface. The same interface is presented (with minor variations) to users on all platforms, including on thin clients.

The specific client components include a word processing, spreadsheet, charting, drawing, and personal information manager. Corel's WordPerfect for Java is a WYSIWYG word processor that offers the subset of functionality used by the majority of users. Additional features are being added by Corel and other software developers and can be downloaded by the client as needed.

The client components also include Quattro Pro for Java, a

robust spreadsheet application with several hundred built-in functions, and Corel Chart for Java, a charting application with 2-D and 3-D chart and graph capabilities. The Corel PIM is an e-mail client, address book, scheduler, calendar, planner, calculator. These components are tightly integrated within the other applications. For example, the address book can be accessed from all applications of the suite and all components can make use of the e-mail facility to easily send documents. The e-mail client supports common e-mail standards such as POP3 and IMAP4, allowing organizations to take advantage of existing e-mail back-end servers. In contrast to the other components of the suite, the PIM has its own user interface when it is launched as a separate application.

COREL OFFICE FOR JAVA: THE SERVER SIDE

Because Corel Office for Java is a server- and network-centric suite, the server provides an important component of the overall enterprise solution. It makes it possible to accomplish the goals of security and low maintenance by providing central document storage, version control, groupware scheduling, and communication.

To be more specific, Corel Office for Java provides Lightweight Directory Access Protocol (LDAP) directory services, database connectivity, and productivity modules on the server. LDAP is used on the server to provide file management, security, name spacing, and printing services. These LDAP services were licensed from a third-party partner of Corel, Novera Software Inc. of Burlington, Massachusetts, at www.novera.com.

Without LDAP, it is not possible for the user to download an application from one server and save a document to another server, because only one-to-one relationships are established. LDAP, in conjunction with Novera's EPIC, or Enterprise Platform for Internet Computing, removes this limitation, allowing organizations to establish multiple connected servers with separate functions. For example, one server could be used exclusively as a document server. Office for Java users would then download the required applet from the application server and save documents to the document server. The user does not need to know about the two different servers; they are transparent. They are presented as directories available, and the saving process can be directed automatically to the chosen document server. The user profile grants users access to appropriate network resources regardless of their location, making it possible for users to move without having to move desktops.

These three tables outline the server modules:

Table 14-2. LDAP directory services modules

File management system
   Server file system mapping
   Folder/directory
   Document revision control
   File I/O
	File management provides the user with centrally controlled access to folders and directories on multiple network servers, handles file input and output and document revision control.

Security
   User log-on and user profile
   User grouping
	Security is accomplished through user log-on and customizable user profile, controlling not just which server can be accessed, but also which files and directories can be accessed per user and per server.

Name spacing
   Corporate resources
   Address storage
   (e-mail, etc.)
	Users can be grouped into workgroups to jointly collaborate on documents. The necessary groupware capability is also part of Corel Office for Java.

Printing services Network printer addressing	In Corel Office for Java, printing is a server-centric process. The user sends his or her Java document to the central server, where it is printed on one of the available network printers.

Table 14-3. Database connectivity modules

Database connectivity JDBC (Java database connectivity) to SQL servers or other databases	Connectivity to relational databases, address lists, and meeting rooms is possible with the database connectivity of Corel Office for Java.
Scriptable front end Groupware scheduling and e-mail administration Document and Information workflow	

Table 14-4. Productivity modules

Spell checking Global search and replace Import and export filters Printing format conversion On-line help	Productivity modules are put on the server rather than the clientside, saving hard-drive space for occasionally used materials.

As Table 14-3 indicates, Corel Office for Java offers a broad range of database connectivity features. Through Corel's licensing agreement with SANGA (also of Burlington, Massachusetts, at www.sangacorp.com) for its SANGA Pages product, users of Office for Java will be able to access a wide range of databases from the client components, create new database-driven Java front ends to databases, and incorporate a groupware system into the overall deployment. Compared to Lotus Notes, which requires the installation of a proprietary Notes server, SANGA Pages groupware can be built on any number of ODBC compatible databases. This allows organizations to make use of existing database installations by providing both access to the Java clients as well as groupware functionality.

In a thin client environment, the architecture has to account for the memory restrictions on the client. While it is feasible to download and execute individual components on the client, certain components need to reside on the server. This means that documents get submitted to these services.

Import and export filters provide connectivity to legacy applications in the intranet environment. Documents can be converted from a wide range of standard applications into the Office for Java format and vice versa.

Corel Office for Java is not just a complete set of office applications with the requisite back end: it is built on a Java-based application framework that makes the suite completely extensible and customizable.

The client/server architecture of Corel Office for Java is designed to optimize overall performance. Most functionality is executed on the client side, which takes the burden off of network bandwidth for unnecessary transfer and communication. The architecture is highly scalable and works well within an organization's existing intranet infrastructure. Effective version control, the use of just-in-time compilers, and the ability to update distributed technology all contribute to high performances. Future network computers will have higher power processors and less overhead in the operating system, so that performance will be more than just acceptable.

BEYOND THE OFFICE SUITE

Because all of Corel's client components are JavaBeans, this not only provides a full suite of integrated office applications for the Java platform, but also gives developers the opportunity to reuse components in a new environment.

The JavaBeans API, or Application Programming Interface, is the component architecture for the Java platform. JavaBeans enables developers to write reusable components once and then run them anywhere. For example, a corporate developer or a third party could use a spreadsheet component, along with database connectivity and toolbar widgets, to produce a new vertical market application.

As a result, Corel Office for Java will be marketed both as a full suite of applications as well as a collection of JavaBeans, ready for innovative reuse across the Internet and intranet environments.

THIRD-PARTY DEVELOPMENT: COREL APPLICATION FRAMEWORK

The Corel Application Framework for Java, the framework on which all Corel Office for Java's applications are based, is a library of integrated Java classes and interfaces designed for the rapid development of platform-independent GUI applications. The Corel Application Framework is written entirely in Java. Applications based on this framework will therefore run on all Java Virtual Machines and are portable across different platforms. These are the key components of the Corel Application Framework:

- Application framework classes set up the main architecture of Corel Office for Java.

- Java Object Interfaces (JOI) provide the communication between a container and the components contained therein. Common user interface classes augment the Java AWT package to provide UI components that have been adopted by most state-of-the-art GUI applications.

- Advanced Graphics is an imaging model composed of a set of powerful graphics extensions, with support for coordinate mapping, Bezier objects, outline and fill patterns, among others.

- Persistent classes provide file and directory service (the conversion of the document objects into server object for storage and vice versa).

Furthermore, the Corel Application Framework is fully compatible with the upcoming release of JavaBeans, and provides an application framework whose open architecture design will complement the Java Beans' technology. This common architecture, together with the streamlined feature set accounts for the low overall footprint of Corel Office for Java. The beta version of Corel Office for Java occupied less than 5 MB and the fully loaded commercial version is scheduled to reside within a 5 to 8 MB range.

PUTTING YOUR OFFICE ON THE NETWORK: BENEFITS

Corel Office for Java is one of the first applications to take full advantage of the Java computing platform. The server-centric architecture contributes to a much lower cost of administration. Software resides centrally on the application server and is updated centrally as well. Application distribution no longer means installing the software permanently on fat clients. In the past, this has contributed both to rising costs and rising complexity of administration, as installation procedures varied from desktop to desktop.

This architecture also means that users can begin work on one machine, and continue their work on another desktop, independent of platform or physical location. Corporations that are deploying thin client environments will also realize substantial cost savings in hardware acquisition and maintenance, since network computers are less complex than PCs. At the same time, these machines can feature the same class of powerful processors (200 MHz) and offer the same capabilities users are accustomed to. The latter functionality is, of course, provided by Corel Office for Java—either standalone or in conjunction with any numbers of JavaBeans.

The Corel Office for Java, then, offers a number of advantages for businesses. Since it works with thin clients and fat clients, has built-in groupware functionality, and connects to back-end databases, it offers a complete enterprise solution. With transparent distribution of updates and version-control possible with the Corel Castanet channel, administrative and maintenance costs are reduced. There are also some built-in security advantages with Java. The cross-platform capabilities of Corel Office for Java means that files and documents are sharable across multiple platforms in any computing environment. Users can create office documents that are immediately publishable to their printer, the intranet, or the Internet. No conversion or reformatting is required.

DEVELOPMENT EXPERIENCE

When Corel set out to develop Office for Java, the programming language had been used predominantly to create applets like animations for Web pages and some single-use applets like forms. No other developer had attempted to create a full suite of office components and the widely held belief was that Java could not be used for a project of such scope.

After starting development in April 1996, Corel showed the first prototype, already with a rich GUI, to an audience of Java developers during JavaOne, the premier conference for Java developers and clients. It became obvious that Java could indeed be used for this type of sophisticated application. The prototype featured a Windows-like user interface and compound document capabilities, and surprised many with its already acceptable speed. The beta version has further improved speed and overall performance.

With the commercial version in late summer 1997 and the current progress for Java Virtual Machines and just-in-time compilers, we believe that performance will cease to be an issue in the development and deployment of Java applications.

Also contributing to the overall positive experience with Java development is the ease of development. Developers familiar with object-oriented languages like C++ have found the learning curve to be extremely short and steep. Many of Corel's programmers learned the basics of Java in a matter of days and became productive very quickly. The properties of Java itself contribute to an amazingly high speed of development: the preview version with word processor, charting, and spreadsheet functionality went live on the Web on October 16, 1996, a scant four and a half months after the unveiling of the initial prototype. The speed of development has been continuous at the same rate.

Overall, Java allows programmers to be highly productive.

DEVELOPMENT ISSUES

When development started, Java did offer a lot of excitement and increasing momentum, but no integrated development environment. Symantec Visual Café was chosen by Corel's developers as the primary development platform. Many of our developments were focused on providing capabilities common in other development environments. The basic AWT (Advanced Windowing Toolkit) of Java 1.02 does not offer GUI widgets, sophisticated graphics, etc. These were developed separately by Corel and have become part of our Corel Application Framework.

MARKETING AND PRICING A NETWORK-CENTRIC OFFICE PRODUCTIVITY TOOL

The development of a cross-platform, downloadable, modular, extensible, network-centric office suite has raised some interesting questions on pricing and distribution. Other Java developers, particularly developers of JavaBeans components, are facing much the same questions: How are the applications distributed? How are they priced? Are retail boxes necessary or should one rely exclusively on electronic distribution. Currently, these issues have not been finalized. However, several general observations can be made:

- Corel Office for Java will be marketed in a number of ways. These include possible bundling the suite with network computers, like Sun Microsystem's JavaStation, NCI's (NCI is an Oracle subsidiary) or IBM's network computer.

- Corporate installations will be implemented by system integrators and corporate resellers. In these cases, licensing remains reasonably straightforward. The corporation may purchase server license and the right to use the software and a certain number of clients.

- A third channel is beginning to emerge. Internet service providers can install the software on their central servers and allow their customers use of the software for a monthly fee. To date, the main stumbling block remains bandwidth. However, many progressive service providers are currently experimenting with high bandwidth solutions like ISDN or cable modems. With this infrastructure in place, it becomes entirely feasible to make Corel Office for Java available through this channel. End users would then download the components on an as-needed basis, regardless of their computing platform or physical location.

- JavaBeans will be packaged in a suite of components to provide developers with a starting point for their application development. These components are targeted mostly at corporate developers wishing to use components for rapidly deploying intranet applications.

WRITE IT WITH JAVA

The preview and beta versions, as well as the early feedback from potential clients and developers alike, has not only proven that Java can indeed be used for the development of general purpose applets and applications, but also that there is a market need for these applications. Organizations have started to rethink their corporate information infrastructures, deploying intranets instead of proprietary networks and testing thin clients for vertical applications and single-task environments.

Corel Office for Java offers these organizations the productivity applications they require, the necessary integration with legacy systems, innovative new features such as database access and groupware functionality across platforms, and at the same time allows developers to take full advantage of sophisticated Java components developed by Corel Corporation.

CHAPTER 15

MITSUBISHI: JAVA IN SILICON*

Ivan Greenberg, Systems Marketing Manager, Embedded Solutions, VSIS, Inc., Mitsubishi Electronics America, Inc.

Kazunori Saitoh, Ph.D., LSI Development Manager, Microprocessors and Embedded System Solutions, System LSI Laboratory, Mitsubishi Electric Corporation

Mitsubishi was the first company to port Java to silicon and demonstrate its potential utility for consumer electronic devices. At JavaOne in 1996, Mitsubishi presented several examples of next-generation consumer product applications, including satellite global positioning systems, local and streaming audio recording and playback, streaming audio download, and real-time drawing functions using its new M32R/D chip—with Java. These types of application systems require high-performance computation with low power consumption and minimal cost. PIMs (personal information managers), intelligent cellular phones, NCs (network computers), and digital cameras are systems with similar requirements. The major advantages of Java for these types of applications are its computing power and network-centricity. Relatively low development costs and fast development cycles are also a factor. The major advantages of Mitsubishi's M32R/D chip for these types of applications is its combination of random access memory and microprocessor core on the same piece of silicon; this provides the infrastructure for high-performance computing and low power consumption, and offers cost advantages. Mitsubishi will begin vol-

*Chapter 15 Mitsubishi: Java in Silicon © 1997, Mitsubishi Electronics America, Inc. All rights reserved. This material provided by MELA is published with the prior written permission of MELA. No warranties, express or implied, are granted by MELA as to this material. Broadcast or republication is not permitted without MELA's prior written permission. "eRAM" is a trademark of MELA. "eRAM-enabled" is a servicemark of MELA.

ume production of the M32R/D microprocessor in the second quarter of 1997 and plans to complete porting the Java Virtual Machine to the M32R/D for volume production by the end of the year. In 1998, Mitsubishi plans to increase the on-chip memory size and performance of the M32R/D so it can better execute Java applets.

In his May 1996 JavaOne keynote address, James Gosling, Java-Soft's chief scientist and architect of the original Java programming environment, had this to say about Mitsubishi Electric Corporation's M32R/D microprocessor:

> "This is actually my personal winner for the coolness category for hardware. This is a DRAM chip from Mitsubishi. It's a 16-megabit DRAM. And if you look at the center of it, there's this little patch, and that patch is actually a 67-megahertz RISC CPU. This whole thing sucks very little power, and it's a really fast device, and the next revision coming apparently is in 64-megabit DRAM, where the CPU is about twice as fast. So you've got 100 megahertz in something about the form factor of your fingernail. And once you've got stuff like this, it really changes the kind of things you can build. You could build a complete speech recognition system into a doorknob."

Mitsubishi Electric's presence at JavaOne came as no surprise. In December 1995, Mitsubishi Electronics America licensed Sun Microsystems' Java language and HotJava browser—second only to Netscape Communications Corporation—to build cost-effective, high-volume, digital networked products for consumer, industrial, and commercial applications.

What made Mitsubishi Electric's presence notable at JavaOne was it established itself as the first company to port the entire Java Virtual Machine to a general-purpose microprocessor specifically designed for consumer embedded applications. This porting presented the world with a Java engine that could act as a black box to the embedded development community, hiding a significant portion of the low-level hardware and assembly code from embedded application developers, to whom time to market is of paramount importance.

The microprocessor receiving the port, the M32R/D, is an example of Mitsubishi Electric's eRAM, embedded high-density Dynamic Random-Access Memory (DRAM) technology, which helped the company establish itself as the first in the industry to successfully integrate a microprocessor and DRAM together on the same piece of silicon. Mitsubishi Electric integrated the two technologies in response to market pressure on its customers—high-volume Original Equipment Manufacturers (OEMs)—to design more intelligent and sophisticated consumer embedded products. By exploiting eRAM technology, a large amount of random-access memory can be placed on the same silicon die as the microprocessor core and be cost-effectively manufactured in high volumes. As a result, Mitsubishi Electric's microprocessor-DRAM integration achievement has enormous significance in microprocessor applications for the consumer embedded market as well as for Java-enabled consumer embedded applications.

To support the eRAM technology and the M32R/D microprocessor in the North American marketplace, Mitsubishi Electric is using two of its semiconductor-systems-based business units that are part of its North American affiliate, Mitsubishi Electronics America, Inc.— Electronic Device Group and VSIS, Inc., both based in Sunnyvale, California. The Electronic Device Group is Mitsubishi Electric's semiconductor distribution arm in North America, and it drives Java applications for Mitsubishi's microprocessor customers via its applications engineering, marketing, and sales groups.

VSIS, Inc., is a separate, entrepreneurial organization that is also a semiconductor systems development arm of Mitsubishi Electric. VSIS is close to the emerging Java product market in North America and focuses on developing intellectual property and emerging applications of Java in chips. One of VSIS's main projects is to drive the eRAM technology employed in the M32R/D microprocessor, particularly as it is coupled with Java, as a means of enabling consumer embedded applications.

TRENDS IN THE CONSUMER ELECTRONICS MARKET

Mitsubishi Electric is one of the world's largest producers of microcontrollers and memories, and the company has developed significant core competencies in both integrated circuit process technologies. Focused on the technology needs of its OEM customer base, the company's major strategy is to enable consumer embedded electronics applications through integrating several functions previously associated with separate process technologies into the same piece of silicon to create system-on-a-chip solutions.

The market for consumer embedded applications is enormous. For example, in 1995, 1.6 billion central-processing-unit (CPU) chips were shipped to the embedded computing market, compared to only 20 million CPU chips for the personal computer (PC) market.

Historically, Mitsubishi Electric's 8-bit and 16-bit microcontrollers have served the embedded market as controllers, rather than processors. Controllers contain a limited amount of on-chip embedded read-only memory, often in the 2-kilobyte to 16-kilobyte range, which gives them the intelligence to perform specific limited functions. Examples of the functions a controller might perform include operating a liquid crystal display's drive controls; operating personal computer joysticks and peripherals; and operating the on-screen display, closed captioning, and channel selection systems of televisions, videocassette recorders, and cable television converter boxes. Processors, on the other hand, have a high degree of computing power and access a large amount of off-chip RAM—usually DRAM in the megabyte range—to perform complex and sophisticated applications such as 3-D graphics rendering, communications, and networking functions, as well as to perform the CPU function in personal computers and workstations. These processor applications could use Java.

During the past five years, data-processing functions have appeared in the consumer embedded-microcomputer market in such applications as global positioning systems for car navigation and personal digital assistants with on-screen bitmap displays. Along with the intelligence of these devices comes the strong demand from consumers for a richer embedded-system feature set enabled by faster CPU-to-DRAM transfer processing speed.

The strong demand for a richer, embedded-system feature set is causing 16-bit microcontrollers based on complex instruction set computing (CISC) architecture to become displaced by 32-bit microprocessors employing a reduced instruction set computing

(RISC) architecture. RISC processors generally outperform CISC processors. One reason cited for this performance disparity is pipelining.

Pipelining is a process in which the execution of an instruction is divided into several steps, each one requiring the same amount of time to complete. Once the pipeline is filled, instruction execution proceeds at the speed of each step. Hence, if the pipeline comprises n stages, execution speed is improved by a factor of n.

CISC processors require instruction decoding into unbalanced microcode. CISC instructions map into varying numbers of microcoded instructions, which in turn require varying numbers of intermediate clock cycles to execute. For example, the first CISC instruction might map into four microcoded instructions, the next might map into eight microcoded instructions, the next into three microcoded instructions, the next into one microcoded instruction, and so on. In contrast, RISC instructions are hardwired into the architecture and, hence, require the same number of intermediate clock cycles to execute. As a result, the RISC scheme makes pipelining possible, and results in generally faster processing speeds.

JUMPING THE MEMORY WALL

For the past 20 years, microprocessor vendors and DRAM vendors have both successfully evolved their integrated circuit process technologies for higher yields—meaning that an ever increasing percentage of silicon dies survive the manufacturing process without fatal defects—but otherwise they have followed distinctly different paths. Microprocessor vendors have pursued ever higher performance logic with relatively short design cycle times, while DRAM vendors have aimed for ever increasing memory density with relatively long design cycle times.

Unlike microprocessor vendors, DRAM vendors cannot evolve their manufacturing processes for high-performance logic because of the constraints imposed by a DRAM cell. A DRAM cell is the element of a DRAM device that stores one bit (binary digit) of information. Each DRAM cell must have a fixed capacitance associated with it to reliably store one bit, and this fixed capacitance is linked directly to the physical area of the cell. DRAM vendors have created exotic cell structures as a means of both increasing memory density and accommodating fixed cell capacitance. However, such structures have no place or value in the pure logic process used for microprocessor development.

In essence, since microprocessor and DRAM process technologies have conflicting goals both technologically and economically, they have each evolved separately and developed their own respective economies of scale.

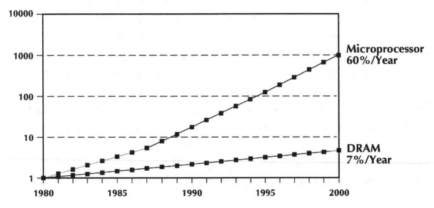

Adapted with permission from *Computer Architecture: A Quantitative Approach,* second edition, by David Patterson and John Hennessy, 1996, Morgan Kaufman Publishers, Inc., Figure 5.1, page 374.

Figure 15-1. The widening performance gap between microprocessors and DRAMs contributes to marginal system performance growth.

One could raise the argument that both processes should be kept separate to give customers the best cost/performance ratio. However, VSIS believes this is a shortsighted philosophy and sees it as an opportunity to capitalize on Mitsubishi Electric's eRAM embedded DRAM technology. Next-generation microprocessors demonstrate significant performance growth over their predecessors when using industry-standard benchmarks, but achieve only marginal improvement when placed in real systems because of the huge performance gap between microprocessors and DRAMs. No matter how fast a microprocessor runs, it still must fetch its code from DRAM, which is painfully slow. The eRAM technology successfully bridges this performance gap by bringing the microprocessor and DRAM process technologies together on the same piece of silicon.

After overcoming the technical hurdles of microprocessor-DRAM integration, the industry will achieve exponential improvements in microprocessor system performance.

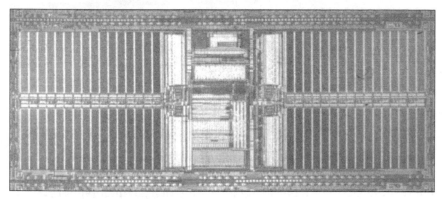

©1997 Mitsubishi Electronics America, Inc. Used with permission. All rights reserved.

Figure 15-2. Die of Mitsubishi Electric's M32R/D microprocessor with on-chip DRAM. Putting memory and a microprocessor on the same piece of silicon increases the intelligence of consumer embedded devices as well as offering performance and cost advantages.

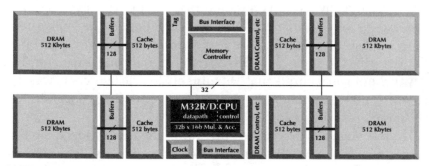

©1997 Mitsubishi Electronics America, Inc. Used with permission. All rights reserved.

Figure 15-3. Layout of Mitsubishi Electric's M32R/D microprocessor with on-chip DRAM. No matter how fast a microprocessor runs, it needs to fetch its code from DRAM, which is painfully slow—an autobahn ending in a crowded toll booth. Mitsubishi's M32R/D microprocessor bridges this performance gap.

MITSUBISHI'S M32R/D

The M32R/D microprocessor is an example of Mitsubishi Electric's eRAM technology. Mitsubishi Electric gave a technical presentation on the M32R/D microprocessor in February 1996 at the IEEE International Solid-State Circuits Conference in San Francisco, California. Mitsubishi Electronics America formally announced the product to the press the following month.

The M32R/D is a general-purpose microprocessor featuring a small 32-bit RISC CPU core, 2 megabytes (16 megabits) of integrated DRAM, Digital Signal Processing (DSP) functionality, and on-chip memory support. The 32-bit RISC core features 4 kilobytes of SRAM cache memory, a memory controller, and peripheral circuits.

The M32R/D microprocessor features an unusually wide 128-bit internal bus with a maximum operating speed of 66.6 megahertz. The internal bus connects the microprocessor core, SRAM cache memory, and DRAM together. Using the on-chip DRAM, the M32R/D microprocessor has a performance rating of 52.4 million instructions per second, based on Dhrystone version 2.1 benchmark software.

DRAM was selected over SRAM as the process technology for the M32R/D microprocessor because of its cost advantages for consumer embedded applications. SRAM has the advantage of higher performance, making it ideally suited for cache memory, which allows it to quickly swap data to and from a CPU. However, SRAM is too expensive to implement in high densities and is bulky compared to DRAM. SRAM requires six transistors to store one bit of data; storing the same bit in DRAM requires only one transistor. The key technological hurdle that Mitsubishi Electric overcame was discovering how to embed a 32-bit RISC microprocessor core within a DRAM process technology.

Even though DRAM is inherently slow, the extra-wide 128-bit internal bus of the M32R/D microprocessor gives its CPU core extremely fast access to memory. It takes only five clock cycles, or 75 nanoseconds at 66 megahertz, for the M32R/D microprocessor to access four 32-bit words. If the same microprocessor had to access 70-nanosecond commercial DRAM off-chip, it would take about 20 cycles for it to access the same four 32-bit words. On-chip access to DRAM gives the M32R/D microprocessor a major performance advantage, provided all the memory required for access can be stored in 2 megabytes of DRAM.

Accessing DRAM internally also allows the M32R/D microprocessor to have lower power consumption than microprocessors that access DRAM off-chip, and low power characteristics are of key importance to battery-powered consumer embedded applications. Typically, the M32R/D microprocessor draws only 275 milliwatts of power from its 3.3-volt power supply when it accesses the on-chip DRAM—approximately one-fourth of what a comparable 3.3-volt microprocessor would draw if it was accessing the DRAM off-chip. When the CPU is not running (in standby mode), the M32R/D microprocessor uses less than 2 milliwatts.

Table 15-1. The M32R/D chip is designed to meet the computing performance, power consumption, and cost requirements of these types of consumer electronic devices. Java, embedded in the M32R/D, offers significant advantages for device connectivity as well as multimedia and dynamic capabilities.

Applications of M32R/D

    Personal digital assistant (PDA)

    Intelligent data pager

    Printer system configuration based on M32R/D

    Web browsing phone

    Web browsing television

    Future camera application

    Set-top box

    Multimedia processing system

Excluding the multiply-accumulate (MAC) unit, the M32R/D microprocessor's CPU core size is tiny when compared with existing RISC CPUs—about 4 square millimeters. The small size of the CPU core makes possible the integration of high densities of DRAM (such as 2 megabytes) on the same chip. However, even with these high memory densities, the M32R/D microprocessor's die size is small enough to attain high yields. High yields ensure that a chip can be manufactured cost effectively in large enough volumes to satisfy the price constraints of the consumer embedded market.

The M32R/D implements a five-stage RISC pipeline: fetch, decode, execute, access memory, and write back. It also features compact code because it uses both 16-bit and 32-bit instruction formats. Using 16-bit instruction format allows code size to be compressed for effective use of the on-chip DRAM. The 32-bit instruction format allows direct access to the 32-megabyte address space.

The M32R/D microprocessor also supports DSP instructions with its MAC unit. This allows the M32R/D microprocessor to perform modem, data compression and decompression, filtering, and other DSP applications. It accesses 32-word-by-16-bit and 16-word-by-16-bit DSP instructions in only one clock cycle.

The M32R/D microprocessor has 4 kilobytes of SRAM cache memory, which temporarily stores CPU instruction entries. The CPU maintains an instruction queue with two 128-bit entries, which usually represents 8 to 16 instructions. When one of the entries is empty, another 128-bit entry transfers from cache memory in one clock cycle. The on-chip DRAM will fill cache misses in five clock cycles.

Normally, an embedded application's system bus is shared by microprocessor memory traffic and also by the processor input-output (I/O) traffic. Assuming the embedded application has all of its dynamic memory requirements fulfilled by the on-chip DRAM, its external bus will have interaction with peripherals and no need to access off-chip DRAM. As a result, the expectation of greatly reduced off-chip traffic requirements allows the M32R/D microprocessor to afford a 16-bit external data bus that operates at 16.7 megahertz.

The M32R/D microprocessor's use of the eRAM embedded DRAM technology reduces the size, chip count, and cost of consumer embedded systems. For example, an embedded system in which a microprocessor accesses DRAM externally might use a chipset consisting of a microprocessor, a digital ASIC that is designed for a specific embedded application, two pieces of 512-kilobyte or 1-megabyte DRAM, and an analog ASIC. The same system using the M32R/D microprocessor would require only one additional chip—a digital/analog ASIC. A microprocessor which uses external DRAM typically fits in a plastic quad flat pack (PQFP) that has 160 to 200 pins. The M32R/D microprocessor fits neatly within a 100-pin thin quad flat pack (TQFP) package. Incorporating the M32R/D microprocessor's small RISC CPU and DRAM on the same chip increases DRAM die size by only 16 percent.

JAVA IN SILICON

Mitsubishi Electric was among the first companies involved with the Sun Microsystems team, code named Green, which was formed in 1991 and developed Oak, Java's predecessor. James Gosling, then a Green team member, designed Oak to be a replacement language for C++ that would work in a distributed manner over networks. Oak was also an operating system.

The Green team spoke with Mitsubishi Electric about using Oak-based interfaces in cellular phones, televisions, and home and industrial automation systems before Sun Microsystems established the team as FirstPerson, Inc., a wholly owned subsidiary, in October 1992. Since Oak was targeted for consumer applications, like the Web browsing phone, personal digital assistant, and digital set-top box, Mitsubishi Electric was interested in applying Oak to consumer embedded applications—areas where Mitsubishi had experience and had developed core competencies. This was somewhat different from Sun Microsystems, FirstPerson's parent, which had developed its core competencies in UNIX-based workstations and was more naturally oriented toward Internet applications.

In March 1994, Mitsubishi Electric began working with FirstPerson on the five-month task of porting Oak to the M16, then Mitsubishi's most advanced microcontroller, so that Mitsubishi could evaluate Oak for possible future consumer embedded applications.

Mitsubishi Electric benefited from porting Oak to the M16 microcontroller because it made the subsequent porting of the Java Virtual Machine to the M32R/D microprocessor, two years later, a rather simple two-month engineering job. Like Java, Oak used threads to manage its basic libraries, so porting multithreading in Java took only two weeks. The majority of the work involved porting the Java Abstract Window Toolkit (AWT) and Java's network capabilities to the M32R/D microprocessor. AWT features much more sophisticated graphics capabilities than Oak, and the network capabilities allow users to download Java applets from the Internet.

Mitsubishi Electric also learned that the performance of script operating systems such as Oak would be significantly increased if the CPU could have faster access to high-density memory. It presented an opportune time for the company to introduce a 32-bit

RISC processor with 2 megabytes of on-chip DRAM for implementing intelligent embedded applications.

JAVA IMPLEMENTATION CHALLENGE

Although Mitsubishi Electric proved at JavaOne that it could port the entire Java Virtual Machine to the M32R/D microprocessor, implementing Java in consumer embedded applications is currently one of the major challenges facing Mitsubishi Electric and its affiliated business units, Electronic Device Group and VSIS, because Java currently is too large for the types of embedded applications Mitsubishi is targeting. Mitsubishi Electric's M32R/D demonstration at JavaOne was performed with a system that had 8 megabytes of memory (2 megabytes of internal DRAM, 4 megabytes of external DRAM, and a 2-megabyte SRAM PC Card), and like other microprocessors geared for the consumer embedded market, the M32R/D microprocessor will execute Java applications slowly. However, when compared to other microprocessors, the M32R/D, by virtue of its on-chip DRAM, is the most suitable engine for executing Java applications on embedded consumer devices.

The capability exists today to build a complete system powered by JavaOS™, an operating system written in C and Java, with a total of 4 megabytes of ROM and 4 megabytes of RAM. Typically, the ROM contains the microkernel, drivers, Java Virtual Machine, and standard Java classes; plus the JavaOS windows, graphics, and networking components; as well as the HotJava browser code.

If one considers a system comprising the M32R/D microprocessor with 4 megabytes of on-chip RAM and 4 megabytes of external RAM, the M32R/D could execute the complete JavaOS out of on-chip memory; 2.5 megabytes of external RAM could be used for dynamic requirements of JavaOS and HotJava, leaving 1.5 megabytes of external RAM for downloaded HTML pages, applets (or applications), and images. The majority of consumer embedded system applications, which do not require robust windowing and browsing environments, could run Java in half the total memory space just described—2 megabytes of ROM and 2 megabytes of RAM—which would all fit in the 4 megabytes of on-chip memory space of a next-generation M32R/D microprocessor.

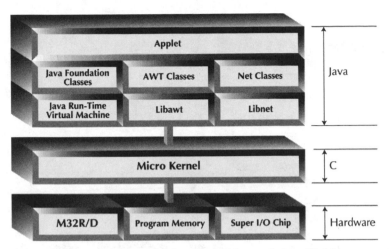

©1997 Mitsubishi Electronics America, Inc. Used with permission. All rights reserved.

Figure 15-4. Java ported to Mitsubishi Electric's M32R/D microprocessor.

Unlike the desktop space, many consumer embedded applications must operate with less than 4 megabytes of memory. Furthermore, in many cases, consumer embedded applications require real-time performance, which translates into extremely fast execution speed. Hence, Mitsubishi Electric is currently investigating different ways of improving the performance and size of JavaOS.

Mitsubishi Electric is using a two-pronged approach to resolve these issues: increasing the amount of on-chip memory and reducing the size of the JavaOS needed for running consumer embedded applications. VSIS believes that once these two challenges are met, Mitsubishi Electric's eRAM-based microprocessor will feature lightning fast execution of Java applications while drawing a mere trickle of current. Since this device would store the complete Java run-time environment and Java application on the chip, it would represent the quintessential Java chip for consumer electronic devices.

CONSUMER DEVICES ON-LINE: WEB BROWSING PHONE

Currently, Mitsubishi Electric has targeted consumer embedded applications that fit the present DRAM capacity of the M32R/D micro-

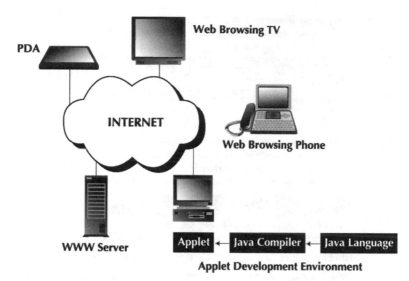

©1997 Mitsubishi Electronics America, Inc. Used with permission. All rights reserved.

Figure 15-5. Users of Java-enabled Web browsing phones, Web browsing televisions, and personal digital assistants will be able to connect to a wealth of interactive Internet applications. This connectivity is a key benefit of embedding Java in consumer devices.

processor, such as the Web browsing phone and the Web browsing television.

If the Web browsing phone adds only two simple features to existing phones, such as e-mail and World Wide Web browsing, it will have an immediate and substantial effect on people's lives. The Web browsing phone will need a simple base user-interface application that would allow users to navigate through the World Wide Web, e-mail, and telephony. To satisfy marketing's "holy grail," the Web browsing phone's features must provide useful and exciting features/functions and be cost effective enough to manufacture so the end product will stay within the consumer market price point.

Adding Java will enrich the Web browsing phone even further. When people use a Java-enabled Web browsing phone to browse the World Wide Web, they will not be restricted to merely viewing information; they can download meaningful applications to interact with the information. People can do home banking, download audio and video clips using audio/video streaming applications, and conceivably run any application that fits within the Web browsing phone's environment, including its memory footprint, display size, and keyboard ergonomics.

For example, let's say a person installs a Web browsing phone in his bedroom. Before he goes to sleep at night, instead of setting his alarm for the following morning, he could download a Java applet that would enable the Web browsing phone to perform several functions at different times the following morning. He could interact with the Java applet to set the Web browsing phone to download a compact disc at 6 A.M. so he would wake to his favorite music, then download weather information at 7 A.M. so he would be able to dress appropriately, and finally download audio traffic information so he could determine the fastest route to work during his rush-hour commute.

What makes Java in the Web browsing phone so useful is that the application would not need to be purchased from a software store and installed on the device; new applications could be downloaded from the Internet. In addition, a locally resident application layer would aggregate exciting applications or applets from appropriate Internet sites, further increasing the Web browsing phone's usefulness.

JAVA-ENABLED PERSONAL DIGITAL ASSISTANTS

In the near future, next-generation wireless personal digital assistants will be able to run most or all of their application suites in Java. They will have a personal information manager (PIM), calculator, to-do list, and a World Wide Web browser. They will also employ special services, such as agent-based Internet searches and next-generation e-mail that has voice, data, and fax capability, and they will have a built-in mechanism to aggregate appropriate Java applications from appropriate Internet sites.

Like the Java-enabled Web browsing phone, users of Java-enabled personal digital assistants will be able to connect to a wealth of interactive Internet applications, and be able to manipulate their stock portfolios, play games, and use interactive travel services that will show them the best route to travel from point A to point B in a given metropolitan area.

Since the next-generation, Java-enabled personal digital assistant will have all the applications written in Java, the lower-level details of the platform will cease to be a development issue and a new class of Java-based personal digital assistants will proliferate throughout the industry. Personal digital assistant manufacturers will choose the microprocessor platform that has the lowest cost/performance and power/performance ratios.

JAVA—A BLACK BOX FOR FUTURE SOFTWARE APPLICATIONS

The Java environment holds the promise of converting the consumer embedded hardware platform into a black box for software developers. Unencumbered by hardware idiosyncrasies, embedded application developers will swiftly develop Java applications that will run on all platforms. The winning hardware platform in this new marketplace will offer the lowest cost/performance and power/performance ratios. Mitsubishi Electric believes its eRAM-based microprocessors will enable a winning Java embedded platform for the consumer market.

JavaSoft, JavaOne, Java, Java Virtual Machine, JavaOS, and Hot-Java are trademarks or registered trademarks of Sun Microsystems, Inc.

eRAM is a trademark of Mitsubishi Electronics America, Inc.

BIBLIOGRAPHY

Bernard Cole, "Embedded Systems: Searching for Standards," Electronic Engineering Times, December 18, 1995, pp. 39, 79, 81.

Microprocessor-DRAM Performance Gap" diagram (gap.tif). Adapted with permission from *Computer Architecture: A Quantitative Approach,* second edition, by David Patterson and John Hennessy, Morgan Kaufmann Publishers, Inc., 1996, Figure 5.1, page 374.

REFERENCES

Jim Turley, "Mitsubishi Mixes Microprocessor, Memory," *Microprocessor Report,* May 27, 1996, pp. 10-12.

David Bursky, "Combo RISC and DRAM Solves Data Bandwidth Issues," *Electronic Design,* March 4, 1996, pp. 67-68, 70-71.

Toru Shimizu, et al., "A Multimedia 32b RISC Microprocessor with 16Mb DRAM," IEEE International Solid-State Circuits Conference, *Digest of Technical Papers, vol. 39.* February 1996, pp. 216-217, 448.

JAVA
RESOURCES

The early business adopters of Java in this book are a great place to start seeing Java in action. Directories of Java applets and links are available on-line. For business the JavaSoft and IBM Java pages are information-packed. This list is by no means exhaustive, but these resources will get you informed and keep you informed.

URLS OF ORGANIZATIONS IN *JAVA FOR BUSINESS*

www.millipore.com
www.economist.com
www.cherwell.com/cherwell/chemsymphony
www.marimba.com
www.trilogy.com
www.entertainnet.com
www.excite.com
www.sportsline.com
www.reuters.com
www.csx.com
www.nandotimes.com
www.hotwired.com
www.netscape.com
www.dtai.com
www.imservice.com
www.bah.com
www.acl.lanl.gov/TeleMed
www.roche.com
www.ergon.ch

www.national.com
www.home.com
www.sun.com
www.virtualvin.com
www.homeaccount.com
www.corel.com
www.mitsubishi.com

CHANNELS OF ORGANIZATIONS IN *JAVA FOR BUSINESS*

talk.hotwired.com
trans.corel.com
trans.marimba.com
trans.sportsline.com
trans.entertainnet.com
trans.excite.com

JAVA BUSINESS RESOURCES

www.javasoft.com
www.sun.com
www.ibm.com/java/home.html
www.netscape.com
www.gamelan.com
trans.earthweb.com

JAVA SECURITY

www.cs.princeton.edu/sip/
www.javasoft.com

JAVA NEWS

www.javaworld.com
www.radix.net/~cknudsen/javanews/

JAVA BOOKS

http://lightyear.ncsa.uiuc.edu/~srp/java/javabooks.html

ABOUT THE
CONTRIBUTORS

JAVA FOR BUSINESS

Thomas Anderson is Director of Corporate Communications at Millipore Corporation, a Boston-based science and process engineering company with a sophisticated Web presence. Tom has in-depth experience with Internet strategy and execution, and was a contributor to Mary Cronin's *Internet Strategy Handbook* (Harvard Business Press, 1996). At Millipore, Anderson has championed the use of relational catalog databases, narrowcasting, multimedia, and traditional communication tools to reach scientists, physicians and technical audiences worldwide. His enthusiasm for Java is from a marketing and communications perspective. He holds a BA in Chemistry from Holy Cross College and an MA in English Literature from Boston College.

MARIMBA: BUILDING THE NEW CUSTOMER CHANNEL

Kim Polese is the CEO and one of the co-founders of Marimba, Inc., a Java-oriented start-up founded to develop next-generation technologies for deploying network-aware Java applications. Prior to Marimba, Polese worked at Sun Microsystems for seven years, first as product manager for C++ than then as product manager of Oak— now known as Java. Kim was the driving force behind developing and promoting the Java brand, including business strategy, the coining of its new name, branding, OEM licensing, marketing communications and developer evangelism. Before Kim joined Sun, she worked as an applications engineer for IntelliCorp Inc., consulting with engineers in the development of expert system application frameworks. She holds a BS in Biophysics from the University of California, Berkeley and studied Computer Science at the University of Washington, Seattle.

REUTERS: USING JAVA IN THE TRADING ROOM

Dave Weller is a Technical Manager working for Reuters, based in London. He is currently responsible for the development of the infrastructure to support the Reuters Web—an extranet for the financial community. He joined Reuters in 1989 and has worked in a variety of software development roles. Dave has a BSc in Geography from Salford University and an MSc in Social Philosophy from the London School of Economics.

Glenn Wasserman has been working at Reuters since the summer of 1983 in various capacities within software development as well as within Reuters international product management and marketing groups. Prior to joining Reuters, he worked as a programmer in the government systems division of General Instrument Inc. Glenn has a bachelors of science degree in computer science from Hofstra University on Long Island.

CSX: CUSTOMERS ON-TRACK

John F. Andrews is President of CSX Technology and Senior Vice President, Technology for CSX Transportation, and is a member of CSX Corporation's Commercial Board. CSX Technology, a business unit of CSX, provides data processing, information systems and telecommunications in support of CSX's transportation companies and their customers. Andrews joined CSX in 1993 from GTE where he served most recently as the Vice President and General Manager of several business units, serving the health, government and telecommunications industries. During his career at GTE, he also held positions in engineering, planning, operations and finance. Andrews holds a BA degree in Business Administration/Finance from Whitworth College and a Masters Degree in Business Administration from the University of Puget Sound. He currently serves on numerous boards and national committees for organizations such as the Association of American Railroads, Harvard School of Government and the Conference Board. He was a candidate for 1996 CIO of the Year in *InformationWeek* and was a 1997 Visionary Award winner in *CommunicationsWeek*.

Marshall A. Gibbs is Assistant Vice President—Enterprise Solutions for CSX Technology. CSX Technology, a business unit of CSX, provides data processing, information systems and telecommunications in support of CSX's transportation companies and their customers. Gibbs joined CSX in April 1994, from Price Waterhouse, where he was with the Management Consulting Services organization. He specialized in large-scale workstation and distributed computing solutions for the Enterprise, implementing more than 15 systems during his tenure. His formal education includes a BA degree in Business Administration/Computer Information Systems and a Masters Degree in Business Administration, both from the University of Florida.

NANDO TIMES: FAST-FORWARD TO NEWS

James Calloway has been general manager of Nando.net since the spring of 1994. Before that he had served as the Programming Manager for *The News & Observer* in Raleigh, NC, for four years and as a programmer/analyst there for another four years. He began his career at *The News & Observer* as a staff writer in 1978. Calloway has a masters degree in communications from the University of North Carolina at Chapel Hill and a bachelor of journalism degree from the University of Missouri at Columbia.

HOTWIRED: NEW TECHNOLOGIES, NEW MARKETS

Ed Anuff is responsible for the operations and direction of HotWired's Advanced Products Group. In this role, he is responsible for designing the strategy for the company's new interactive services. He led the launch of the company's search engine, HotBot, the Java-based chat service, Talk.com, and the personalized news search agent, NewBot. Ed has more than eight years experience in computer software and interactive multimedia. He was the founder of Vision Software International, publisher of the popular Camera-Man QuickTime multimedia tool and the first company to ship products using Microsoft's Video for Windows. In 1993, Anuff joined Motion Works as vice president of product marketing, supervising product management and marketing for that company's multimedia tool products including ProMotion, AddMotion, MediaShop, and Multimedia Utilities. He is the author of the best selling *Java Sourcebook,* published by J. Wiley and Sons, as well as the forthcoming *New Media Manager,* published by HarperEdge. Anuff received a BS degree in management from Rensselaer Polytechnic Institute.

NETSCAPE: JAVA FOR THE NETWORKED ENTERPRISE

Ammiel Kamon is a senior product manager at Netscape Communications Corporation, focusing on applications development technology and application strategies. Prior to Netscape, Kamon spent six years at Oracle Consulting building custom applications and the massively parallel processing (MPP) consulting practice. Prior to Oracle Kamon did research in trusted databases. Kamon holds a Computer Science and business degree from Carnegie Mellon University.

NATIONAL JEWISH CENTER FOR IMMUNOLOGY AND RESPIRATORY DISEASES/LOS ALAMOS NATIONAL LABORATORY: BETTER PATIENT CARE WITH JAVA

James Lowell Cook, M.D., is Vice Chairman, Department of Medicine, and the Head, Division of Infectious Diseases, at the National Jewish Center for Immunology and Respiratory Medicine, Denver, Colorado. Cook is also Professor of Medicine, Microbiology and Immunology at the University of Colorado Health Sciences Center, Denver, Colorado. Dr. Cook conceived and chaired a series of international symposiums on Frontiers in Mycobacteriology in 1990, 1992 and 1994. He has served on a number of public advisory committees including NIH and American Cancer Society committees. Dr. Cook has a BA from Baylor University and M.D. from the Baylor College of Medicine and did post-graduate work at the NIH and the Utah College of Medicine.

David Forslund, a fellow of the American Physical Society, is a theoretical plasma physicist who has worked in a broad range of plasma physics, from space plasma physics, to magnetic fusion to laser fusion and, more recently, in computer science. As deputy director of the Advanced Computing Laboratory at Los Alamos National Laboratory, he has helped guide the installation and operation of one of the largest massively parallel supercomputers in the world and led a research project in the practical applications of distributed computing. He has over 50 publications in refereed scientific journals and has given numerous invited talks in plasma physics and computer science. He has been directing a major research project aimed at developing integrated technologies for the National Information Infrastructure. This includes developing a fully functional, distributed graphical patient record system in use by radiologists at the National Jewish Center for Immunology and Respiratory Medicine in Denver, Colorado. He has also directed a project designed to enable portable massively parallel scientific applications. Dr. Forslund has a BS in Physics from University of Santa Clara and MA and Ph.D. in Astrophysics from Princeton University.

James E. George is a computer scientist at the Los Alamos National Laboratory and has been a member of the Sunrise/Tele-Med/Teleflex project team since 1994. The team is focused on applying distributed object and multimedia tools to various application areas of interest. The most developed is the TeleMed project which developed a prototype in cooperation with the National Jewish Center for Immunology and Respiratory Medicine. Currently, the team is focusing on applying leading edge tools for interoperable distributed objects and dynamically downloaded user client tools via Java on physics/engineering projects. George has a Ph.D. in Computer Science from Stanford University, and MSEE degree from New York University and a BSEE degree from the University of Oklahoma.

Mimi N. Hackley is the NTM Registry Director, Mycobacterial Service, Infectious Diseases Division, National Jewish Center for Immunology and Respiratory Medicine. Hackley has worked as a public health educator, research consultant, and research assistant. She has publications in infectious diseases, exercise and worker safety. Hackley has a BA in Social Work from the University of California Irvine and a Masters in Public Health from San Diego University.

Richard L. Phillips is a Technical Staff Member, Computing, Information and Communications Division, Los Alamos National Laboratory. Recent experience has been in computer graphics hardware and software development, computer animated film production, interactive environmental mapping systems, computer aided design, database management systems, interactive query languages, low cost computer graphics systems, raster graphics algorithms, distributed graphics systems, graphics-based user interface management systems, microcoded image synthesis algorithms, graphics based workstations, systems integration, window systems, multimedia digital publication and networking. Prior to LANL, Phillips was a Professor of Aerospace engineering at the University of Michigan. Philips has BS in Engineering and Mathematics and a Ph.D. from the University of Michigan.

F. HOFFMANN-LA ROCHE: JAVA FOR THE PHARMACEUTICAL INTRANET

Enrico Bondi works in the Corporate Safety and Environmental Protection department at F. Hoffmann-La Roche AG in Basel, Switzerland. Since the beginning of the Seismo warehouse and information project in 1989, Bondi has been responsible for system and database administration. Bondi started at F. Hoffmann-La Roche as a laboratory technician in 1960 and then moved to the department of safety and environmental protection.

Gabriela Keller completed a masters degree in computer science at the Swiss Federal Institute of Technology at Zurich, Switzerland in 1993. After that she came to Ergon Informatik AG, where she has been responsible for the F. Hoffmann-La Roche Seismo project since 1995. This work includes database design and application development under C and Java.

NATIONAL SEMICONDUCTOR: ACCELERATING TIME TO MARKET FOR DESIGN ENGINEERS

Phil Gibson is Director of InterActive Marketing at National Semiconductor. Phil has managed various marketing roles in Telecom, Networking, and Personal Systems for National for the last 12 years. He is currently in charge of National's marketing intranet and external worldwide Web site. National's external Web site is rated as the number one semiconductor site by design engineers and Phil and his Team are merging that site with all of National's legacy systems. Lotus Notes is the primary workflow agent for Sales Force Automation, and streamlining communications from the Factory to the Field and back is Phil's primary objective. Phil holds a BSEE from UC Davis and an MBA from USC.

Saif Kantrikar is currently working at 3Com as an Intranet Application Development Manager. Prior to this, he worked at National Semiconductor as a Senior Web Architect and Application Developer for National's External Web site. Saif holds a Bachelors Degree in Computer Science from Bharath Institute of Science and Technology, India and a Masters Degree in Computer Science from the University of Southern California.

@HOME: CABLE JAVA

Mark Neumann is Director of Content Engineering for the @Home Network, a high speed Internet Service Provider focusing on cable modem services to the home and business. Prior to @Home Mark helped develop Apple Computer's eWorld on-line service, which was based on America Online technology. Over his 19 year career, he has focused on the development of large, network distributed systems.

VIRTUAL VINEYARDS AND SUN MICROSYSTEMS: THE NAPA VALLEY WINE AUCTION, LIVE, ON-LINE

Carl Meske is Internet Architect, Internet and Networking Products Group for Sun Microsystems Computer Company. As Internet Architect, Carl Meske works with Marketing, Engineering, and Sales Development to provide strategic input and direction for the development of the Netra product line for INPG. He also works with Bob Bressler, the Chief Scientist of Networking, to evaluate and test new Internet and networking technologies, as well as how to utilize and integrate INPG and Sun technology in today's business environments. Such efforts have included the "Napa Valley Wine Auction" and the "24 hours in Cyberspace" projects. Carl Meske holds a BSCS from the University of Washington, 1988, and a BS in Forestry from Washington State University, 1979. Ask him some day about his trial and tribulations of being a forester in the Pacific Northwest.

Rob Reesor is Senior Software Developer and Webmaster at Virtual Vineyards, a Web-based purveyor of fine wine, gourmet foods, and accessories. Prior to Virtual Vineyards, he was a software engineer and TIBCO, a Reuters company, and an engineer and project manager at IntelliCorp, Inc. Rob holds BS and MS degrees in Computer Science from the University of Oregon.

HOME ACCOUNT NETWORK: BANKING ON JAVA

David J. Brewer is currently the Chief Technology Officer for HOME Account Network and is an Officer and Director of the company. Dave is a retired Lieutenant Commander/US Navy with over 17 years of Internet (Arpanet) experience. He managed the design and implementation of FDDI networks in all public naval shipyards, networking over 60,000 civilian and military personnel using state-of-the-art Cisco networking products. He retired in 1992 and started SolTech Systems Corporation and merged his company with HOME Account Network in 1996 after 3 years of high volume Sun Microsystems, Oracle, and Cisco sales and professional services.

Charles A. Atkins is President, Proprietary Financial Products. In 1986 Mr. Atkins formed Proprietary Financial Products, Inc. (PFP) to develop, patent and license consumer financial service products.

The firm filed patent applications for its first product in April 1987 and was awarded its first patent with 33 separate claims in August 1990 (US Patent #4,953,085). As President of PFP, Mr. Atkins has been responsible for the operation of the company and for the filing of patent applications with more than 350 claims for product and systems innovations in the consumer financial services industry. PFP was the first independent firm that was awarded a patent for a consumer financial product by the United States Patent and Trademark Office.

COREL CORPORATION: THINNING DOWN THE OFFICE SUITE

Chris Blber is currently the Director of Strategic Alliances at Corel Corporation. In this position, he has been closely involved in the evolution of the Corel Office for Java project and its presentation in the marketplace. He joined Corel in 1989 to oversee European sales and marketing with a special concentration on the German, Austrian and Swiss regions. After leaving in 1994 for another company, Chris rejoined Corel in 1995.

MITSUBISHI: JAVA IN SILICON

Kazunori Saitoh has been in the forefront of integrated circuit research and development technology during his 20 years with Mitsubishi Electric Corporation. He was first engaged in the development of basic control software for electron and ion-beam lithography research and development. He then went on to work in the microprocessor department of Mitsubishi Electrics System LSA Laboratory and was involved in the development of basic software for microprocessors. He now leads Mitsubishi Electrics embedded DRAM microprocessor (M32R/D) and VLIWmultimedia processor (D30V) development projects. In his present role, he seeks to provide system solutions for consumer embedded applications via the optimized codesign of hardware and software, such as the M32R/D and Java. He holds bachelors and masters degrees in electrical engineering from Waseda University, Tokyo, Japan, and a doctorate in electrical engineering from Osaka University, Osaka, Japan.

Ivan Greenberg strategically markets system-on-a-chip solutions for VSIS, Inc., that leverage Mitsubishi Electric Corporation's eRAM technology in the emerging mobile computing, personal communications, graphics acceleration, and embedded Java markets. At Raytheon, he did advanced radar systems test engineering and training. At GTE Government Systems, he designed and developed digital communications hardware and firmware as well as designed and tested ASICs, software algorithms, and DSP-based boards for CDMA spread-spectrum modems. At Mitsubishi Electronics America, he developed, executed, and managed innovative sales strategies for the Lucent Technologies account, and secured an unprecedented microcontroller design win with Lucent's wireless PBX. He has a bachelors degree in electrical engineering from Northeastern University and has nearly completed his masters degree in the same discipline from the same university.

INDEX